PETER APPLEBOME

Scout's Honor

A Father's Unlikely
Foray Into the Woods

A HARVEST BOOK/HARCOURT, INC.

Orlando   Austin   New York   San Diego   Toronto   London

For Ben, who showed the way

Library of Congress Cataloging-in-Publication Data
Applebome, Peter.
Scout's honor: a father's unlikely foray into the woods/
Peter Applebome.—1st ed.
p.   cm.
ISBN 0-15-100592-3 (alk. paper)
ISBN 0-15-602968-5 (pbk.)
1. Boy Scouts. 2. Father and child—United States—Case studies.
3. Boy Scouts of America.   I. Title.
HS3313.A66   2003
369.43'092—dc21   2002155933

Text set in Fairfield Light
Designed by Linda Lockowitz

Printed in the United States of America
First Harvest edition 2004
A C E G I K J H F D B

"Peter Applebome's view of America from the inside of a pup tent is funny, moving, informative, and, above all, inspiring. *Scout's Honor* will have you laughing like 'City Slickers' and cheering like 'Bad News Bears.'"

—Bruce Feiler, author of *Walking the Bible*

"In this refreshingly schmaltz-free account of what a father can learn from his son, 'committed indoorsman' Peter Applebome becomes a dedicated Scout father and traces the sometimes controversial but still endearingly unhip history of the Boy Scouts."

—*New York Magazine*

"*Scout's Honor* is at the same time a hilarious outdoor odyssey, a moving glimpse of a father's heart, and the best commentary ever on the Boy Scouts and their touchingly awkward history. When I was a Scout, the ultimate approbation for a job well done was something called 'Three and a Half Hows.' So here's to you, Peter Applebome: How! How! How! Hhhhh!"

—Stephen Harrigan, author of *The Gates of the Alamo*

"A sweet-hearted account of the author's adventures, as well as a reasoned critique of institutional shortcomings."

—*Kirkus Reviews*

"A fascinating parallel journey. As Applebome, the 'committed indoorsman,' is suffering the frigid, rain-soaked rafting trips, bonding with Ben in the way only shared misery can accomplish, Applebome, the knowing chronicler of the zeitgeist, is exploring Scouting's Edwardian headwaters and charting its course."

—*St. Petersburg Times*

Contents

Year III

Acknowledgments

One of the greatest pleasures of doing a book is getting a chance at the end to thank the people who helped along the way. Thanking them all might double the size of the book, so these are just some of them.

First and foremost were the grownups and kids of Troop 1—and your guess which was which is as good as mine. As noted elsewhere, most of the names have been changed to protect everyone's privacy, but the troop is the result of an extraordinary amount of work by both the adult leaders—the dads who helped out and the moms who did much of the organizational work—and the Scouts themselves. I owe a debt to each and every one of them.

As with my last book, I owe a special debt to Steve Harrigan, Eagle Scout and Alamo-ologist extraordinaire. He served as the world's best sounding board via our daily e-mail, and somehow took the time to read the first draft of every chapter, no matter how lame, I sent his way. Also invaluable readers and critics were Matt Purdy, Dan Pedersen, Bruce Feiler, Dave Watson, Bill Flank, and my brother, Edward Applebome.

At the *New York Times*, I'm particularly indebted to Jon Landman, once described as the greatest leader since Moses, or some such thing, who generously cut me a few weeks' slack at the beginning and end of this process, first to prime the pump, then to have some time to see the book whole. Without his support, I would never have been able to make this work. Of my many friends and colleagues on the *Times*'s Metro Desk, Susan Edgerley, Joe Sexton, Gerry Mullany, Kate Phillips, Mary Ann Giordano, Joan Nassivera, Jeanne Pinder, Bill Goss, Anne Cronin, Tony Marcano, Wendell Jamison, and others, I owe particular thanks to Patrick Farrell, who was always there to step in whenever needed and helped make it possible to somehow get this done during the most excruciating year of newspapering any of us expect to live through.

My agent, Esther Newberg, though not exactly the Boy Scout type, was a diligent, efficient, and even enthusiastic advocate for the book. At Harcourt, I owe particular thanks to André Bernard, who was a great supporter of my last book and from the start saw the potential in this one. I was extraordinarily lucky to have as my editor Andrea Schulz, who was as helpful and enthusiastic as an editor can be and was unfailingly, almost annoyingly, accurate in seeing what needed pruning or elaborating. If something goes on too long, you can assume I ignored her counsel.

My parents, Jerome and Sydel Applebome, were, as always, an enormous, irreplaceable source of support, especially during my time off when I used a bedroom of their house as my writing cottage.

At home, I would be remiss if I did not put in a heartfelt word for Wally, the world's most loyal dog, who stayed up with me every single late night I worked on this book. My daughter, Emma, was, as always, a source of joy and support. I am, of course, indebted in countless ways to my wife, Mary Catherine, who deserves most of the credit for the fact that both of our kids turned out to be such jewels.

And without Ben's humor, patience, wisdom, and grace there would be no book. Thanks, Ben, for letting me come along.

Truth in Advertising

This is the true story of the author's belated introduction to the world of Boy Scouts. All the events played out as described here—with discreet deletions and amendments for taste and tact. The three leaders of Troop 1, Bill Flank, Marc Toonkel, and Chuck Johnson, are identified by their real names, as are figures from the troop's past. All the Scouts are identified by pseudonyms to protect their privacy. Most of the Scout characters are based on real kids in Troop 1. A few of the Scout characters are composites, using the attributes and experiences of more than one kid. And the names of most of the other adults, both in Troop 1 and elsewhere, as well as the names of some of the other troops, have been changed as well. For parents or their agents trying to determine the identities of the more mischievous characters here, a simple rule should suffice: If there's anything remotely, possibly, conceivably less than perfect expressed or implied about any character here, it's not your kid.

Introduction: My Unexpected Detour

In the final year of the last tired old millennium, the year I turned fifty, I found myself doing something I hadn't quite planned on. I joined the Boy Scouts.

If we want to get technical here, I was almost four decades too old to officially join Chappaqua Troop 1, which was founded in 1913, three years after Scouting began in America. And as a committed indoorsman, whose camping experience consisted of one night sleeping in a borrowed tent with my son Ben's Cub Scout pack in a backyard in Atlanta, where we had lived before moving north, I'm not sure the troop would have taken me anyway. I'm all for sensible aerobic pursuits like tennis or running, and had a fair jump shot and first step to hoop in my basketball prime hundreds of years ago. But Grizzly Adams I am not. I can barely swim, having never quite figured out the breathing part of doing the crawl. I cannot tie a knot more complicated than the one it takes to tie your shoelaces and couldn't tell a floor lashing from a shear lashing if the fate of the universe depended on it. I've never made a fire in anything other than a gas grill. The allure of sleeping in some cold, wet, mosquito-infested tent, with bears, lethal deer ticks, coyotes, rabid skunks, beavers, snakes, muskrats, jaguars, cougars, and bears lurking around, when you could be safely at home watching a ball game, an old movie, or the Countdown of the 100 Best Songs of All Time on television—or even just sleeping in your own bed—remains one of life's enduring mysteries.

But the troop had taken Ben, and for various reasons—love, guilt, terror at how fast he was growing up, curiosity—I decided to come along for the ride. And before long I found myself poring over the Boy Scout Handbook pondering the mysteries of the square knot, tautline hitch, and clove hitch, and learning the manly art of one-pot cookcraft, the tenets of no-trace camping, and the moral code of the Scout Law. Before I knew it, I was joining Ben and his troop on countless hikes, camporees, trekorees, canoe trips, nature walks, camp-outs, bird-cage cleaning expeditions, Christmas tree sales, the annual Klondike Derby, and three week-long sojourns at beautiful Camp Waubeeka at the Curtis S. Read Scout Reservation in upstate New York.

It would be hard to overstate how unlikely all this was. I was hardly unaware of the primal role Scouting played in the lives of many boys and the mythic, Norman Rockwell way it served as a repository of enduring American values. I have since been regaled by many friends' stories—glorious and awful—of how Scouting helped define their youth. I've heard of their memories of majestic sunsets on West Texas camp-outs, being tormented by sadistic Eagle Scouts, guzzling cherry vodka smuggled into their Scout canteens, having girls laugh at their Scout uniform, smoking pieces of grapevine, and finding themselves in a canoe with an angry cottonmouth. I've heard them go on and on about their Scoutmasters—some distinctly creepy, others revered mentors and surrogate fathers, of learning skills they still use forty years later, of blowing up tents with propane stoves, of learning how to be a leader, of learning an admirable code of conduct, and of learning how to fart in Spanish, fill a fellow Scout's backpack with rocks, or score a six-pack of beer.

But as a child in suburban New York, Boy Scouting was about as much a part of my childhood as castrating calves. I vaguely remember visiting my cousin Ricky in the Bronx and going to some Cub Scout event in what seemed like a dingy urban school. I remember the odd-looking uniforms, particularly his yellow neckerchief, an item of apparel as unlikely and vestigial as pantaloons. I sat with my Aunt Hannah in old wooden auditorium seats as the Scouts were awarded mysterious badges and awards and swore abstruse oaths. It all seemed as arcane, musty, old-fashioned, and inscrutable as a Masonic initiation rite.

No one I knew in the town on Long Island where I grew up was interested in Scouting. Why would you be? On our block, in the Cretaceous Era of the 1950s and '60s, every day was game day. Everyone sentimentalizes his youth, but when I think back to my childhood on Tanners Road what strikes me most is the sense of freedom that I took for granted and that my own kids have never known. Every day after school, we all gathered at our suburban cul-de-sac for whatever sport was in season— baseball at the high school intramural field behind our house or the big lot at the bottom of the hill, football in the street with the goal lines from the Mohrs' driveway to the Zalks' tree, basketball in the Biblowitzes' driveway. (It was so long ago that today's two essential suburban sports, soccer and computer games, had not yet been invented.) We came up with our own customized local variations of certain sports—a whiffle-ball golf game played in the plantings around the birches and shrubs at the Bretts' next door, an indoor game with no rules called wrist muscles that consisted of hitting a basketball with a baseball bat into a bunch of cushions, a two-person baseball game without a bat called Giants and Dodgers, a winter basketball game in the snow that devolved into a contest to see who could throw the most snowballs into the open window of my parents' bedroom (that proved very much a one-time experience). It was all pack-like, unplanned, and innocent (well, maybe not the snowballs), and it never crossed our minds—or our parents'—that anyone needed to keep an eye on us or worry about our safety.

If I thought about Scouting at all, it was with an instinctive, dismissive snort of disapproval. The drab, hopelessly uncool uniforms! The borderline fascist marching! The hilariously goofy grownups in those ridiculous shorts, neckerchiefs, and high socks! And the world around us had the same low-level disdain. Not for nothing did the author Paul Fussell note the contempt with which "the right sort of people" view Scouting. After all, he wrote, "a general, the scourge of the Boers invented it; Kipling admired it, the Hitlerjugend (and the Soviet Pioneers) aped it. If its insistence that there is a God has not sufficed to alienate the enlightened, its khaki uniforms, lanyards, salutes, badges and flag worship have seemed to argue incipient militarism, if not outright fascism. . . . Then there are the leers and giggles triggered by the very word scoutmaster, which in knowing circles is alone sufficient to promise comic pederastic narrative."

Back then we weren't privy to that particular narrative, and truth to tell, it wasn't really the faux fascism of Scouting that turned us off; it was the dorky superfluity of it. Why put on those silly uniforms and go hiking with someone's father when we could wander off by ourselves into the woods behind our house, have crab-apple fights to our heart's content, or rocket—helmetless, of course—down Cardiac Hill on our bikes? Why join a pack when we already had one?

Still, Scouting seemed a quaint and harmless enough diversion when Ben ventured first into Tiger Cubs in first grade, then into Den 4, Pack 370, in Atlanta, the first steps in the progression from Tiger Cubs to Cub Scouts to Webelos to full-fledged Boy Scouts. Actually, Ben's initiation into Scouting passed me by: My wife signed him up with a bunch of his friends. But I realize now that when he made us purchase a flag and flagpole and fly the flag on patriotic holidays, when he passed a Red Cross first-aid class in fourth grade, when he delivered impromptu lectures on how to crawl on your belly out of a burning house or what to do on the occasion of a fall through ice—not a huge problem in Georgia, but you can never be too prepared—it was all part of the journey down the Bobcat Trail, which lays out the skills Cub Scouts have to master to advance in Scouting. Every now and then I dutifully participated. I went with Ben to the Pinewood Derby, where kids make little racing cars from a kit and then see which ones roll downhill the fastest. Unlike the dads who had fancy sets of Craftsman tools and a knowledge of how to use them, I was little help, and our rickety car with its wobbly wheels invariably brought up the rear. For our troubles, we got a blue Cub Scout ribbon reading I DID MY BEST and the booby-prize designation: BEST OLD-FASHIONED. I picked Ben up after the pack meetings at the Peachtree Presbyterian Church. I scribbled my name a few times to show he'd completed activities in his manual, the Big Bear Cub Scout Book, a Cub Scout version of the Boy Scout Handbook ("Tell what to do in case of a school bus accident"), and went to the annual pack dinner. It all seemed harmless enough. And in a world defined by play dates—a concept my neighborhood friends would have found as alien as Kurdish poetry—it did seem to offer broader social interaction than his usual activities. But it all seemed like a trifling sideshow to my parenting life, something like the Teenage Mutant Ninja Turtles or the Mighty Morphin Power Rangers, that would have its brief day and then drift into the past.

My heart was in the Darwinian competition of soccer and basketball, and, most of all, the green pageant of Little League—keeping score, hits and misses. I loved every moment of batting practice or playing catch on the front lawn. When Ben evolved from fumbling rookie to an equal partner, I was usually the one trying to drag things out before going back inside. Helping out with all his teams from second grade to fifth—the triumphal march of the invincible Braves, the Oedipal drama of the tormented Astros, the Zenlike amity of the Giants, our one moonlighting expedition into fall baseball with the scrappy River Dogs—was to me the essence of dad-dom. My travel schedule as a journalist covering stories across the South made it hard to be the main coach—my highest rank was co-coach of the River Dogs. But just bringing my antique Rawlings Ken Boyer Trapeze glove out of retirement felt like a kind of rebirth, and every time a kid called me "Coach" I got a tiny, surreptitious jolt of pleasure. So whether hitting fungoes to the outfielders, warming up the relievers, serving as first-base coach, or yelling encouragement from the dugout, I felt so right in Little League I could even put up with the over-the-top dads who were already pushing their kids toward their dates with destiny in the bigs.

One year, when I'd been traveling too much, I was invited to a cultural event—something on the order of a celebration of American poetry—at the White House on a day when Ben had a big play-off game. Half out of guilt, half out desire (hell, I really didn't want to hear a night of poetry anyway), I chose the game. Ben wasn't the star, and I wasn't really essential personnel, but I just wanted to be there. He thought I was completely crazy at the time, but was more pleased than baffled by my choice. Ben still calls it the Gold Standard of Good Dad-dom, though I did it as much for me as for him.

Ben loved Little League too, but more with a sense of enjoying the camaraderie, the uniforms, and the postgame Gatorade than with a manic passion to win every game or become a star. All his friends were Braves fans, so he became one too in a casual way, but he never studied box scores and sports-page agate the way I had when I was a kid and never suffered unduly when they lost. I thought we had bonded on my terms forever when Ben was five and danced around with me like my little soulmate during perhaps my ultimate ecstatic experience as a fan, Christian Laettner's miracle last-second shot that allowed Duke to beat Kentucky in the 1992 NCAA Basketball Tournament. But, in fact, the moment came and went in his life without leaving a trace.

Instead, it turned out, he really loved Scouting. He'd pore over the Wolf Cub Scout Book, the Big Bear Cub Scout Book, and the Webelos Scout Book: handbooks filled with a heady mix of Kipling and Indian lore, the practical (knot tying, fire safety, first aid), and the principled (patriotism, religion, respect for nature) with the requisite paranoia—even for eight-year-olds!—about drugs and child abuse. In the summer after fifth grade, I drove Ben up to Scout camp in the foothills of the North Georgia mountains. He and his friends seemed tiny and utterly innocent next to the pimply and vaguely thuggish middle school Boy Scouts who drove up with us, the screeching guitars and THUMP THUMP THUMP of Dr. Dre, Nirvana, and Puff Daddy leaking out from the headphones of their Discmans like premonitions of the dark mysteries of teenagerdom to come. The rudimentary, military green army surplus tents on their wooden pallets seemed an invitation to a horrid week of heat stroke and poodle-sized Georgia mosquitoes. Two men in Scout uniforms were spending the week there as Cubmasters or packmasters or whatever they were called. I couldn't tell if they were saints or lunatics, but whatever my outer limit of good daddom was, it sure as heck didn't stretch that far. Ben came back glowing with tales of wondrous rafting trips on perilous rapids, fabulous all-protein and carbohydrate dinners, and amazing experiments in minimalist personal hygiene.

So when we moved to New York when he was eleven, one way to ease his transition seemed to be to join the local Scout troop. And I had particular reason to see that the transition worked. There is a dreaded moral abyss to which all modern men are in danger of descending—the fallen state of being a bad dad. Some dads are indeed failures as fathers and as humans—bigamists, family deserters, wife beaters, Type A jerks who never stop barking into their cell phones at Little League games. But caught between hellish demands at work and a vague ideal of the nurturing New Age Man, many men feel like they're guilty no matter what they do. And moving one's family, with its potential to wreak grievous and irreparable psychic harm to frail juvenile psyches, can be seen as prima facie proof of bad dad-dom. So I was thrilled to find a new Scout troop for Ben, and even willing to participate a bit to ease the transition. I was excited to sign him up for his new Little League, but he had only a year left to play. So if the main event was going to be Scouting, I figured I'd give it a try too. Better the dorkiness and potential social ostracism of Scouting than the eternal damnation of being consigned to the circle of hell reserved for substandard dads.

In that spirit, after my wife had done some investigative reporting on the two Scout troops in town, I found myself one September evening at our town hall attending Troop 1's annual organizational meeting. It reminded me of nothing so much as my cousin Ricky's inscrutable pack meeting. A handful of dads and moms were gathered in the tan upholstered chairs in a meeting room. As I walked in they were poring over the proposed schedule for the upcoming year, checking every date against the school calendar, discussing the order of camp-outs and camporees and hikes with Jesuitical precision and seriousness of purpose. At the front of the room was a man who looked to be in his midsixties with a bristling white beard and steelrimmed glasses, wearing a Boy Scouts of America T-shirt, a red Boy Scouts windbreaker, and olive pants with a tooled leather

Boy Scouts belt. There were long discussions about whether the Clear Lake camp-out would conflict with Young Writers Day or whether the canoe camp-out could be held on the same weekend as the eighth-grade social. The man at the front of the room pondered each scheduling dilemma with an aggressively professorial mien. He'd cock his head, check his legal pad, and posit solutions ("What if we held the Court of Honor on the twelfth and move the overnight canoe trip to the weekend of the fifteenth?") like a general plotting strategy for a winter offensive. After much animated discussion, they'd go on to the next event. I did my best not to nod off and scurried out when the meeting finally ran its course. If passing up the White House for Little League was largely for me, this was definitely for Ben.

What happened over the next year was not at all what I was expecting when I left that meeting room. But, to my utter surprise, I soon found myself sucked in to Scouting. I liked the way it brought kids and dads together in a totally noncompetitive way. I liked the skills and values—well, most of them—that it taught. I liked being in a group that, in the end, wasn't about whose kid was going to be treated like royalty because he had the best fastball and whose was just tolerated because he wasn't a star. I loved the hiking on the Appalachian Trail or in the myriad forests just up the Taconic Parkway, and I came to tolerate—sometimes—the camping that came with it. And before too long I found myself wanting to know more about Scouting, the boys in it, and how its retrograde rituals fit into the hyperactive, jaded lives kids live in contemporary suburbia. Scouting could not recreate for my son what I liked about my childhood. But in some ways it offered a different version of the same experience, one so many kids lose out on now as they shuttle between music lessons, soccer games, religious school, SAT tutoring, and whatever else they start doing by middle school to make their résumés look good for the Ivy League.

And once I got involved, the venture seemed to offer a lot. A way to learn about the too-rich-for-my-blood town to which I had moved, a place that soon became semi-famous as the residence of the Clintons, those plucky avatars of timeless values. A way to grab hold of my son as he plummeted way too fast toward the terrifying maw of teenagerdom and the real separation not far beyond that. A window onto something that seemed at once a defining slice of Americana—square and traditional in the best sense—and a lunkheaded anachronism intent on rendering itself totally irrelevant.

And finally, it seemed an oddly appealing way to contemplate my diminishing place in the cosmos. Barreling toward the big Five-O, and facing the predictable demon of self-doubt and the specter of closing doors, Scouting seemed an intriguing vehicle for taking stock as I navigated the shoals of midlife angst. Rather than get divorced, quit my job, move to Montana, buy a cherry-red Porsche, study Buddhism, or take up the flute, I decided to hike into the woods with a bunch of kids and try to figure out what Lord Robert S. S. Baden-Powell was up to when he founded Scouting in 1907. I'm not saying this was the smartest choice in the world. I'm not even saying it seemed like such a great idea at the time. I'm just saying it's what I decided to do.

"Adventure, learning, challenge, responsibility—the promise of Scouting is all this and more," my Boy Scout Handbook read, following the greeting from Chief Scout Executive Jere B. Ratcliffe, who beamed out at us with a beefy air of congenital affability. "Are you ready for the adventure to begin?" Well, as things turned out, I wasn't ready at all. Not for the latrines at Camp Waubeeka. Not for the Scouts' gourmet Beefaroni/ramen noodle/mystery meat/oatmeal campfire stews. And certainly not for the Scouts' proclivity for kicking up ugly controversies and ill will by choosing to expel gays and atheists—even if they had achieved Scouting's top rank as Eagle Scouts. Having finally bought in to the virtues of Scouting, I was immediately forced to confront its vices and to wonder whether Scouting was destined to become just another cultural battleground in American life, charged turf in which you had to take sides for or against them.

And that turned out to be one more thing that I wasn't ready for. Because having grown up a card-carrying member of the Scouting-averse constituency, and disagreeing with their expulsions of gays and atheists, it should have been easy to know which side I came down on. It was not. Scouting may be an anachronism, a holdover from Edwardian England and the dying days of the American frontier that's rapidly losing out in the vast new suburban marketplace of kid-oriented events and attractions. But if it's a throwback, it's still a resonant one that over the years has enrolled more than 100 million American boys, evolved into a global movement that now includes 25 million boys in 217 countries and territories, and become so much a mirror of the way Americans see themselves that many people are amazed that Scouting began in Britain, not the United States.

Scouting has always been a conservative organization, and in the past several years those conservative instincts have seemed to be driving the organization off a cliff. Still, the more time I spent around Troop 1, the more I came to feel that if the corporate bureaucrats who run Scouting from their bunker in Irving, Texas, have a lot to learn, the members of the liberal thought police who managed to turn Scouting into a hate crime do too. And, to my surprise, in the end what was admirable and worthy about Scouting seemed far more important than what was stupid and narrow about it.

But all that came later. First I had to figure out how to tie the damn knots.

Year I

1: Canoeing at Jerry's

Since 1976, Troop 1 has been coming to Jerry's Three River Canoes and Campground on the Delaware River between New York and Pennsylvania for the 13.5-mile canoe trip from Pond Eddy, New York, to Matamoros, Pennsylvania, that begins the Scouting calendar each September. It was easy to see why.

When the Delaware was discovered—at least by white guys—by Henry Hudson in 1609, he described it, a bit redundantly, as "one of the finest, best and pleasantest rivers in the world." And from the time the Lenni-Lenape Indians first began plying it in hollowed chestnut logs, its 330 miles, and particularly the 73.4 miles of the Upper Delaware, have been viewed as some of the most scenic stretches of navigable river in the Northeast. Once polluted, the river is now full of brown and rainbow trout, smallmouth and striped bass, walleye, pickerel, panfish, carp, catfish, and white suckers, and the Upper Delaware, which is burrowed into the Appalachian Plateau, has become the most popular canoeing river in the Northeast. The river begins near Hancock, New York, at the edge of the Catskills, and meanders down past tiny riverside hamlets like Buckingham and Lordville, Kellams and Callicoon, which had their heyday in the era of the Erie Canal. It makes its way in artful twists and turns past spectacular shale and sandstone cliffs rising several hundred feet in the air and finally empties into the Atlantic Ocean at the mouth of Delaware Bay.

Ben and I joined the assembled masses of Troop 1 on a crisp September morning at the troop's traditional meeting place at Roaring Brook Elementary School. We caravaned up the Taconic Parkway, across the Bear Mountain Bridge, through the desultory town of Port Jervis. As we arrived at the river, I had two conflicting thoughts.

The first thought was that, all things considered, this didn't seem too bad. Ben had been to one of the troop's weekly Wednesday-night meetings and seemed almost instantly at home there. One father I knew in Atlanta had referred quite proudly to his bratty kid, who found something to whine about at every birthday party, Little League game, or school trip, as "oppositional"—as if his kid's fits, snits, and tantrums bespoke some glorious inner reserve of independence and creativity. Ben was not oppositional. He tended to assume that the natural order of things was benign, not malignant, and that other kids were likely to be benign too. So while he didn't really know anyone in the troop, he was immediately a part of it, happy to plop down on the floor with the other kids intently listening to the Troop 1 Scoutmaster, Dr. Flank, the white-haired gentleman from my introductory session, give pretrip instructions on gear, garb, and canoeing technique. And truth to tell, what was there not to like in spending a gorgeous fall day canoeing down the Delaware River? Even for me, who was maybe a tad oppositional, this trip felt like a felicitous, wholesome introduction to our new life as rugged venturers into the great outdoors, especially since it was not likely to entail sleeping outside, forgoing indoor plumbing, or coping with animals better viewed at the zoo or in wildlife videos than in the wild. The trees were showing the first reds, yellows, and golds of fall. Our fellow Scouts and Scout dads, in their Timberland, Columbia, and Patagonia outdoors gear, seemed full of virtuous vigor and good cheer. Jerry's World Headquarters, a ramshackle wood frame cabin with a Direct TV satellite dish on top and canoeing safety instructions and photographs of visiting bears on the walls, had a pleasantly behind-the-times quality that seemed worlds away from our immaculately manicured little slice of suburbia in Westchester County. Two golden Labs and one black Lab jumped in and out of the water nearby and a crew of beefy young men took your money, carried canoes on their head, and transported adventurers in vans old enough to have survived Vietnam. And it was either this or rendering myself inept at some household chore, so it wasn't like I had a better alternative.

The second thought was that maybe I should have paid more attention to the waiver I had signed from the Three Rivers Canoe Corporation. I had absentmindedly skimmed the legalese acknowledging that I was fully aware that canoeing down the Delaware River carried inherent risks, dangers, and hazards that might result in "injury or illness including, but not limited to, bodily harm, disease, fractures, partial and/or total paralysis" and other things that I was disinclined to experience. The waiver added that there was, of course, the danger that the guide might misjudge terrain, weather, and water level; and the risk of unforeseen events like falling out of my canoe and drowning. (At one time, an average of ten people a year drowned in the Delaware, a number that has declined to two or three a year since the National Park Service took over management of the upper part of the river in 1978.)

As Dr. Flank, a retired chemistry professor, stood in the tall grass down the hill from Jerry's World Headquarters building, waving his paddle above him like Crazy Horse brandishing his rifle as he prepared to attack the cavalry, a third disquieting thought began to nag at me: I didn't have the slightest idea how to paddle a canoe, especially down the rapids clearly marked on the mimeographed map we had been given. And the more Dr. Flank went on, the more I found myself thinking about the helpful hand-lettered sign next to the pay phone: "Any serious life threatening or medical emergencies 911 in effect in this area."

True, Ben and I were lined up next to perhaps twenty kids, some brawny high school kids, most scrawny little twerps barely out of elementary school, and if they could do it, I guessed I could. Of course, like all good Boy Scouts, we were prepared. We had our balers, made by keeping the handle and bottom but cutting the top off one-gallon plastic milk jugs with our Swiss army knives. We had tied the baler to the seat of the canoe using some knot or another that the kids knew even if I didn't. We had on our bright orange personal flotation devices. We had our spare clothes, extra pair of wool socks, and bag lunch all tucked into the hermetically sealed waterproof bag Ben and I had purchased at great expense earlier in the week. Most of us had compasses just in case. I'm not sure in case of what—my guess was you were going to paddle downstream whether it was E-SE or E-NW—but we had them anyway. We had our first-aid kits with assorted bandages, creams, poultices, scissors, and tweezers. We were led by Dr. Flank, who at sixty-seven had only done this about a thousand times. He was aided by his able assistants: Mr. Johnson, a middle school science teacher; Mr. Toonkel, who owns a business that sells plumbing and heating supplies; and our Dudley Do-Right, all-star Scout, Senior Patrol Leader Todd Davis, who was only in tenth grade but gave off an air of imperial confidence as he walked around checking kids' life vests and conferring with Jerry's minions.

But the more Dr. Flank went on, the more I started wondering if this was such a great idea, especially since, as Dr. Flank helpfully reminded us, a drowning is eight times more likely in a canoe than in any other form of aquatic conveyance.

"Listen up!" shouted Dr. Flank, glaring at the kids like some kind of Old Testament prophet on a bad hair day. Dr. Flank had various forms of address, I came to learn, and this was his full-throated "YOU-BETTER-LISTEN-VERY-CAREFULLY-TO-EVERY-WORD-OR-YOU'LL-PROBABLY-DIE" mode. First, he told us that the water temperature was about 50 degrees and went on and on about how fast hypothermia, which can be fatal, would set in if we found ourselves under water for any length of time. The body loses heat 240 times faster in water than in air, and a person capsized into water below 55 degrees Fahrenheit can face hypothermia, which causes disorientation, drowsiness, and lack of coordination, within fifteen minutes or so. I wasn't all that happy to jump into a cold swimming pool on a hot summer day, much less face death by frigid dopiness like one of the first hapless city slickers to die in a wilderness horror movie, stumbling through the forest in a dull, chilly haze until falling nose first to the ground stone dead, too addled even to check his stocks before dying.

Then he ran through the proper technique for the J stroke, which allowed the person in the rear of the boat—me—to use the paddle as a rudder to steer the boat as we moved downstream. The idea, as any idiot who has ever paddled a canoe knows, is to begin with a forceful stroke, propelling the canoe forward, then to bring the paddle around behind the canoe as if forming a J. We all mimicked the J stroke, our paddles whooshing through the air on cue. I stroked dutifully, hoping the mere motion would turn me into an accomplished canoeist.

"Follow the black snake," Dr. Flank went on, meaning the clear ribbon of water indicating there were no rocks underneath. "If you see an inverted V, it means there's a rock straight ahead. You want to steer away from the rocks. If you don't, if you find yourself stuck on a rock, this is what you do. First thing," he said. Then he repeated it louder in case any of the kids were already drifting off into other frequencies. "FIRST THING! You need to lean hard on the downstream gunwale to raise the other end of the boat above the waterline. It takes four to six seconds to fill a boat with a half ton of water. That happens today, you're in big trouble. Then, when you're stable, use the grip of the paddle, not the tip, to push yourself off the rocks and back into the water. If you do tip over, let the boat go first. You don't want the boat behind you ramming into you from behind, especially when it could slam you into a boulder. A boat full of water can squash you flatter than a pancake. You can literally be crushed to death. And then float down feet first, with your feet as high as you can get them. You don't want to get your feet caught on a rock and get pulled under. And when you go through the rapids, get off the seat and kneel down on the bottom of the canoe to bring down your center of gravity and keep the canoe stable. Leave about twenty yards between one another, and be sure to go where it's smoothest. Don't try to be a hero or you'll be a wet hero."

Ben seemed oddly oblivious to the potential disasters at hand, but my head was swimming, which was more than I could probably do if I ended up in the water. I briefly considered suggesting that he go with a more experienced partner, but then I realized that half the adults looked as spooked as I felt. *They didn't get it either!* Forget the lawyer's language about partial and/or total paralysis, which seemed terrifying but rather abstract. As we pushed the canoe into the water, getting dangerously wet and cold suddenly seemed almost inevitable.

We clambered in, Ben in front, me in back, and shoved off from the muddy banks of the river, at which point it became clear my incipient panic was not misplaced. I still had no idea how to do the J stroke. I felt like a duck with Alzheimer's—what exactly was I supposed to do?

Ben was in the front earnestly paddling away under the assumption that I knew what I was doing as our navigator. But despite my ineffectual efforts at J stroking, the boat seemed to be going where it wanted to. Maybe the better thing was to paddle on the right when I wanted to go left and paddle on the left when I wanted to go right. That's how the Indians did it in every movie I had ever seen, and if it was good enough for them, it was surely good enough for me. We tried that and splashed around for perhaps ten seconds. Other Scouts and dads, no matter how befuddled they had seemed on land, were sailing merrily down the stream, with the lads, no doubt, comforted by the assured competence of their old man. Mr. Toonkel, who was wearing a black wet suit and paddling around imperiously in a bullet-shaped kayak as he looked out for the stragglers at the rear of the flotilla, watched us from a distance, obviously sizing us up as the class dunces.

After paddling, stroking, splashing, and floundering around for another few seconds, I heard an unmistakable metallic grinding sound. Then I felt a dull, ominous thud. Then we ground to a dead stop. I didn't know much about canoeing, but, though my mind raced frantically for alternative possibilities (We'd dropped anchor? I'd accidentally activated a braking system no one had told me about? We'd been attacked by river sharks?), I quickly realized what had just happened. In my first fifteen seconds of sanctioned Boy Scout activity, I had managed to land the canoe on a rock, almost certainly setting in motion one of the cataclysmic scenarios Dr. Flank had so grimly outlined for us. Hypothermia? Flattened against jagged rocks by a runaway half-ton canoe? Drowning as our feet were being crushed under subaqueous boulders? Our old standby of partial and/or total paralysis? It was bad enough to put myself at risk, without imperiling my son as well, and the thought passed fleetingly through my brain that if I managed to drown us in our first fifteen seconds, I'd almost certainly go down in history as the single worst Scout who ever lived.

Ben shot me a look that bespoke mild annoyance, a distinct

lack of confidence in my canoeing abilities, and/or tempered amusement, rather than serious concern for life and limb. He apparently didn't realize the gravity of our peril. "We're on a rock, Dad," he said helpfully.

"Thank you for sharing," I replied, trying but failing to affect an air of blithe, I've-got-it-all-under-control unconcern. "I'm well aware of that."

"Do you know how to get us off?"

"Of course I do," I lied.

My first concern was for the risk of our boat being swamped by that half ton of water Dr. Flank had told us about. But before we could adjust our weight toward the downstream gunwale, whatever that was, something surprising happened: Nothing. The canoe did not fill up with water. We were not pitched perilously into the swirling river. We did not have to worry about floating downstream with our feet in front of us or slipping into a fatal hypothermic torpor.

Dr. Flank had made it all sound so dire and perilous back on land. But now that I had almost instantaneously put us in harm's way, it was quite clear that short of panicking and standing up in the canoe, it was going to be pretty hard to sink it. Despite the water rushing by, we seemed fairly secure in our temporary roosting place on the rock. So first we kind of shimmied the canoe off its resting place. And then, with a minimum of pushing with the paddle handle, we were able to slide off the rock, into the water, and back to our ineffectual floundering around. I had learned a little about canoeing, but a lot about Scouting. Indeed, my first Scouting epiphany was: IT'S GOOD TO BE PREPARED, BUT, IN TRUTH, THINGS ALMOST NEVER TURN OUT AS BAD AS YOU FEAR THEY WILL.

I resumed our journey with a new sense of vigor and purpose, having proved that my son was safe, after all, under my command. Ben continued paddling away. Mr. Toonkel, looking like a mustachioed mallard in his kayak, shouted out a little encouragement about proper J-strokemanship, and I gave it another go. Let's see, paddle forcefully, bring the paddle behind in a J, then straighten it out like a rudder to steer. Push it toward the left and the canoe goes to the right. Push it to the right and the canoe goes to the left. It wasn't nuclear physics. Sure enough, this time it made sense, and almost instantly I became the master of my canoe-bound domain. Before long, we were seriously hauling butt in an effort to catch up with everyone else. Within a few minutes we were in the thick of our armada. This turned out to be a pretty varied group. Two canoes held boys and their moms, which we were told was a first-ever female incursion into Troop 1's little male world. In one canoe a man with blond hair seemed to be arguing nonstop with his son. You could hear them all the way to Port Jervis.

"PADDLE, KENNETH," the man hollered.

"I AM PADDLING, DAD. MY ARMS ARE TIRED," the kid hollered back.

"THIS IS THE LAST TIME WE'RE DOING THIS, KENNETH."

"GOOD, DAD. IT WAS YOUR IDEA ANYWAY."

Several canoes were captained by older Scouts, high school kids in muscle shirts and do rags. Todd was with one of the smaller kids and Dr. Flank was with another. We were all spread out across perhaps a 150-yard stretch of river in a haphazard flotilla, joined by an occasional raft, tube, or canoe full of college kids from Pennsylvania, Hasidic Jews on an outing from communities in Rockland County, or nurses celebrating a birthday.

Once I had mastered the J stroke, our trip turned, with amazing dispatch, into a thing of quiet, surprising bliss. By midmorning the temperature was in the low 60s. The sun was bright. The sky was a vivid, cloudless blue. There was no wind and no humidity. It was a perfect day for canoeing. We paddled along, sometimes pushing the tempo to pass another canoe, sometimes trawling at a leisurely pace. The river was relatively high, which meant it didn't take much work to keep up with the group, and the canoe slithered effortlessly over most of the rocks beneath us. The air was thick with wildlife, here a turkey vulture, there a hawk. We spotted a bald eagle within the first hour and watched the Canadian geese squawking overhead.

Before long, we passed our first rapids, which turned out to be a blink-and-you-miss-them affair known as Staircase Rift. It presented us with pleasingly churning water that felt like a very mild version of the wave machines at landlocked water parks. So much for the horrific rapids. (See Epiphany #1 above.)

Before long, it was time for lunch. We paddled our canoes to the shore and pulled them out of the water at a brushy gravel bar called Mongaup Island. Ben and I found a commodious rock to sit on, opened up our waterproof bag, which looked like a small body bag, and pulled out our lunch—two peanut-butter-and-jelly and two turkey sandwiches, a bag of sesame sticks, chocolate-chip granola bars, carrot sticks, and, the *pièce de résistance,* a Snickers bar for each of us.

The big kids largely hung out together under a big pin oak tree, the two women and their sons ate under another, and everyone happily unveiled a profusion of modest delights—giddy bags of brightly colored M&Ms; gaudy deli sandwiches of turkey, pastrami, and ham; coveted containers of Pringles; plastic bags full of pretzel rods; one kid's famous homemade teriyaki beef jerky; assorted trail mixes or "gorp" of peanuts, walnuts, Craisins, raisins, dates, apricots, Rice Chex, Cheerios, chocolate drops, and Lord knows what else; Cokes and big plastic Nalgene jugs of water and Arizona Iced Tea and drink boxes of toxic but irresistible Yoo-Hoos.

We all pretty much ate what we brought, but the snacks like the trail mix and pretzels got passed around. When we got ready to get back in the canoes, Mr. Toonkel walked through the group with a big bag full of red, green, purple, and orange Tootsie Roll Pops, which he gave out to grownups and kids alike. Fortified and sucking happily away, we packed up our bags, wrappers, and debris, emptied it all into garbage bags stowed in our waterproof bags, climbed back into the canoes, and shoved off.

The rest of the way was even better. The rapids past Mongaup Island and Butler Falls were more challenging, and after the river bent sharply to the right about three-quarters of the way through our route, we turned into the most spectacular scenery of the trip—250-foot sheer cliffs rising from the left banks of the river, which made us feel like agreeably inconsequential bit players at the bottom of a sublime aquatic canyon. We waved jauntily to the onlookers up on the bluffs. It was by now hot enough for everyone to take off their jackets and fleeces and make the trip in T-shirts, many of which soon got very wet. I'm not sure who fired the first splash, probably some of the younger kids trying to aggravate the older ones, but as we sailed under the cliffs about half the boats started splashing each other, a use of the paddle that Dr. Flank had not mentioned in our initial briefing but now seemed to tolerate as acceptable youthful exuberance.

Ben would have been perfectly happy to be a combatant, but I opted for a safe, dry distance from the hostilities. Instead, we got ourselves wet in the exhilarating final plunge down Sawmill Rift, where you were supposed to hug the right side of the stream while avoiding a bunch of massive boulders strewn casually around in the middle. We bounced on through, not exactly candidates for some PBS white-water rafting epic, but feeling we'd got our money's worth nonetheless. Then we exited the canoes—Jerry's minions were on hand to turn them over, dump the water out, and affix them to the top of the ancient, rusted-out vans. We'd been on the river, counting lunch, for about five hours.

We'd made the trip largely as a solitary pair, sharing a canoe and sharing a lunch, so it felt more like a father-son outing than a Scout outing. But once we all hit land, we became a group, like returning explorers who now had our perilous journey in common. We all helped Jerry's men lift the canoes and compared notes about this or that rapid or rock. Todd Davis came over to us to see how we did. Todd had a way of walking that made him look like he was bouncing off the soles of his feet and a gift for talking to younger kids as if they were his equals instead of the awed squirts they felt like.

"This your first time canoeing?" he asked Ben, who nodded. "You guys did good then," Todd said. "And you were smart enough to stay pretty dry." Then Dr. Flank came over, checked on our progress, and told us he was glad we had joined the group. We all milled around, then piled into the vans in anticipation of being repatriated to mere civilization and bounced and rocked our way merrily back to Jerry's. From there, we recovered our gear, threw it in the car, and stopping only to worship at the shrine of the Golden Arches, headed for home. Despite myself, I'd liked every part of it—the trip to a place I'd never been, the physical exertion of the canoeing and the meditative bliss of floating down the river, and the sense of being a part, however tenuously, of this armada of dads and kids. I loved the idea of Mr. Toonkel handing out the Tootsie Roll Pops to the kids and dads—who pampers dads in this world? And what I liked best was doing it with Ben, and on his turf, not on mine.

2: Trustworthy, Loyal, Helpful

"Guys. Guys. Keep it down. Guys. Guys. Pay attention, OK?"

There were many things that could be said about Bob Heller, most of them having to do with his remarkable ability to stay asleep. He was legendary in the troop for the four alarm clocks he used to wake up each morning, the three beepers he needed to rouse him for nighttime calls from the Volunteer Ambulance Corps, the way he could be blissfully snoring away in his tent at nine in the morning as all around him younger Scouts who had been up since seven were brewing up some dubious concoction for breakfast, loudly debating the fine points of Starcraft, the favored computer game, or yelling about just who was to blame for bringing to camp the seven-inch butterfly knife Mr. Toonkel had just confiscated. But though he was a high school junior overseeing a bunch of middle school kids, one thing you could not say was that he had any ability at all to keep the others quiet or to get them to pay any attention to him as he was trying to impart various essential truths of Scouting wisdom.

The troop met every Wednesday evening from 7:30 to 8:45 at the Roaring Brook Elementary School. And it took only a few meetings to get a sense of the cast of characters and the way each meeting was a delicate balancing act between the forces of chaos and the forces of light. There had been some semblance of order at the beginning of this week's meeting, held three weeks after we returned from canoeing. The dramatis personae waltzed in, affecting the odd mix of adolescent bravado and pallid ghetto style ("Yo!" "What's happenin?" "'Sup dude?") that has become the mark of the suburban teenager. A few shot baskets in the gym with its eight-foot-high hoops. One threw a rubber ball against the wall. A few sat down and leafed through their Scout Handbooks.

After a while, Dr. Flank barked out, "All right, let's get going," and the kids lined up in three rows. These represented the three patrols, the basic unit of troop organization. At the top of the troop pecking order was the Senior Patrol Leader—Todd Davis, of course. Below him were Bob Heller and Jack Larson, the two assistant Senior Patrol Leaders. All of them were high school juniors. Each patrol had a Patrol Leader, usually an eighth or ninth grader. The patrols were filled out by the rest of the kids in the troop, most of them in sixth and seventh grades. The meeting began with a reasonably earnest recitation of the Pledge of Allegiance. That was followed by an equally respectable version of the Scout Oath ("On my honor, I will do my best / To do my duty to God and my country / and to obey the Scout Law / To help other people at all times / To keep myself physically strong, mentally awake and morally straight") and the Scout Law ("A Scout is trustworthy, loyal, helpful, friendly, courteous, kind, obedient, cheerful, thrifty, brave, clean and reverent"). Neither, of course, is to be confused with the Scout Motto ("Be Prepared") or the Scout Slogan ("Do a Good Turn Daily").

But within a few minutes, all that sense of civility and order was forgotten in the face of a series of unspeakable disasters that had apparently afflicted the troop. Soon Scouts were strewn like wreckage from an accident across the wooden floor, each one facing a peril more dire than the next. There was Louis, lying on his back, his right arm apparently immobilized by some fall from a tree, errant axe blade, marauding bear, portage mishap, spelunking dunking, rock-climbing fall, wild-dog mauling, unexpected blow from an improperly lashed tree limb, or any other rogue catastrophe. The rest of his patrol gathered around. Their task was to make a sling out of a Scout kerchief, an item none of them had ever been known to wear or carry, which may have explained why, even in this desperate hour of need, Louis was clearly fighting off the urge to break out laughing.

"Guys. You tie an overhand knot in the largest angle of the triangle," Bob said, reading from the newest version of the venerable Scout Handbook. "Now place the sling over the chest with the knot at the elbow of the injured limb and one end over the opposite shoulder. Guys. Pay attention. Guys? Guys. Guys!"

"I did not have sex with that woman, Miss Lewinsky," said Louis, his eyes closed, apparently delirious from his injuries. "She was only there to deliver the pizza."

"Guys. Be serious. OK. OK. It's cold out. He's turning blue. What do you do?"

"One of the inaugurated presidents died of hypothermia from a cold Inauguration Day."

"No he didn't, you idiot. He died of pneumonia."

"Guys, cut it out. We're doing first aid. Not presidents."

"McKinley."

"Not McKinley. He was shot."

"At his inauguration?"

"No, not at his inauguration. Years later."

"Guys. Guys. Cut it out."

"So who got pneumonia at his inauguration?"

"Garfield."

"The cat?"

"No, not the cat. James A. Garfield. The president."

"No, he was shot too."

"Guys. Guys. Guys."

And so it went, with no one ever paying appropriate tribute to the memory of William Henry Harrison, who at the age of sixty-seven delivered an endless 8,500-word inaugural address hatless and coatless in a frigid drizzle, caught cold, and died of pneumonia thirty-one days after entering the White House in 1841 as the ninth president. Had the Boy Scout Handbook been around at the time ("Getting chilled during an outing can be miserable and sometimes dangerous . . . you should always be equipped for a surprise storm or cool evening winds"), he might have had a happier and lengthier term in office.

But we digress. As did most of the other Scouts around the room, where similar scenes of potentially fatal carnage were also playing out. The theme for the meeting was first aid, as opposed to nights reserved for canoeing or Jeff Gottlieb, the suburban frontiersman who came every year and showed the Scouts his deerskin moccasins, skins from roadkill, and homemade stone tools. All around the room, in clumps of five or six kids, Scouts were preparing splints for lower-leg and thigh fractures and treatments for hypothermia, frostbite, and heatstroke. They were practicing the walking assist, one-person carry, four-handed seat carry, and two-person carry, all of which enabled Scouts to transport their fellows around with no gear necessary. They used wooden poles (though of course strong saplings, tool handles, oars, and tent poles would have done in a pinch) to fashion a stretcher out of a blanket (a tent fly or a sleeping bag with the bottom corner seams opened would also have sufficed). Oddly, no mention was made of the fallback position of lashing together three metal pack frames. Amid the general chaos, Scouts were responding to shouted questions about treatments for burns, bleeding, poisoning, snake bites, bee stings, jellyfish stings, heat exhaustion, frostbite, blisters, sprained ankles, and fish hooks stuck in your skin.

"How do you tell a third-degree burn?"

"Charred flesh! Skin may be burned away!"

"Do you remove clothing?"

"Yes!"

"No! It might be sticking to the flesh."

"Right!"

"Do you apply creams or medicine?"

"No! Wrap him in a blanket and get him to the hospital!"

"Yes. Good."

"Now, bites and puncture wounds..."

Troop 1 membership in recent years had gone up and down between about fifteen active Scouts to about forty. At the moment the figure was near the higher end. It was not exactly a spit-and-polish assemblage. At the first meeting of the year in early September, Dr. Flank had given a stern lecture about coming to the meetings appropriately dressed. As it turned out, he gave the same lecture every year, to only modest effect. For Troop 1, "appropriately dressed" did not mean, say, coming with your Scout neckerchief properly held in place with a slide. It did not mean any kind of headgear—whether a mesh cap or a broad-brim number—or Scout socks or belt. It basically meant showing up looking reasonably neat wearing the traditional field uniform shirt and khaki pants, which these days usually meant cargo pants with many hundreds of pockets large and small.

Troop 1 was a somewhat motley assemblage in other ways as well. The constant factor was the adult leadership. Dr. Flank, Mr. Toonkel, and Mr. Johnson all had kids who had graduated from the troop years ago. Dr. Flank had a long commitment to Scouting; he had been active ever since he was a Scout in Philadelphia in the 1940s. Mr. Johnson, whose title was Troop

Committee Chairman, and Mr. Toonkel, the Assistant Scout-master, were both former Scouts who had drifted into it as volunteer leaders when their kids were in Troop 1 and then stayed. Dr. Flank had a Ph.D. in chemistry and a fierce, bristling quality that inspired respect and a bit of fear from the kids. Mr. Johnson was laid-back and laconic, more likely to roll his eyes at the kids than to bark at them. And Mr. Toonkel, who sported a bushy mustache he sometimes waxed up for an amiably villainous quality, was a study in perpetual motion who always seemed to have some project he wanted the kids to tackle. The three men were like old fishing buddies, who knew each others' favorite recipes and quirks so well that they ran the troop with a sort of telepathic empathy. The other dads, like me, who showed up at the weekly meetings, mostly just hung around and watched, or chatted quietly among themselves, until it was time to take their kid home.

The troop composition varied from year to year depending on how many new kids were recruited and how many older ones stayed around, but it was usually structured like a pyramid, with a sparse crop of senior boys at the top and larger classes of younger kids at the bottom. Most kids joined at eleven or twelve and dropped out by sixteen or seventeen, as Scouting was replaced by high school sports and social activities or squeezed out by the crush of schoolwork. So the goal was to keep at least two or three older high school kids around to keep the younger kids quiet at the meetings, share the teaching, and serve as role models. Next came the younger high school kids and older middle school ones, peach fuzz beginning to crop up on upper lips, who had been around the troop long enough to attain the status of veterans. This meant either that they (A) knew a little and shared it, or, more commonly, (B) conferred on themselves the status of aspiring wise guys and shared that too. At the bottom were the younger middle school kids like Ben, new to the troop and often to each other, who mostly watched in awed, cowed, respectful silence. The older kids had often achieved the coveted rank of Eagle Scout. The younger ones were dutifully collecting their merit badges and working on advancement from Tenderfoot, to Second Class, to First Class, to Star, to Life. It all had the quality of an adolescent anthill, at once chaotic and quite rigorously organized.

A casual inventory of the cast of conspicuous characters would have begun with Todd, the third Davis brother to make Eagle, whose blond good looks, trim build, consummate Scout skills, and air of energetic self-confidence stood in sharp distinction to the awkward and unsure younger kids still trying to find their way. It's yet another indicator of Scouting's diminished status in American life that the term Eagle Scout is as likely to evoke suspect inferences (goody two-shoes, repressed straight arrow) as glowing ones (high-achieving, All-American kid). But it was hard to find much not to like in Todd Davis. At various times he was on the varsity soccer, swimming, and track teams. His house was full of musical instruments—piano, vibraphone, cellos, clarinets, saxophones—and he was an ace trombonist who played or sang in six different musical assemblages ranging from all-state and county jazz bands to rock garage bands to the high school a cappela group called the Acafellas. He was photo editor of the student yearbook and an accomplished photographer on top of being a master of sundry Scouting skills. It was not clear when he slept and, indeed, he often had the slightly bleary look of someone trying to cram twenty-four hours of activity into seventeen or eighteen hours of day.

Becoming a Scout was an easy choice for Todd. The middle Davis brother, Jeff, a senior, was an Eagle Scout, and the oldest sibling, their brother Robert, is still a troop legend: He earned an astounding fifty-one merit badges (it takes twenty-one to make Eagle), more than any boy in memory and almost certainly more than anyone in the history of the troop. Todd's thirty-eight may well have been second. When the Scoutmasters sized up kids for their outdoors skills, Todd was the standard they judged against. You did not have to attend many meetings to start hearing Todd Davis stories. When he cooked, the Scoutmasters were quick to remind newcomers and the other Scouts, it wasn't some pedestrian one-pot stew. He liked to cook dishes with Spanish rice, or elaborate pizzas, or apple pies for dessert. For breakfast, he brought vanilla frosted cinammon rolls that baked in an Outback Oven, sort of a Mylar dome perched on top of a Coleman stove, or pancakes or a cheese omelet he'd bring in a plastic bag and then cook. He'd bring a hunk of sausage and cut the meat in neat slices and then cook it up in a skillet, while the younger kids waited like supplicants to get a slice. He did too many things to be fixated on Scouting, but it was an important part of his life. He wasn't self-conscious about Scouting the way some kids were. If people didn't appreciate it, he figured that was their problem. He worried where Scouting was headed and took his role in the troop seriously. He was aware that for some kids Scouting counted mostly as a credential, like those kids who made Eagle—one more item for their college résumés—and then more or less disappeared. It offended his sense of what Scouting was supposed to be. But, that aside, he had liked being a little Scout, and he also liked being a big one, helping the kids set up their tents or learn to cook on their Coleman stoves, giving a hard time to the wise guys, watching the new kids come into the group. Trustworthy. Loyal. Helpful. Friendly. Courteous. Kind. Obedient. Cheerful. Thrifty. Brave. Clean. Reverent. I had no way of knowing how he stacked up on all the twelve elements of the Scout Law, but as far as I could tell, he was doing pretty well.

If Todd Davis was one version of contemporary boyhood, the Polo Boy was another. The image of the Polo Boy had stuck with me ever since I first saw him staring out with a glazed expression of cool disdain from an advertising poster in the Boy's Department of Bloomingdale's in White Plains. He's got the exquisite, sexually ambiguous WASP features of the Polo cosmology and wears a Ralph Lauren Polo for Boys denim shirt ($37) over a white T-shirt, the two top buttons on the shirt and the two buttons on the collar unbuttoned. He has long dirty-blond hair cascading down over his shirt collar, one strand of which tumbles over his face obscuring his right eye. He's holding an old brown wooden baseball bat with frayed black tape on the handle. It's a ridiculous art director's conceit. Kids use metal bats and have for twenty years. And if they occasionally use wooden ones, they're sleek Louisville Sluggers or something comparable. No kid has used a bat vaguely resembling this one since 1972.

Still, if the image doesn't reflect reality, it does ooze attitude. Polo Boy's eyes are narrowed into little slits, his lips pursed. Who knows what he's so mad about? Maybe he had a learning disability or severe attention-deficit disorder. Maybe he can't read. He killed his investment-banker father. He's a runaway from a sadistic Parisian boarding school. He's a brilliant computer geek whose brain processes information at too high a level to allow him to talk to anyone. His mom's a movie star with a drinking problem who left him with a bored Danish nanny, who does her nails and talks to her friends on the phone all day. Or maybe he's just mad that he's supposed to bat and all he has is this ridiculous wooden antique. Who knows? Something's definitely awry. But the point is not that he's a mess, but that he's so cool, *it doesn't matter!* He's not a cautionary figure, but a study in style, Madison Avenue's idea of a hip contemporary kid, and he's as likely to be a Boy Scout as he is to have Glenn Miller or Benny Goodman CDs in his Discman.

As I hung around the troop I began to see Todd Davis and the Polo Boy as two poles of contemporary boyhood. It wasn't quite like the old comic stock image of the angel in white with halo on one shoulder and the devil in red with pitchfork on the other. Todd was not without a bit of attitude himself, and both types have their place in the psychic makeup of adolescent boys. But the media are full of celebrations of gifted-but-screwy variations on the Polo Boy—surly athletes, profane rappers, druggy actors, bored scions of famous families. All the positive images we have of Scouting are as antique as the Polo Boy's ridiculous prop of a bat. Try to come up with an advertising campaign or contemporary pop culture image that makes use of Scouts in a nonironic context. It can't be done. Even when Madison Avenue wants to portray an all-American scene, it might be a kid and his floppy-eared dog or a soccer mom and her happy brood or Little Leaguers or almost anything other than a Scout in his uniform. Now when Scouting shows up in popular culture it's often as an arch or campy effort in mockery, like the February 2000 issue of *Out* magazine, which features on the cover a too-pretty Scout with thick lips and a pink sleeveless Scout shirt and inside features a fashion spread ("Snap to it, boys. Scout camp's in full swing, and your old beige uniform just won't cut it anymore.") of Scouts in $128 khaki industrial poplin shirts and $115 pale rose short-sleeve sweatshirts.

So if Todd was at one end of the scale and the Polo Boy at the other, the sixth, seventh, and eighth graders who formed the heart of the troop seemed like an intriguing laboratory of unchanneled adolescent possibility, all floating barely formed somewhere between the two. Halo or pitchfork? Todd or Polo? Trustworthy, loyal, helpful or cool, detached, ironic?

For now, the great middling masses of Troop 1 defied easy categorization. The youngest ones, just out of elementary school, were too cowed to affect much more than an air of respectful solicitude. The older ones included samples of almost whatever Boy Scout stereotype you wanted—nerd, straight arrow, misfit, jock, all-American kid, unpretentious average Joe.

Some of the kids came in matched sets. Hal and Herb were identical twin eleven-year-olds with identical braces and identical T-shirts showing a TV remote control and the words "IT'S A MAN THING. YOU WOULDN'T UNDERSTAND." They were in constant motion, usually either conspiring with or sniping at each other, and no one ever had the slightest idea which twin was which. Sam 'n Eric, who only seemed like twins, were SUV-sized football players and world-class hams who liked to play at being the class clowns. Knowing that they were guaranteed an amused and appreciative reception from their peers, they'd be the ones to ask, in mock bewilderment, what *Russian Water* was when Dr. Flank was talking about canoeing down *rushing water*. Though only a year older than Hal and Herb, they seemed ready for high school and were partial to metal music, dirt bikes, acting tougher than they were, and acting totally shocked, baffled, and hurt whenever any of the adults called them on their behavior. Barrett, Jonah, and Mark, the Three Amigos, were pint-sized motormouths who had been in the same Cub Scout pack since third grade. Left to their own devices, they tended to rattle on about an amazing mix of subjects—meteorology (Barrett's specialty), computer drives, the Simpsons, rocketry, James Bond, fighter jets. Les and Rick were clearly visitors from another planet, dropped off at the meetings or driven to camp by well-meaning parents, but totally uninterested in Scouting. They spent the meetings huddled together like refugees, watching from a distance and occasionally glancing at their watches to see how soon they could go home. The only question about them was how long they would last before dropping out.

Others were very much one of a kind. Elliot, who had brought the homemade beef jerky to the canoe trip, was a science and math whiz who never seemed to go anyplace, summer or winter, without a heavy fleece, and whose measured air of bespectacled gravity always reminded me for some reason of the older of the two Darling boys in *Peter Pan*. Bernie mixed an utterly cherubic mien and a fondness for technology with a blithe disregard for anything the Scoutmasters ever said. If he wasn't showing off a forbidden weapon in his best Homer Simpson voice, he was climbing a tree while the Scoutmasters were trying to keep the troop organized. Doug had the most advanced case of computer lust in the group. He always seemed a bit lost and forlorn offline, rattling on and on about strategy for Terrans, Zergs, and Protoss in Starcraft like an emigré pining for the plugged-in Old Country. Allen, a blend of Chef Emeril and Napster, wore Teva sandals with wool socks summer and winter, rain or shine. He was usually either cooking up a respectable quiche or breaking into the kind of show tunes or early Beatles songs no kids listen to anymore. George was a blur of stray ions, unable to slow down or sit still, who drove even the other kids a bit crazy with his air of perpetual puppy-dog excitement. Louis was small and serious with round glasses, and looked and acted like Harry Potter. Jimmy was the biggest seventh grader on the planet, a hulking football player with an intense, serious air and a wry, cutting wit. Tommy, even at twelve, seemed ready to outgrow the whole thing, as if the only test he really worried about was the one for his driver's license. There were sons of lawyers and sons of doctors, sons of auto repair shop owners and sons of teachers. There were Jews, Catholics, Baptists, and Methodists, but only a smattering of Asian kids and, as was pretty much true of the town as a whole, no blacks, though years ago Milt Williams, a local trumpet teacher and the father of the singer Vanessa Williams, had had a son go through the troop and was Scoutmaster or assistant Scoutmaster for many years. There was a grandson of Woody Guthrie, who attended meetings in his Scout shirt and black seaman's cap.

And then there was my son. We like to think of our kids as extensions of ourselves, but already at eleven Ben was getting to be his own person. His best quality, I thought, was an impeccable inner compass. He seemed strikingly detached from most of the world's social currents, oblivious to rap and pop music, uninterested for the most part in pro sports, sort of agreeably square. He'd go from one interest to another—space travel, the Civil War, an endless profusion of books, favorite films we watched together like *The Godfather I* and *II, Airplane,* and, a little later, *Dr. Strangelove*—at his own pace, not all that concerned about whether it was fashionable or cool or on anyone else's radar screen. Which, no doubt, was one reason he liked Scouting. For all the kids in the troop, it took a certain degree of self-assurance to do something that didn't bring much social reinforcement. But Ben loved the outdoors, and he was far more cooperative than competitive. Scouting fit his temperment. I sometimes asked him who was the smartest or the best athlete or particularly popular among the kids he knew, but he just shrugged. He didn't seem to think in terms of comparisons. Even his biased father knew he wasn't perfect. He was an average athlete—he did fine at soccer and baseball—but didn't have a passion to compete; and at eleven he had a modest ring of baby fat and needed to be in much better shape. If I worried about anything about him, I worried a little he'd end up a wuss. And, though no father should say this, I wished he had just a small bit of Polo Boy's ironic, knowing cool in him sometime. I loved all kinds of music, particularly jazz and the more ragged varieties of country. He'd pick up on a song I played every now and then, usually something with a sense of humor. But while his sister knew every pop group out there, he seemed mostly oblivious to music. It was a place, like sports, where I was looking for a connection between us that wasn't there. And sometimes I worried that Ben was too nice for his own good. Every father wants to shelter his kid, and I was glad he was eleven going on twelve, not sixteen. But I also know it's a competitive world out there, probably more so where we lived than most places. I watched him sometimes and worried that he needed just a little bit more of a jagged edge. At the same time, I was thankful to have found this amicable oasis for him to attach himself to after our move.

The meeting was coming to an end. We began with a calm pageant of ceremony and tradition and devolved predictably into adolescent disorder and mass confusion; the trick was to bring the meeting back to an even keel before it broke up. This was not an easy thing. By then the energies of the evening had often reached a manic peak. There were jokes to be continued. Alliances to be nurtured. Rivalries to be picked at. Fun still to be had. But between Dr. Flank's fish-eyed stare, Mr. Toonkel's no-nonsense traffic management, and some firm words from Todd Davis, it usually got done.

So at 8:35, after the splints and dressings had been peeled off, the first-aid equipment had been stowed, and the Scout Manuals closed for the day, Dr. Flank looked around, checked his watch, and commenced to bring order to the chaos.

"All right, make a circle. C'mon, it's time to finish up," Dr. Flank barked, in the same stern tones that got the meeting going. He put up his right hand in the Scout sign, the three middle fingers upright, the thumb folded over the pinky, and barked, "Signs up," in the Scout's fairly civilized signal for silence. Most of the kids did the same. Sam 'n Eric and Hal and Herb continued chattering away for a moment, but after Todd walked over in front of them and shot them the evil eye they quieted down too. The whole group dutifully formed a circle and joined hands, their arms crossed right over left, each Scout clasping the hand of the Scout or Scoutmaster on either side of him.

"I think we learned a lot tonight—at least I hope so," Dr. Flank began. "You should have learned something both about how to do first aid and how to take it seriously, because when you need it, it's very serious business indeed."

There were a few more announcements—about an upcoming merit badge seminar, the date of the next camp-out, an older Scout needing help on his Eagle Project. They all said together: "May the Great Master of All Scouts be with us until we meet again." They shook their linked arms, like a chain bouncing up and down. Then they let go. It was time to go home to homework, to familial amity or familial dysfunction, to the Yankees or Mets on television, to the Internet, to Harry Potter or Tom Clancy, to the real world, to sleep.

3: Troop 1 and Other Chappaquacks

When asked how kids had changed over his half century in Scouting, Dr. Flank invariably shrugged his shoulders and said, "Boys are boys. There's not much difference." But whether or not the kids had changed, Scouting certainly had. Troop 1's story is a microcosm of that change.

Chappaqua, the largest hamlet and main population center of the Town of New Castle, lies thirty-five miles north of Times Square in Westchester County. The name, pronounced CHAP-a-kwa, comes from the town's earliest denizens, the Indians of the Wappinger Confederacy, part of the Algonquin language group of the Mohicans. As best as anyone can tell, Chappaqua derives from *Shapeqwa,* an Algonquin word translated—depending on who's translating—as "running water," "boundary," "place of separation," "laurel swamp," or, most lyrically, "place where the wind rustles through the leaves."

The descriptions are not idle verbiage. When the land around the town and most of Westchester County was purchased by an Englishman named Colonel Caleb Heathcote for one hundred pounds from the Indians' Chief Wampus in 1696, it was described as "gardens, orchards, arable lands, pastures, feeding woods, underwoods, meadows, marshes, lakes, ponds, rivers, rivulets, mines and minerals." Its first white settlers were

Quakers, drawn from Long Island in the 1720s by the abundance of water, and the Meeting House built in 1752 still stands on Quaker Road. Even today, the town looks impossibly green and pastoral—like a place where the wind rustles through the leaves. If you look past the suburban bustle and harried lawyers pacing back and forth as they bark into their cell phones at the railroad platform in the morning, it can take your breath away.

The village grew hardly at all, existing as an obscure farming outpost of less than 1,500 people, until 1846, when the New York and Harlem Railroad came to town. Suddenly farmers could get their wares to New York by train rather than horse-drawn stagecoach and people from New York, for better or worse, could get to the town. Chappaqua's first commuter and most famous pre-Clinton resident was the crusading newspaper editor Horace Greeley, who bought his dream house and farm there in 1854. He came up from New York almost every weekend back when the train ride took two hours and eighteen minutes each way. He farmed, shot the breeze with the guys hanging out on Main Street, and gave Chappaqua its first taste of fame when he ran for president against Ulysses S. Grant in 1872. His opponents called his supporters Chappaquacks, and Greeley's race was a disaster. He won only six of thirty-seven states and died a few weeks after the election. Best known for proclaiming, "Go West, young man," his last words had the same tightly edited, aphoristic quality: "It is done. I have fought the good fight. I know that my Redeemer liveth." His statue now stands forlornly by the access road to the Saw Mill River Parkway, which split the town in half when it was built in 1934.

Thanks to the new railroad, the town of New Castle, the governmental unit that includes Chappaqua and the much smaller village of Millwood, grew from 2,401 in 1900 to 3,573 in 1910 and 5,176 in 1920. But it wasn't until the great suburban boom of the 1950s, when the town mushroomed from 8,802 in

1950 to 14,338 in 1960—it's about 18,000 now—that Chappaqua changed fundamentally from an isolated village in northern Westchester to an upscale suburb. And today it's like much of suburbia only more so, with more SUVs, bigger and more expensive houses, and one nail salon per female resident. The current wisdom is that Chappaqua is really the Indian word meaning "high taxes." It has terrific schools that residents continually obsess about, eight million organized activities for kids, and an air of competitive bustle that's in dramatic distinction to its genuinely lovely stone walls, verdant greenery, rushing streams, placid ponds, and country serenity. I had never heard of it before we moved there. But after the arrival of the Clintons in 1999, Chappaqua became well enough known that most people around New York, at least, have learned to put the accent on the first syllable instead of pronouncing it cha-PA-kwa, and most realize it's not the place where Teddy Kennedy drove his car off that bridge. In recent years, we've even come up with enough of our own misbehavior to put the town on the map. One school year ended with a furor over a little black book assessing the sexual habits of high school girls that was circulated on the Internet by high school boys. The next began with a preseason party for the high school football team for which some really thoughtful parents had hired a stripper to entertain. It's a nice place to live, but, to tell you the truth, it could probably use a bit more of the Scout Law somewhere in its collective suburban unconscious.

The village now shares geography and little else with the community that existed in 1913 when the first group of boys in town put on khaki uniforms and campaign hats and called themselves Boy Scouts, three years after the Boy Scouts of America was incorporated. There were ox-drawn carts, animal droppings, and simple frame buildings where ninety years later suburbanites would buy Tuscan cannellini beans, walnut raisin biscotti, and Key lime tarts at the Chappaqua Village Market. And Scouting's evocation of community, service, nature, and faith, which now can seem quaint and dated, hit the town like a bracing summer squall.

The Scouts' philosophy and organization was a blend, and as we shall see not always a natural one, of the work of Lord Robert Baden-Powell, the British war hero, author, and youth leader, and Ernest Thompson Seton and Daniel Carter Beard, two American naturalists and prosyletizers for the virtues of the outdoor life. Seton and Beard, it turned out, had Chappaqua ties. Both were members of the Camp Fire Club, a pioneering group of naturalists and outdoorsmen that included Teddy Roosevelt, Buffalo Bill Cody, and Gifford Pinchot, the father of the U.S. Forest Service. The Club purchased the land on which it built its permanent home in Chappaqua in 1917, which meant Seton and Beard were regulars in town at the time Scouting was beginning in the United States.

During Troop 1's first few years, nearly every boy in town between the ages of twelve and seventeen belonged. The Reverend Otis T. Barnes was the first Scoutmaster, and the First Congregational Church, which had recently seceded from the Society of Friends, was the first sponsor. Meetings were held in Carleton Quinby's father's five-room barn. The activities were more for fun and public service than for advancement—no one had the time to work on merit badges or imagine going for Eagle. But the troop grew enough by 1930 that a second troop was formed, beginning a process in which Troop 2s formed and folded over time. In December 1941, the troop rented the one-room schoolhouse built in 1914 at the top of Old Roaring Brook Road and christened it the Scout Hut. The boys raised money to fix the floor, redo the roof, install lights, and purchase an oil burner. Families donated old furniture. And before long, the Scouts had something that's hard to imagine today—a home of their own, sitting on what today is some of the priciest residential real estate in Westchester County.

It was perhaps the peak of Scouting in town. The troop was so popular it had to set up a waiting list. There were well over one hundred kids in troops 1 and 2, and there was talk of starting a third troop. The local newspaper regularly gave spirited reports of each hike and the citations the troops won at each camporee. "Under a cold sky lit by a full moon," the *New Castle Tribune* reported on January 14, 1955, "the scouts of Troop 1 Chappaqua on Saturday January 8 held an all-night campout in temperatures that went to 16 degrees above." The Scoutmaster, George Kron, known as Jerry, owned a four-hundred-acre slice of wilderness on a mountain in Vermont, known as Beaver Valley, and the troop went there for the camp-out that began the Scout year then the way the canoe trip on the Delaware begins it now. The kids hiked; the dads and Jerry's fellow Scoutmaster, Rick Barns, hung around Jerry's cabin playing cards.

Kron retired in 1961. Barns stayed until 1967 and developed the policy that still stands—that the boys, not the adults, should plan the activities and run the meetings. In 1970, a man named Don Vanderbilt took over the troop. Vanderbilt is still Troop 1's most enduring link between the past and the present. And he's a reminder that for all the high-minded Scout rhetoric about selfless Scoutmasters and all the cheap, wink-wink, nudge-nudge insinuations about their real motives, sometimes the interactions between men and boys that form the heart of Scouting remain mysterious and unknowable.

You could not dream up a character like Donald Maxwell Vanderbilt Jr. He was a squat, never-married man who lived with his mother, worked as a mortician (in the pre-euphemism era, he listed his occupation in troop records simply as "undertaker") at a funeral home in Queens, and brought the funeral-home pillows along on camp-outs for kids who needed them. He smoked four packs of Benson and Hedges a day, quietly sharing them at times with the older kids who were already smokers. Perhaps five feet, six inches tall and weighing about 260 pounds, he was balding and drove a tiny yellow Alfa Romeo. Vanderbilt could barely squeeze his bulky body behind the wheel, and when he finally got in the whole car tilted to the side like a boat in danger of sinking. He also had a dark green Cadillac with the license plate "Scout 1," which he drove to camp-outs or when anyone else had to ride along. The kids never called him anything other than "Don," and he made it clear to any overly respectful new Scouts that was the way he wanted it.

Vanderbilt, who when asked claimed a distant relationship to the swells of the same name, grew up in Greenwich, Connecticut, and was a Scout as a kid, making it all the way to Eagle. But in Troop 1 he was not much for hiking, climbing, or any of the more strenuous elements of Scouting. Instead, he was like a combination of mother hen, favorite uncle, and the character who ran the chuckwagon in a Western movie. He loved to bake bread and cook, and a culinary highlight of every year was the full turkey dinner he'd prepare for the annual winter cabin camping trip. At the other hikes, while the kids trooped off, he'd be back cooking up a huge pot of stew. He was a connoisseur of fine cheeses—Stilton, Brie, and the choice Goudas that Bill Flank brought back from business trips to Holland. His wines tended to be good Burgundies and Bordeaux. His Scotch was Chivas Regal. This was well before anorexia became a fashion statement, and if Vanderbilt, a diabetic, felt his belly was something to be ashamed of, he never let on. Instead, he could talk about food for hours, happily proclaiming, "I'd eat shit if it had cheese on it."

He viewed Scouting as both fun and serious business, and he expected the Scouts to behave that way too. A September 1976 report from the Troop Committee read, "Our experience shows that the morale of the troop is boosted if all boys wear a complete Scout uniform." Vanderbilt expected each boy to show up in a Scout shirt, pants, neckerchief, and cap with visor. Though the kids were expected to dress in uniform, Vanderbilt never ran the troop entirely by the book. He was not above turning profane every now and then, particularly with the older kids. When he got mad enough, like the time one of the kids set a tree on fire at camp, he would end his disquisition with the words "you stupid fuck," which only managed to send the kids into spasms of glee. But he was also a great listener, with an instinctive sense of fairness and respect for kids and for how they differed and what they needed.

For almost two decades Vanderbilt went to Scout camp in the Adirondacks, taking the kids in leadership positions out to an expensive steak dinner in Lake George before camp began. Then, the kids carried his voluminous gear—bed, desk, fly net, etc.—to the campsite while he looked on like a pasha. He loved all kinds of music, and each summer brought a collection of tapes ranging from Bach and Vivaldi to ABBA. He had one of the best collections of Scout patches in the country back before collecting patches caught on in a big way, and he also collected stamps, coffee mugs, knives, and black powder rifles. He always had a short Japanese knife like a little samurai sword, and he always gave a special knife to each departing Senior Patrol Leader. Vanderbilt liked to do fancy rope splicings, where you weave the ends of two ropes together or one rope back into itself. When he was in the mood he'd sometimes teach the simple ones to the kids, who would usually gather around his tent to hang out in the evenings. When he was in a different mood, he would remove his dentures and shine a flashlight up his face, turning himself into something like a deranged, toothless pumpkin, which particularly horrified the new kids who thought his teeth were real. You didn't need Jason or *Friday the 13th* to get scared at night when you had Don Vanderbilt.

One summer, some kids found a racy magazine in his tent. No one remembers just what it was—hard core, soft core, boys, or girls—but people remember kids laughing and whispering as they passed on the news and Vanderbilt sitting on something on his bed looking very embarrassed and refusing to budge until the kids left him alone. Sometimes, when the kids milled around his tent, he would secretly record their conversations, and sometimes he would play old tapes for the troop as a way almost to summon up kids who had long since gone off to college. To the contemporary mind, the combination of single man, Scoutmaster, and anything suggestive adds up to something obviously suspicious. Once one of the older boys, John Rescigno, now a neurologist in Connecticut, asked Vanderbilt if he had ever been to a gay bar. He said he had. But, without exception, the Scouts of the 1970s and '80s said he never did and never would do anything inappropriate. He dated—women—every now and then, but admitted to friends he knew he didn't cut the world's most dashing figure.

In truth, Vanderbilt didn't have any romantic life. His life was his job at the mortuary, his home with his mother, and his extended family with Troop 1. If it wasn't suburban life by the textbook, it was a full life nonetheless, and Vanderbilt lived it his own way, handling the troop's voluminous paperwork at the funeral home while waiting for the Grim Reaper to deliver up the next cold body.

But it wasn't the 1950s anymore, and Vanderbilt was entirely aware of Scouting as a depreciating asset in American life. Scouting had became so uncool that the Scouts in the 1970s adopted a self-conscious slogan: "Scouting today's a lot more than you think." Vanderbilt would grouse about the ever-expanding panoply of organized activities for kids. "I remember when there was nothing but fishing and Scouting," he'd complain. But throughout the 1970s and '80s he still took his duties as seriously as Otis Barnes, George Kron, or Richard Barns did, showing up at a kid's doorstep, for example, if he missed three or four meetings. He sent each kid a birthday card each year. When boys left the troop, they or their parents wrote him neat, regretful letters thanking him for his help and explaining why they were dropping out.

Still, if Scouting was losing favor in the world at large, within the troop life at the Hut moved along by its comfortable old rhythms. The Hut was a squat white stucco building, one story high, with a display of the troop's Eagles and its Scoutmasters beginning with Reverend Barnes in the front foyer. There was a large main meeting room, a quartermaster room where the troop kept its camping gear, a senior patrol room (which was really more of a closet), and a staff lounge, where the adults and older kids usually hung out during meetings. Underneath was a dark, spooky basement with a dirt floor and stone walls, where the troop stored sleds and gear. The Hut was technically only open for meetings, but all the senior kids had keys, and they would sometimes hang out there after school or on weekends. The Hut was a rat's nest, but it was their rat's nest.

Troop 1 and Don Vanderbilt may have been dinosaurs, but they were taking on a mildly imperial quality, with a home that had lasted almost a half century and a leader who had been in place for two decades. But, of course, nothing lasts forever, including Don Vanderbilt. On September 25, 1990, at his dinner table at home, he suffered a heart attack so massive that he was dead before his big body hit the floor. He was fifty-one years old. A huge crowd showed up for his funeral in nearby Pleasantville, where he was decked out in an open casket, wearing an Eagle badge that the other troop leaders permanently borrowed from one of the kids in the troop.

Seen in the light of prevailing suburban fashions, it's hard not to see him as a somewhat comic figure—a rotund, balding bachelor in a Scoutmaster uniform driving that little yellow Alfa Romeo or big green Cadillac. But Vanderbilt was, at heart, serious in the best sense. Once he gave a copy of Baden-Powell's *Scouting for Boys* to Rick Barns. "To Rick," the inscription read. "My 'father' in Scouting. To he who inspires Reaps everything." And when his former Scouts talk about him today, there's a palpable sense of Don Vanderbilt as a friend, teacher, mentor, and, in his own way, an inspiration as well. Doug Rohde, a Scout who researched Troop 1's history for his Eagle project, had to add an addendum to mark Don's death: "Troop 1 can never be the same, but one can only hope that the memory of Don's optimism and devotion will inspire the troop to continue to forge ahead. Once when asked if he ever regretted not having a family of his own, Don remarked that he had the greatest family a man could want, the Scouts of Troop 1. We have truly lost a great father and a great friend."

4: Gathering of the Tribes

Our first camp-out was no mere routine expedition where the troop camped alone. Instead, it was the Paul Bunyan Camporee, a gathering of troops for which Scouts came from across Westchester County—from Ossining and Tarrytown, from Hawthorne and Yonkers, from mighty Scarsdale, New York's wealthy *Ur* Suburb—to muck through the woods, camp out in the chilly autumn air, and hone their Scouting skills.

The good news was that our Boy Scout Handbook had many pages of helpful information on how to prepare for a camp-out. "Pull on your Scout shirt and lace up your hiking boots. Grab your grub and gear. You're a Scout now, and that means you're going camping!" it began. Subsequent pages reported on where to camp and how many of us should come along. Will there be water? Are campfires allowed? There was a long checklist on the Scout outdoor essentials—pocketknife, first-aid kit, extra clothing, rain gear, canteen or water bottle, flashlight, trail food, matches and fire starters, sun protection, map and compass.

The bad news was that I had not read our Boy Scout Handbook. And despite observing a month or so of Wednesday night meetings where kids worked on their knots and learned what to take and what not to take on a hike, my Scouting skills had not progressed at what anyone would term a dramatic rate. So while Ben had done a reasonable job of packing for himself, I woke up on a distressingly cool and cloudy October morning to realize that the wool socks, extra pair of underwear, fleece, shaving kit, and other necessities I had hurriedly thrown into my bag, a modest external-frame backpack that was a hand-me-down from Ben, were not all that would be necessary.

First, I had forgotten to purchase his cans of Sprite, the sine qua non of outdoor activity in our house. We were, amazingly, almost out of toilet paper, an item that seemed likely to come in handy during twenty-four hours in the great outdoors. And, when I belatedly checked our pack of AA batteries, it turned out we didn't have enough for one flashlight, Maglite, Mini Maglite, or whatever we were bringing along, let alone two.

It was 7:45—*just 45 minutes before we were supposed to meet the troop in the Roaring Brook parking lot!!*—and I had just finished slapping together the requisite peanut-butter-and-jelly and turkey sandwiches when the depths of our lack of preparation caught up with me. So I put the sandwiches aside, tore out of the house, jumped in the car, raced to the nearest A&P, scooped up the Sprites, double-ply toilet paper, and a four-pack of AA batteries, and frantically thrust my money at the sleepy-eyed checkout person. Then, no doubt looking like an insomniac terrorist with a colon problem or a Sprite addiction, I ran to the car and sped back home. Precious seconds were ticking away, and I'd never hear the end of it—*more bad dad points!!*—if I caused us to miss our first camp-out. I finished the lunch and feverishly threw more gear in my backpack. Fat Nalgene jars of water? Check. Insect repellent? Check. Charleston River Dogs baseball cap? Check. We'd been advised that the expedition was leaving at 8:30 sharp, so we hurriedly threw our packs into the back of the station wagon, slammed the doors, and roared off to Roaring Brook Elementary School.

Luckily, we arrived at the parking lot at 8:28. *Two minutes to spare!* Or maybe not. Because, as the seconds ticked toward the time when we would presumably synchronize our watches and head out, it was clear we were no more likely to leave at 8:30 than we were to take the Concorde to the Clear Lake Scout Reservation on the east side of the Hudson Highlands. At 8:30 cars were still pulling up, and the gathering felt more like a pregame tailgate party than a tightly wound commando operation. In fact, as we soon learned, our schedule operated on Troop 1 time, in which 8:30 meant maybe 8:40, perhaps 8:45 or so. Men ambled across the lot in hiking boots, camouflage pants, fancy North Face shells, and old flannel shirts to discuss hiking and camping gear, favored fishing locales, and the weather. Kids jumped out of their parents' cars, vans, and SUVs and started climbing on top of the boulders just off the lot or comparing Magic cards.

Least hurried of all was our ringmaster, Dr. Flank, who had formed half of an odd couple with Don Vanderbilt during Don's tenure as Scoutmaster and then taken over after he died. A Supreme Being with a sense of humor must have picked Dr. Flank to follow Vanderbilt. During Vanderbilt's tenure, Flank had been Mr. Outdoors to Vanderbilt's more sedentary role. At sixty-seven, Flank still got excited about every hike and led the annual High Adventure trip, on which a handful of dads and older, more accomplished kids took off for a week of canoeing in the wilderness of northern Canada. Where Vanderbilt was slow and heavy, Flank was edgy and wiry, about five foot nine with a slender build, an erratically trimmed white beard, and a fringe of white hair surrounding not much on top. Vanderbilt was a political conservative, who supported the war in Vietnam; Flank was a liberal who opposed it. Vanderbilt was a connoisseur of guns and a member of the National Rifle Association; Flank didn't like *axes* let alone guns. Instead of Vanderbilt's sporty Alfa

Romeo or boxy Cadillac, Flank drove a sensible blue Volvo with a "BLAME GE" sticker on the back windshield, in reference to a decades-long controversy about the pollution of the Hudson by PCB contamination from General Electric plants along the river. While Vanderbilt's swearing was a subject of troop lore, no one could remember ever hearing a blue note issue from Flank's mouth. On the other hand, the kids feared and respected him much the way they did Vanderbilt. When angry, he could emit a glare so cold and withering it would turn even the most macho fourteen-year-old into a contrite, apologetic penitent responding with humble "yes sirs" and "no sirs" that must have been summoned up from somewhere deep in his unconscious. And though he had a wife and two grown kids, Flank viewed Troop 1 as a family in much the way Vanderbilt did.

Flank was born in Akron, Ohio, in January 1932. His parents moved to Philadelphia before he was three, then separated, and his father died soon after of what was termed blood poisoning—Flank assumes it was tetanus. Flank grew up taking care of himself by day while his mother worked. He loved the city's enormous Fairmount Park and often played hooky and hung out in the woods all day, figuring he could learn more there than in class. He'd build a fire and cook a meal, observe animals, trees, and plants, then scurry off to the library to figure out what he'd seen. And when his friends joined the Boy Scouts he did too; it struck him as a way to camp and hike and do what he enjoyed doing.

Back then troops were often huge—sixty kids or more—and led by military veterans who inclined toward more marching and drill than he would have liked. But even as an urban Jewish kid, Flank found himself taken both by the outdoors activity and by the—how to put it?—moral code of Scouting. He couldn't claim to be wholly expert in living his life in accordance with the Scout Law. Obedience in particular was never a strong point. But like Vanderbilt, he saw Scouting as something serious and worthy as well as just fun. Flank continued through school, studying chemistry and eventually getting his doctorate after doing his dissertation on "The Geometric Factor in Ethylene Oxidation Over Gold-Silver Alloy Catalysts," but he stayed active in Scouting. In Philadelphia, he helped develop a groundbreaking experiment in Block Scouting, recruiting inner-city residents, often women, to develop troops based around city blocks as a way to avoid conflicts over gang turf. He scouted out sites for troop meetings, showing up with his chemistry set and putting on a magic show to get the kids excited. And when he moved to Chappaqua in 1971 after being hired to work for Union Carbide in Tarrytown, he immediately hooked up with Scouting, first with the district, the administrative office that oversees the local troops, then with his son's Cub Scout pack, and finally with Troop 1. His personal quirks and habits—the maple walking stick he brought on camp-outs, the signature campfire tales of Lenni-Lenape Indian lore, the spectacularly bad collection of Scout couture—was not, perhaps, as eccentric as Vanderbilt's. But when Vanderbilt died, there was no question that Dr. Flank would step in. There was one speed bump about a year after he took over: The School District finally condemned the Scout Hut, which had been deteriorating for years and was deemed an accident waiting to happen. The troop printed up T-shirts and hats with the Hut in the middle of the troop seal, hauled out all its gear, and took to meeting across the street at the school instead.

Now, after ten years as Scoutmaster, Flank had made Troop 1 as undeniably his as it had been Vanderbilt's. This entailed a reverence for nature and the outdoors that bordered on the doctrinal. It reflected an ability to be stern and fear-inducing that was balanced by what some parents saw as a tendency to be overly forgiving of malefactors. Dr. Flank was as likely to help the kids with their chemistry or calculus as with their knots, and when Todd Davis had to do a photography and writing project for school, he did an artful photo essay of Dr. Flank at home and a long verbatim transcript of his wisdom on fishing, Scouting, ethics, and philosophy. Dr. Flank's influence showed up in the troop's studied disregard for many of the traditional trappings and conventions of Scouting, hence the hit-or-miss uniforms. And he clearly cared more about some elements of the Scout Law (trustworthiness and loyalty, for example) than others (obedience and reverence). "This is what happens when an aging peacenik takes over a Boy Scout troop," one of the dads once said—much more approvingly than not, but not 100 percent approvingly either.

So as we milled around, everyone knew what time we would leave—whatever time Dr. Flank wanted us to leave. Finally, he called everyone over and made sure the twenty or so kids had a ride with one of the eight dads making the trip. I ended up driving the Amigos, Barrett, Mark, and Jonah. This seemed like a stroke of luck to me, since the Amigos seemed more like Ben than the football players, would-be weapons specialists, or high school kids, and the forty-minute drive might be a chance for Ben to make some new friends.

The Amigos took the backseat. Ben and I were up front. But instead of mingling, the trio in the backseat immediately launched into a mile-a-minute barrage of Amigo talk. As in the old joke about the comedians' convention where everyone knew the material so well they just yelled out the numbers for the jokes, almost all the talk seemed to flow from previous agenda items in Amigo-land.

So first came much rapturous yakking about the SR-71, an alleged spy plane that apparently flies on the edge of the atmosphere. Then a stretch on whether test pilots still throw up after being whirled around in vomit-inducing machinery once they've done it a few times already. And which amusement park rides are most likely to produce the same result. Then Seinfeld: who would be worse to have as a neighbor, George or Kramer? Then a discussion of the "Like a Rock" song on the Chevy truck commercials ("Now let me get this straight. We're supposed to believe that driving a rock is a good thing?" asked Mark), which segued into the nature of tectonic plates, how fast they can shift and whether we could ever have an earthquake in Westchester County. Other topics included the eternal question: Which is better, Florida or California? And the tragic death of Princess Diana, which remained surprisingly disquieting and sad to them more than two years after it happened—and particularly interesting because it turned out she was the friend of a friend of someone's dad. Jackie Kennedy—Why did they call it Camelot? And did you know her husband was part of the Mafia? Finally, they broke into an impromptu oldies medley— "Lollypop, Lollypop, Oh Lolly Lolly Pop," "Hound Dog," "Barbara Ann."

It was all precociously charming in its way, but I sat there thinking, "Hey, wise guys, what about Scouts being friendly, courteous, and whatever it is they're supposed to be to new kids?" Part of my agenda was to see that Ben made new friends, so I spent the drive wrapped up in paternal paranoia about whether he was feeling left out and pining for his old Amigos, Sam and Michael, from Atlanta. In truth, the only one fretting was me. While I was worrying, he was looking forward to the trip, thinking about gear like the borrowed tent we were bringing along, and enjoying the rapid-fire repartee emanating from the backseat. He was already at home in the troop, even if he wasn't yet friends with the other kids.

But I found that out only later, and as we drove up, the Amigos chattering away like magpies, I began to think about my friend Dan. Even though I had never been a Scout and never wanted to be one, I had a sense of the alleged wonderfulness of Scouting—making friends, learning skills, helping old ladies across busy intersections, knowing which fingers to put up in the Scout sign. This, I was perfectly willing to concede, was a good thing. It just wasn't my thing. Indeed, I was more than willing to see my lifelong Scout-a-phobia as more a failing than a virtue—part of the arrogance of the out-of-touch, northeastern chattering classes, who could never figure out why the country kept electing conservative Republican presidents.

But as I checked around and asked about friends' Scouting experiences, it became clear that though many had fond memories of Scouting, others viewed their days in uniform through a much darker lens. There were those who attended a meeting or two, then got away as soon as their parents said they could. Dan had a more noxious experience, however, and he made it clear that any consideration of the topic should include an acknowledgment of THE DARK SIDE OF SCOUTING. By this, he did not mean the depraved, child-abusing Scoutmasters who periodically popped up in newspaper stories. Instead, he meant the routine jerkiness and cruelty that some kids choose to inflict on others, an experience that formed the heart of his own dismal Scouting career.

"A bit of autobiography is in order here," Dan had said. "Unlike you, I grew up in Nebraska—Scouting's heartland if ever there were one. After a pleasant enough time in Cub Scouts and an apprenticeship in Webelos, I was ready to experience the real thing. I lasted six months as a Tenderfoot. The reason: three Eagle Scouts named Keith, Fred, and Fulgie—out-and-out sadists. Most Boy Scouts, to my knowledge, have a tradition of initiations for new Scouts on the first camp-out—some twisted inheritance from Native American culture, I'm sure. I had to eat garbage that we'd buried in the earth after dinner a few hours earlier, then swallow a bottle of Tabasco sauce.

"The problem was Keith, Fred, and Fulgie were utterly bored after climbing Scouting's last mountain to Eaglehood. They instituted a new practice of initiating each Tenderfoot not just on his first camp-out, but on his first visit to each new campground. Since Nebraska and Iowa have loads of campgrounds, at least a dozen initiations loomed before me. I made it to the third one, which I think entailed pulling down my pants and having my naked bottom stuck with various types of thorns. Appealing to a higher court was not an option. The Scoutmaster believed that K, F, and F could do no wrong. After all, they were Eagles! I decided to pack it in, and have been a left-wing Democrat ever since. But I don't think I'm out of touch—at least with my own past—when I say that fascism, whiffs of the *Hitlerjugend,* and serious psychiatric disorders all need to be addressed in any honest look at Scouting."

Well, the *Hitlerjugend* seemed to be taking things a little too far. But I began to remember that even Ben's sunny foray to Scout camp in Georgia had not been without its moments of modest hazing in the form of towel whipping and illegal wrestling holds inflicted by the big kids on the little ones in their troop. And while the Three Amigos of Troop 1 did not seem to have anything in common with the Three Sadists of the Prairie, this was Ben's first camp-out with Troop 1, so I figured I should be alert for untoward incidents and made a mental note to myself to keep an eye on the hulking high school kids.

Before long, we arrived at the Clear Lake Scout Reservation, a 1,400-acre preserve that used to be the property of a world-famous authority on glaciers named Dr. William B. Osgood Field Jr. We passed a park rangers' house with a great, big wood carving of a bear out front and turned onto a rutted, narrow road now jammed with Dodge vans, rusted-out Chevys, and fancy new Ford Explorers. Compared to Chappaqua, it was relatively light on fancy Acuras and Lexuses and more weighted toward meat-and-potatoes American models with bumper stickers reading "SUPPORT YOUR LOCAL POLICE" or "I'M PROUD OF MY EAGLE SCOUT." We bumped and rattled and bounced our way for a mile or so until we came to a big, open field being used as a parking lot by perhaps sixty cars.

The scene unfolding before us had a manic, tribal quality, one part *Braveheart* and one part *Lord of the Flies*. All it lacked was kids wearing headgear made out of animal hides with antlers and horns sticking out. There were a few pristinely outfitted troops in Scout shirts, pants, hats, and neckerchiefs. But since the weather at night figured to dip near freezing, most kids wore the insignia and coat of arms not of their town or troop but of the booming universe of fashionable outdoors outfitters, of REI and EMS, Eddie Bauer and L.L. Bean, Columbia and Lands' End, Patagonia and, most of all, The North Face, whose overpriced fleeces, coats, jackets, and shells had suddenly become the first items of clothing that Ben expressed a consuming interest in owning. The kids, perhaps 250 in all, spilled into the unpaved parking lot in a great inchoate rush of adolescent testosterone. High school football players with buffed-up chests were throwing a football. Skinny little eleven-year-olds were struggling on rubbery legs with packs as big as they were. There were kids with fresh buzz cuts, kids with great scruffy manes, kids wearing the garb of every sports team ever to play, but particularly those who played anywhere near New York—Yankees and Mets, Giants and Jets, Knicks and Nets, Rangers, Devils and Islanders. Getting out of the car next to us was a creature I did not know existed, a truly radical Scout dude with a shiny nose ring and a half dozen visible body piercings and God knows how many in places I didn't even want to think about. Like a fourth dimension, this was a concept I had trouble wrapping my mind around—*a punk rock Boy Scout!*—as if a mad scientist had tried to cross two utterly dissimilar forms of life, say a zebra and a radish, just to see what kind of unnatural life form he could create.

"Everyone get their packs," Dr. Flank barked. "Make sure you have your lunches and everything you're planning to take with you, because we're not coming back until tomorrow. If you need it, be sure to bring it now."

Ben and I dutifully checked our packs.

"Uh, Dad," Ben said. "Where are the sandwiches?"

"They're in there."

"Where?"

"Somewhere," I said, a bit grumpily. What's the use of having a son to comfort you in your middle age when he can't even find the sandwiches? "Maybe they're in mine."

But, as a few moments of casual rummaging followed by five minutes of frantic digging indisputably proved, they were not in his pack. They were not in my pack. They were not in the car. They were nowhere near the Clear Lake Scout Reservation. They were at home. On the kitchen counter. Where I had left them. As I soon figured out in a doleful accounting of what had transpired when I hurriedly threw our stuff together after making the mad dash to the A&P, I had forgotten the sandwiches. I had remembered the Sprites. I had remembered the four-pack of AA batteries. I had forgotten the double-ply toilet paper. Don't ask how; I just did. All this to dash out in a fevered haste to get there before 8:30 for a trip that did not begin until 8:50 or so. Which was a reminder of Scout Rule #2: AT ALL TIMES, IN ALL ACTIVITIES, NEVER PLAY A GAME UNTIL YOU UNDERSTAND THE RULES.

The whole sequence of events—bratty kids, possible sadistic hazing, pierced-up dude Scouts, incipient food deprivation—was not the optimal beginning for our outing. But, remembering that we had survived our brush with hypothermic death during the canoe trip, I figured we were probably not in imminent peril of starving. And I had skimmed enough of my Scout Manual to at least get a whiff of the can-do positivism we Scouts were supposed to exemplify. We did have various snacks, packed in case we were stranded by a sudden blizzard or lost for days on the trail, so we wouldn't starve. And Scouts had coped with worse disasters, so we pulled on our packs—mine a Camptrails Scout External Frame Pack, Ben's a more elaborate EMS Long Trail ST internal frame pack—and began hiking with the troop toward the campsite about a mile away.

We fell in behind Todd Davis in a clump that included the Amigos, some dads I didn't know, Sam 'n Eric, and a few others. Before long the scuffing of hiking boots on the dirt trail, the gentle clanking of canteens or pots rubbing against packs, and the fraternal greetings to and from other Scouts became rather soothing. As my mood brightened a bit, it did occur to me that I had nothing against hiking, which seemed aerobic and medi- tative enough to qualify in my mind as a worthwhile activity. It was the camping that I could do without.

Our destination turned out to be a clearing in a forest of white and red oak, ash and maple. There was a ring of stones in the middle for a campfire. There were plenty of flat areas in the campsite proper that were suitable for pitching a tent, and everyone set up shop there except for Todd, who was wearing a jaunty shell and an Indiana Jones–style fedora. He took his one- man tent to the farthest reaches of the site and set it up alone, one of the privileges of being a senior Scout and a way to squeeze every sliver of authenticity out of the hike.

Ben and I found a spot and began putting together our tent. This turned out to be harder than expected. We, of course, did not own a tent, an item I had never needed, wanted, or given so much as a passing thought to in my previous forty-eight years on the planet. But it was clear that a tent would come in handy for this particular outing, so I borrowed my friend Jill's trusty REI four-person dome tent. As a noncamper, I thought of tents as old canvas Neanderthal-level shelters on the order of the ones soldiers used, so like a caveman contemplating fire I was quite taken with hers, which was made out of some lightweight synthetic fiber with flexible poles in segments linked by a bungee-like cord in the middle. She had shown us how to put it together, and we had repeated the procedure in our living room at home just to be sure we knew how. But here in the wild, our skills suddenly left us. As the dad, I felt it was my job to be able to do this, but I found myself flummoxed. Which way did the big poles go and which way the small ones? What was the deal with the rain fly anyway, and did we really need it? Was there a ground tarp in there, or were we supposed to bring our own? I was prepared to dispense with the rain fly, the covering on top of the tent that keeps moisture away from the tent proper, until Mr. Johnson walked over and, apprehending the depth of our ignorance, set up the whole tent for us. It took him about two minutes.

"It's a borrowed tent," I said in a lame attempt to convey the idea that we were not total incompetents, only temporarily stymied by this unfamiliar tent. "We haven't used this one before." He gave me a sympathetic but condescending look, making it clear I hadn't fooled anyone.

"You got your bear bag?" Mr. Johnson asked.

"Our WHAT?" I blurted out, in a voice that no doubt betrayed more concern than I wanted to express at that moment.

"Your BEAR BAG," he said twice as loud, the way Americans do in foreign countries when they assume the ignorant locals will understand their English if they just say it loud enough.

"*Holy shit,*" I thought. Now, *this* was serious. I was not unmindful of my lessons from the canoe trip about the relationship between possible peril and the chances of it ever actually transpiring. But even if there was just a small chance of a bear wandering into the campsite, no one had told us anything about trapping him (or her) in a bag. Questions began racing through my mind. What kind of bag could it possibly be? Where did you get one? Did you sneak up behind him and slip the bag over him? Or did you set a trap—presumably with a honey jar—and wait for the bear to wander into the bear bag? What if the bear didn't fit in the bear bag? Shouldn't we have had some bear-bag instruction rather than on-the-job training with one thousand pounds of very hacked-off bear? What if he (or she) got out? What if he (or she) *didn't* get out? Where could you possibly take a bear bag loaded, as it were, for bear? What did loaded for bear mean anyway? Which was the really mean one, the brown bear or the black bear? And would it matter much if you had an angry bear already in your bear bag? Wouldn't either be mean enough?

"You hang it from a tree, Dad," said Ben patiently, realizing the nature if not the extent of my confusion. "You put your food in a bag and hang it from a tree, so the bears can't get it. Bears have a great sense of smell, so you don't want any food in your tent. It's very unlikely there's a bear around, but you do it just in case."

Oh. *That* bear bag. As Emily Litella used to say, "Never mind."

By this point everyone had got their tents up, and it was time for lunch. Of course, we didn't have a real lunch that normal people or children with a responsible parent might eat. But we did have the bag of snacks—Snicker's, sesame-seed sticks, chocolate-chip granola bars—plus our precious Sprites. It had the look of a meal prepared when the inmates were running if not the whole asylum, at least the asylum's kitchen, but we made the best of it as the others broke out their turkey subs, bologna-and-cheese, and tuna on rye. Ben and I ate together, but we were not alone; the outing had already, as if by some form of wilderness osmosis, taken on a comfortable packlike quality reminiscent of our happy armada floating down the Delaware.

Before long the Scouts wandered off to do freelance Scout stuff, which basically meant playing with knives and matches in the woods. Aside from the obvious ones like Todd Davis or Sam 'n Eric, I was still having trouble remembering which Scout was which. The dads, on the other hand, came instantly and rather reassuringly into focus. In fact, as we sat around drinking coffee and waiting for the afternoon's activities to begin, I had the feeling of being in an updated version of a World War II movie, with its assortment of recognizable stock characters updated for contemporary suburbia. So we had our moon-faced Southern Baptist, Dennis, who did market research. We had a Verdi Italian, Vince, who was burly and gregarious and ran an auto repair shop in blue-collar Fleetwood, and a Vivaldi Italian, Robert, who was quiet and precise and taught Italian and Spanish in a middle school in White Plains. We had a divorced dad, Larry, who traveled around the country for one of those high-powered consulting firms and did his best to fly in from Atlanta to attend every camp-out with his son Doug, the video game and computer whiz. Harry, an earnest public relations executive, had grown up in Brooklyn the son of Holocaust survivors. And, of course, we had Dr. Flank, Mr. Toonkel, and Mr. Johnson.

There aren't many places where suburban parents, particularly men, find themselves sitting around with nothing much to do but get to know each other. I guess women do it at the nail salon, the only possible way to explain why anyone would pay perfectly good money to sit around while someone paints your nails the color of a Tootsie Roll Pop. So it felt almost illicit to be sitting around in the middle of the day, with no work and no errands, no fix-it jobs to flub, no garbage to take out or kids to drive or finances to ponder or dog to walk, no light bulbs or hamburger meat or school supplies to buy. I fell in with Vince, whose son was the first half of Sam 'n Eric. Vince had an unaffected, heavy-duty Bronx accent and a funny, laconic manner. He had been born in Muro Lucano, a hill town in south central Italy that dates back to the ninth century, and had come to America—to the Bronx's version of Little Italy around Arthur Avenue—when he was eight. He had moved his family to Chappaqua in 1991 and often wondered if he had made the right decision—the big shot, big-head syndrome in town being a bit much for his tastes. "A friend of mine who lives in Goldens Bridge always says to me, 'What kind of a town you living in, Vince?'" he said. "'When the train stops in Chappaqua, you see them get on like they own the damn thing. The atmosphere changes as soon as they get on, all tense and acting like they're entitled to everything. What are you doing there?' And to tell you the truth, sometimes I'm not sure."

It would have been nice to continue to drift off into our suburban version of *Sergeant York,* but soon Dr. Flank started rounding up the boys for the main focus of the trip, a marathon day of Scouting activities. Each patrol was given a name—Scorpions, Pathfinders, Rebels, Seals, Wolverines, Flaming Arrows, Kings, Road Runners, Eagles—and a list of seventeen stations of the cross we were supposed to visit to witness or perform some Scouting skill. Dr. Flank stressed that each patrol would be judged on how well it did and the scores added up at the end of the day.

"What do we get if we win?" asked Sam hopefully.

"You get a ribbon or patch," Dr. Flank said.

Sam looked disappointed, but even I knew that the only way to get anything better than a ribbon or a patch was to save someone's life, in which case you got the gold Honor Medal, a round medal hanging from a blood-red field. For almost everything else, you got a ribbon or a patch. If you passed basket weaving, famous as the easiest merit badge, you got one. If you mastered snorkeling or completed the mile swim, you got one. If you obeyed the tenets of no-trace camping, if you camped outdoors in below-freezing temperatures, if you showed organ donor awareness, or if you just showed up for the Paul Bunyan Camporee, you got one.

We divided up into our patrols and headed back down the dirt road to the staging area. The first station we reached was manned by a burly man in full Scout regalia. Arrayed around him, ominously, were dozens of tough strands of rope. He looked at the kids with a skeptical appraising eye. "Who knows how to do the timber hitch?" he asked. Right out of the box, we had come to the quintessential test of our Scouting skills—knot tying. As knots go, the timber hitch was pretty elementary. Not so elementary, of course, that I had any idea how to do it, but elementary enough that Scouts past the level of Second Class— the step past Tenderfoot—probably did.

Todd Davis, of course, stepped forward.

"OK," the man asked. "What do we use a timber hitch for?"

"To drag a log across the ground," Todd replied.

"And what does a hitch do?"

"It's a knot that ties a rope to an object."

"Can you show us how to do it?"

In about five seconds Todd had passed the end of the rope around the log and looped the short end around the standing part of the rope. He wrapped the end around itself three or four more times and tightened the hitch against the log. Then he manfully dragged the log ten or fifteen feet to show that it worked. The others, or at least the ones who knew how to do it, stepped forward and repeated Todd's feat.

Next, showing that the Paul Bunyan business was not just for effect, came the two-person saw, in which two kids sawing together cut their way through a log. Next, a dad talked about his cameras and lenses and showed off photos. There was a

Civil War reenactor, a guy in a tattered Union uniform heating up his coffee out of a vintage Civil War–era kettle, showing off his Enfield rifle, and passing around his .58-caliber lead mini balls. What exactly he had to do with Scouting wasn't completely clear, but he rattled on in the present tense like a happy psychotic, allowing how General Sheridan was doing this and General Hood was doing that, and the Rebels weren't going to be able to hold on much longer. He had a supply of hardtack, which he offered to the kids. It wasn't much, but it was better than our lunch had been. Next was archery, where each kid got to shoot five arrows in the vague direction of the target, and then the inevitable compass course, with much incomprehensible talk about true north, magnetic north, and declination.

Then came the all-important flapjack flip. A beefy guy with a beard and a red flannel shirt—he'd obviously taken this Paul Bunyan stuff to heart—greeted us with a suspiciously cheery "Hi, guys." The kids responded with a wary "Yo." On a long wooden table were two thick copper skillets and a stack of pancakes that appeared to be the consistency of hockey pucks.

"How many of you have ever flipped flapjacks?" he asked, in a tone of voice that suggested a query more on the order of "How many of you would like to ride dirtbikes down the Grand Canyon?"

There were a few halfhearted grunts.

"Well," he said, oblivious to the lukewarm responses, "that's what we're going to do today." He picked up his skillet and plopped one of the ossified pancakes in the pan, where it landed like a lead ball on a concrete floor. It would have made the hardtack taste like filet mignon. With a graceful flip of the wrist, he sent the pancake gently skyward, where it turned over twice and landed with a metallic thud flat in the pan. Cirque de Soleil it was not, but the kids each took their turn trying to prove their flapjack competence. It struck me as just about the dopiest exercise in perfecting useless skills I had ever witnessed. Indeed, the whole thing had a good-hearted but makeshift quality. That, I was coming to realize, was Scouting. We increasingly fork over cash for our kids' pleasures—video games, rented movies, Game Boys. Or we pay professionals to do things for them. If they're fat, they get personal trainers. If they're promising athletes, they get their own coach. If they're problematic students, they get a tutor. There are people in Westchester County who are paid to teach your kid how to ride his bicycle. Scouting, by comparison, is largely run by volunteers who do it for various benign, charitable, inscrutable, or suspect reasons. Sometimes it seems admirable, sometimes it seems half-assed. But more often than not it feels like something from another time.

We dutifully finished the last few events: another log pull, a relay race, and an exhibition of chain-saw wizardry—the last definitely a look-but-don't-touch affair. But by this point, we were all ready to trudge back to the campsite. Dr. Flank had a fire going, and we wasted no time getting ready for dinner. Outdoors cooking can be quite an art, and Dr. Flank's voluminous files contained recipes for sweet-and-sour spareribs, chicken, blueberry cobbler, fried rice, and tomato pepper steak. His personal favorite was eggplant in hoisin sauce. But, of course, it can be pretty elemental too, as in the traditional Scout one-pot stew, which exemplified the main cooking style for the evening.

This was a patrol cooking affair, which meant each patrol brought what it needed to cook for its six or eight Scouts and whatever dads needed to be fed as well. Ben's group played it pretty straight. They boiled their water, then put in two three-ounce packages of America's Choice Oriental Style Ramen Noodle Soup. When that softened and turned noodlelike, they dropped in ample chunks of precooked chicken and a package of Birds Eye frozen vegetables. The scene had a slightly Macbethean quality, with the Scouts, wooden ladles in hand, plopping ingredients into the murky brew, but the concoction itself seemed more innocent than not. The same could not be said for the meal made by the patrol cooking nearby. They began with the water and the Ramen noodles and some ground beef, which seemed enough for a respectable stew. But sometimes it's important to go the extra mile, so they added some oatmeal to give it a little texture, then some Craisins to give it that indefinable wilderness *je ne sais quoi*. A little beef stock. Some of Elliot's beef jerky to give it a little flavor. Some salt. Some pepper. A bay leaf. Some tomato sauce. A few garlic breadcrumbs. Finally it was deemed to be ready, and they ladled it out onto plastic plates. It had the mottled look of something meant to be served in another form—freeze dried for astronaut food or ground up and hardened like a vitamin pill. Tom, the one who was twelve going on sixteen, took the first taste and not surprisingly pronounced it "awesome." Like a Greek chorus, the other diners pronounced themselves equally pleased. We all ate like happy cavemen. After dinner there was coffee for the grownups and Chips Ahoy! and other cookies for the whole crew.

We had one more activity, the campfire, where all the troops would gather in one grand, pan-Westchester affair. We hiked toward the site, flashlights beaming bouncing darts of light through the darkness. Scouts seemed to pop out of every hill and gully, in groups of two or three or whole tribes marching through the night, like a gallant boy army gathering for some virtuous crusade. (Of course, it could have been a dubious gang of boy thugs bent on mayhem, but they were Scouts, so I was willing to give them the benefit of the doubt.) We reached an amphitheater carved into a clearing with a semicircle of logs used as seats. They were filled with Scouts facing a huge unlit pyre of thoroughly combustible matter—layers of kindling twigs on the bottom, then modest branches and tree limbs, then big, stout logs, all stacked in a neat pyramid at least four feet high. Everyone was quiet and orderly until all the seats filled up.

Then the chant began—"Light the fire. Light the fire. Light the fire."—first a few kids, then, it seemed, everyone, louder and louder. Now we were really getting to *Lord of the Flies* terrain. Could "Kill the pig, cut his throat, spill his blood" be too far behind? Luckily, two older Scouts finally stepped forward and did the deed. Within minutes, the scene was lit by an enormous bonfire that lit up the sky like a blazing torch. A great plume of yellow flame crackled into the night and above that burning embers climbed upward into the black sky like fiery bugs, the last ones rising fifteen feet above the fire until they finally died out. We all watched the dancing flame and swirling embers in total silence for five or ten minutes, until one of the senior Scouts who had lit the bonfire stepped in front of it. He leaned forward from the waist, hands on both knees.

"You having a good time?" he hollered.

"Yeah," we hollered back.

"I CAN'T HEAR YOU!" he yelled in the inevitable attack of hearing impairment that has accompanied every such oration in history. "YOU HAVING A GOOD TIME?"

"YEAH," we yelled a little louder.

"Awright, that's more like it. We all had a great day. I saw a lot of great Scout spirit out there. Now we've got a great campfire planned, so let's get going."

Once upon a time, this might have meant an old-fashioned sing-along. Scout songbooks from the 1960s included 150 sing-along favorites divided into Opening Songs ("Hail, Hail the Gang's All Here," "How Do You Do?"), Scouting Spirit ("I'm Happy When I'm Hiking," "There's Something About a Boy Scout,"), Patriotic Songs, Action Songs, Quiet Songs, Worship Songs (from "Onward Christian Soldiers" to "Sholom A'ley-chem"), and Closing Songs ("Auld Lang Syne," "Taps"). Today's songbook isn't that much different, but it's hard to imagine too many fourteen-year-olds who want to sit around the campfire singing "If You're Happy and You Know It Clap Your Hands," "Waltzing Matilda," or "Sweetly Sings the Donkey."

Still, the program that ensued did have a remarkably timeless quality. There were skits, most having to do with familiar body odors that follow an imperfectly digested meal, unsightly females, or misunderstandings involving a pickle. Lucky Scouts were recruited to the bonfire to tackle tongue-twisting and memory tricks, the main one requiring the Scout to remember and recite a list of ten items of increasing obscurity and length. I got about as far as "one fat hen, a couple of ducks, and three frigidy frogs" and then lost track.

One skit called for a bunch of kids to act out the parts of a story—a nervous woman, a concerned cop, and a chimpanzee. One kid, a boy of about twelve or thirteen with short dark hair, wearing a dark blue fleece and blue jeans, stood out. His job was to play a chimpanzee. Each time his cue came up, the boy dashed around the fire, the mammoth bonfire serving as a crackling, flickering backdrop. He scurried around making snuffling chimplike sounds, swinging his arms just so, head hunched down, chest out, legs taking clumsy, bow-legged, brisk chimplike strides. The other boys played their parts with a hammy kind of enthusiasm, but this kid stood out to the point I looked forward to his recurring role to see if he could keep up the same primeval level of energy and authenticity, which he invariably did. I wasn't sure what was so striking about the kid until I thought back to the Polo Boy. Who knows? Maybe this kid went home and sat slack-jawed by the television listening to Marilyn Manson on headphones and watching *South Park* all night. But, for this moment at least, he was the un–Polo Boy. There was not a sliver of attitude, no ironic distance, no sense of superior cool, just primal, unadulterated boyhood energy. He seemed everything the Polo Boy's contrived, antique bat was supposed to denote but wasn't—like a kid who had never seen a computer or a video game or a mall and was working from a pre-Microsoft, pre-Napster, pre-Britney, pre-*Simpsons* operating system. I tried to think of a group other than Boy Scouts whose goal was to teach that kid the same kind of values. I couldn't think of any.

The campfire was winding down. We sang a song or two, then stood and linked arms as a kid with a bugle played "Taps." We—or at least the Scouts who knew them—sang the words:

> Day is done, gone the sun;
> From the lake, from the hills, from the sky;
> All is well, safely rest,
> God is nigh.

> Fading light dims the sight;
> And a star gems the sky,
> Gleaming bright;
> From afar, drawing nigh,
> Falls the night.

Somehow my own ironic distance was whittled away as well. We all walked quiet as mice back to our campsites. Ben and I found our tent, opened our sleeping bags, and crawled in. Lying on the plastic mat underneath the sleeping bag wasn't much different from sleeping on cement, and the sweaters I fluffed up under my head to serve as a pillow didn't help. Outside the temperature was dipping below 40. The night was thick with alien noises: hooting owls, kids conspiring in hushed tones, the crackle and crunch of unknown footsteps on dry leaves. It was, in short, all the discomfort and senseless deprivation I had expected. But, that said, inside the tent things were warm and pleasantly cocoonlike. It was a comfortable, intimate thing to be alone, just the two of us, in this strange tent in the woods. Ben took out his flashlight and started to read a Tom Clancy book he'd already read three times, part of his ritual before going to sleep.

"Not too long, OK?" I said. "It's getting late."

"Ten minutes," he replied.

"OK. Ten minutes max."

Maybe it was ten or maybe it was twenty or maybe it was an hour or two. You couldn't have known by me. Long before he finished, I was out like a block of cement, snoring the sleep of the weary dead blissfully into the night.

5: The Hero of Mafeking

Our band of merry adventurers had many fathers, both the troop leaders of the past and the men who almost a century ago gave rise to what has become the biggest voluntary youth movement in history. But the most important figure in Scouting's history was an astoundingly complex man—self-knowing and self-deceiving, ruggedly masculine and sexually ambiguous, a hero of war who saw himself as a man of peace, an imperialist and a universalist—who was one of the most celebrated figures of his time and now is all but forgotten outside of Great Britain.

Born in 1857, Lord Robert Baden-Powell became one of Britain's most admired heroes when his badly outnumbered garrison held off a much larger army of Boers for seven months at Mafeking in South Africa from October 1899 to May 1900. The siege, relentlessly chronicled in the British press, made him a national celebrity. Out of that celebrity he was able to fashion a movement to train boys in outdoor skills and traditional values that swept the nation, and swiftly spread to America and most of the rest of the world.

But rather than a clear-cut exemplar of Edwardian virtue, Baden-Powell was a figure of tantalizing eccentricities and contradictions. While one of the most famous men in Britain, he headed the Boy Scouts for three decades for no pay other than expenses. He rose at five each morning after sleeping alone on his balcony, did five minutes of exercise, peeled himself an apple, did two hours of writing, and at 7:30 took a cold bath, always drying himself with a stiff, partially starched towel. He much preferred what he called "the religion of the woods" to any organized variety, which made him very unpopular with many churchmen. He was called "the inspired mystic of Scouting," and saw himself more as a moral leader than a military one. He was Knight Commander of the Order of the Bath, recipient of the Jubilee Medal and some thirty-seven other medals, decorations, and orders and six honorary doctorates, founder of the Boy Scouts, and Chief Scout of the World.

He also spent most of his life obsessed by a younger soldier he invariably called "the Boy." The two lived together in shared bungalows and exchanged presents and ardent letters when they were apart. When the Boy was held prisoner during the siege of Mafeking, Baden-Powell sent him under flags of truce cocoa, wine, a soft mattress, hairbrushes, books, mosquito curtains, cologne, soup, lemonade, stamps, stationery, and money. Baden-Powell was a talented actor who loved playing women's roles and making his own dresses, and he designed embroidery patterns for regimental wives. Even in the veldt, he insisted on bathing every day with scented soap. Whenever possible, he sought out the local executioner when he traveled. He loved visiting battlefields of all kinds and recording bizarre forms of death, ranging, as one biographer put it, "from a novel form of strangulation in Tunisia, to the fate of a workman who fell down one of the steep metal water-collecting slopes on Gibraltar and burst into flames with the friction." He credited all his success to his mother.

Baden-Powell married in 1912 at the age of fifty-five, and after dispensing with the messy unpleasantness of sex achieved a warm, comradely union with the woman who became his partner in Scouting. Describing in his autobiography the importance of picking the right guide for a Scouting expedition in hostile territory, he wrote: "The selection is one that cannot be lightly made. It is as bad as choosing a horse—or a wife. There is a lot depending on it."

A lot of what people think of the Boy Scouts depends on how they read Baden-Powell, who either sums up the glories of a truly inspired movement for human betterment or reflects its shallowness and hypocrisy. It's not hard to find both views. One worshipful biography, published at the peak of Baden-Powell's fame in 1924, begins:

> In a quiet street, on the north side of Hyde Park, that blessed breathing space of London babies and London birds, was born on the 22nd of February 1857, a baby whose future career was destined to have perhaps more widely reaching effect than that of any man since the Founder of Christianity. No "star of the east" heralded his coming. There was nothing miraculous about his birth and babyhood; yet there are literally millions of people in the world today who are the better for Robert Baden-Powell having been born.

At the other extreme is a 1984 biography by a Columbia University professor, Michael Rosenthal, which casts Baden-Powell as little more than a reflection of the evils of British imperialism. Baden-Powell, Rosenthal stresses, served a crown that subjected "more than 345 million people to the will of Her Majesty's government by threat of force, justified through the moral imperative to bring the blessings of peace and justice to people in need of guidance." And his biggest service to the crown, Rosenthal concludes, was to hatch "an obedience-engendering scheme" whose aim was to "produce efficient recruits for the empire for generations to come." In Rosenthal's eyes, Baden-Powell was a racist and anti-Semite, soft on fascism, who created a cold "character factory" while others tried to build more genuinely humanistic youth movements. One can feel cool derision on every page.

Robert Stephenson Smyth Powell, or Stephe for short, was the eighth of ten children born to Henrietta Grace Powell and the Reverend Baden-Powell, Savilian Professor of Geometry at Oxford. Before his birth his mother had lost three children, which left seven years between Robert and the next youngest sibling. And three years after his birth, his father died suddenly. The result was an extraordinary bond between mother and son. He wrote her two thousand letters over the course of his life, kept elaborate illustrated diaries and notebooks to share with her, and turned motherhood into almost an object of worship. And as he developed into a precocious, imaginative child, a natural actor and a talented artist, a complicated dynamic began to play out. On the one hand, he was utterly devoted to and obsessed with pleasing his mother. On the other, he was struggling to develop a male identity without any father to emulate. The two drives coalesced into his life's work: Baden-Powell became one of the most celebrated and admired men in England by forming an organization built around teaching boys how to become men.

In 1870 he was sent off on a scholarship to Charterhouse, one of the elite English public schools that produced England's leaders. He proved an indifferent student. In 1876 he failed the examination for a university education at Balliol and then at Christ Church. Instead, he did what many others of his class did: He joined the British Army in search of adventure.

At the time, the glory days of Empire, the military was a natural route to advancement, and Baden-Powell took to it with gusto, entertaining his fellow soldiers with plays from his Charterhouse days. He spent two years in India and Afghanistan, came back to England, then returned to Afghanistan, where he perfected the odd balance of jocular stagecraft and imperial gravity that he maintained throughout his military career. On the one hand were mayhem, hangings, and floggings of recalcitrant Indians and Afghans; on the other was the thirteen Hussars mounting a production of *The Pirates of Penzance,* with swords planted in the dirt to mark off the stage and revolvers loaded just in case.

In Afghanistan, Baden-Powell threw himself into two things. The first was the theater—he organized four plays in two months. The second was a friendship with a twenty-year-old officer named Kenneth McLaren, who cut such a striking figure as the female lead in two productions that one subordinate noted: "One of our fellows made a very pretty girl." Their regiment moved to Muttra, where Baden-Powell and McLaren took a bungalow together and where for three years, Baden-Powell's letters home were dominated by one or another diverting snippet about "the Boy." He would praise his friend's fit body and recount a trip to the palace of the Maharaj of Deng, where the two shared a magnificent room and the Boy read a novel to him as they lazed in bed until breakfast time. When the Boy went on leave to Kashmir, Baden-Powell's sunny mood turned to "beastly melancholy," and he wrote home asking his mother to purchase "a nice little present for the Boy—I think a pair of ivory brushes—good ones with M. McL. on the back would be rather nailing." For more than twenty years, they continued a relationship that led Baden-Powell to call McLaren "my best friend in the world."

It is, of course, dangerous to impose one era's values and standards of conduct on another. Intense, even passionate, relationships between men were often celebrated in the nineteenth century, with no sense that the relationship was homosexual. And despite much scholarly picking and digging, there is no real evidence that the relationship between Baden-Powell and

McLaren was ever a physical one. But Tim Jeal, the British biographer whose *The Boy-Man: The Life of Lord Baden-Powell* is the best Baden-Powell biography to date, says that the older man's passionate relationship with McLaren was certainly consistent with the predilections he expressed in his life. He delighted in male nudity, while he found female nudity distasteful and recoiled at overtly sexual women. He enjoyed looking at pictures of naked boys with a friend from Charterhouse. When he finally married late in life, he began to experience agonizing headaches, which disappeared when he took to sleeping outside on the balcony instead of with his wife. It was a different time, with different strictures, but even Jeal, who is inclined to champion Baden-Powell, concludes that the evidence points "inexorably" to the conclusion he was a repressed homosexual.

Baden-Powell's unit did not see any combat until 1896 in Africa. And his military training left him enamored less with warfare itself than with the more cerebral life of the scouts, the wily outriders who became the eyes and ears of the army. Through them, he became a student of what he called "the science of woodcraft"—how to move invisibly through enemy territory, learning the tracks of animals; how to live off the land and read the small details of the natural life of the veldt. And over time, the self-taught virtues of the African tribesmen, the teamwork of the army, the ability to adapt to harsh terrains, and the character-building attributes of the outdoor life began to come together in his mind as something between a discipline and a faith.

Baden-Powell had had some success thus far—at forty, he had become the youngest colonel in the British Army. Still, his career was moving along in a rather conventional path until a combination of fate, guile, pluck, and chance made him a national hero. In 1899 he was sent to South Africa, where relations were deteriorating by the day between the modest British forces stationed there and the Boer farmers hoping to win their independence in a land with the world's richest gold reefs. Baden-Powell was dispatched with the imprecise mission of diverting and engaging some five thousand to six thousand Boers until more British armies could arrive.

His command took him to the small tin-roofed trading town of Mafeking—the name means "Place of Stones"—on a sun-baked rise surrounded by a treeless veldt about 650 miles north of Cape Town. There his force of about two thousand men, most of them untrained, was soon besieged by some six thousand Boers, who were superior fighters and horsemen. It's a measure of how charged Baden-Powell's legacy is that historians are still battling over most elements of the siege, including whether Baden-Powell was there out of necessity or thanks to a tactical error or a carefully staged show of heroism. What is clear is that Baden-Powell, the most theatrical of soldiers, turned Mafeking into a dramatic tour de force, and at the end of 217 days of siege, from October 13, 1899, to May 17, 1900, when relief arrived and the Boers skulked away, he had emerged as one of Britain's greatest war heroes.

Baden-Powell's critics ascribe his sudden elevation to national celebrity to his shrewd instinct for showmanship and, as Rosenthal put it, "a supporting cast of stolid, rather immobile Boers reluctant to take much initiative." His supporters say he survived a truly perilous situation by craft and cunning, and that his fame reflected the perfect match between a romantic military victory and a nation that was ripe for a stirring victory and new hero. But whatever the case, Baden-Powell performed like a man determined to turn his big moment into a Gilbert and Sullivan operetta. He'd sit calmly dictating messages in the market square, like the embodiment of British pluck, as enemy shells exploded around him. "Four hours bombardment; one dog killed," went one published in British newspapers. He went on nocturnal scouting missions behind enemy lines on his own. And, as the siege dragged on, he sponsored regular entertainments of concerts and plays, from Hottentot dances to what he called his "World Wide Show" of singing and dancing and playing the fool. Transmitted by reporters and his own messages sent through enemy lines, every triumph, show of moxie, and display of comic drollery was played up in the papers back home and made his exploits a national sensation.

One aspect of his performance that was not much mentioned was his treatment of the Africans in Mafeking and under his command. Beginning with Thomas Pakenham in 1979, some historians have argued that Baden-Powell's rationing of food so egregiously favored whites over blacks that it amounted to something close to mass murder. It is a complicated discussion, based on different accounts of just what food was available at what time to which African populations, some under his control, some not. Jeal is persuasive in arguing that while Baden-Powell clearly favored whites over blacks in food distribution, the most critical accounts mischaracterized the food available to blacks and distorted the reports made at the time. Still, neither side portrays Baden-Powell in a favorable light, and even Jeal said he was scandalously ungenerous and deceptive in not giving credit to African soldiers and officers in the defense of Mafeking.

It is still a raw issue. In 1999 just before South Africa was scheduled to host the World Scout Conference, which brings together about one thousand delegates from more than 150 countries and territories, African tribal leaders filed a $5.9 million petition with the British government. The Baralong-Boora-Tshidi Tribal Authority said that black Africans were entitled to compensation for damages and for promises Baden-Powell made but never kept. And if many saw a hero, others, even at the time, were not so sure: "He seems to close every argument with a snap," wrote Angus Hamilton of the *Times* of London, "as though the steel manacles of his ambition, had checkmated the emotion of the man in the instincts of the soldier."

Baden-Powell partly benefited from an accident of timing: Britain had just undergone a string of imperial reversals around the world, and news of the undermanned garrison holding out against superior forces played perfectly to the popular mood. It set off a celebration so raucous that the word *maffick* entered the language as a verb, defined by Webster's as "to celebrate with boisterous rejoicing and hilarious behavior." At least nineteen musical pieces were composed in his honor, with titles like "The Baden-Powell Schottische" and "The Hero of Mafeking Valse."

There was a final element of Mafeking that came to loom large in Baden-Powell's life. It did not seem important at the time; he did not even make mention of it in his reports on the siege. But during the siege, the defenders of Mafeking at times enlisted the services of the youths of the town. The boys in question were part of the local cadet corps, something of a military auxiliary. Baden-Powell later said they were trained in scouting, which was apparently not true. They were under the command of two other officers, not him. But in a garrison that never had enough men to do all the jobs they had come in handy, carrying messages, doing odd jobs, and thus freeing the adults to serve as riflemen in the trenches. And when Baden-Powell in 1908 published *Scouting for Boys,* his first tale was of the boy scouts of Mafeking, some of whom rode bicycles under enemy bombardment to deliver letters to distant forts in a town five miles away. He asked his young readers if they would be able to be as heroic. "I am sure you would—although probably you wouldn't much like doing it," he wrote. And then he ended his Camp Fire Yarn No. 1 with the following thought: "But you need not have a war in order to be useful as a scout. As a peace scout there is lots for you to do—any day, wherever you may be."

Of course, one of the perils of heroism and celebrity is coming up with a second act. In March 1903 Baden-Powell returned to England as Inspector General of the Cavalry. His job was to inspect cavalry regiments around the world and rethink the role of the cavalry in the future. It was a perfectly respectable post and one consistent with a successful life as a military officer. But for the thirty-seven years since he had left for India as a nineteen-year-old, he had spent almost all his time abroad in far-flung, adventurous locales. Now, the hero of Mafeking was taking a desk job and moving back in with his mother. It turned out to be something of a comedown. His tour was not viewed as a great success, and his mother was pressuring him to finally find a bride, something he attempted without great enthusiasm.

But he did find something else to get enthusiastic about. As a result of his celebrity, Baden-Powell was often asked to inspect cadet corps and organizations involved with the training of youths. It was the right time: Military reversals in the nineteenth century had set in motion a national hysteria about Britain's incipient decline and industrialization, and the movement of boys from the countryside to the city exacerbated the fears. Anxiety about national decline and the deterioration of the nation's youth is a common note in modern life. But in England, a tiny island of forty million people in 1900 trying to control an empire of 11.5 million square miles and 345 million people, the anxiety had particular sociopolitical throw weight. Baden-Powell, too, worried about the deterioration of the nation's moral fiber and the spread of "loafers and wasters," typically working-class lads who hung out on street corners, drank and smoked, gambled and watched sports instead of playing them, and grew thin and pale. He was also suspicious of public schoolboys, who spent all their time buried in books rather than out in the fresh air. Slowly, Baden-Powell came to see a new challenge—a national crusade to inspire, seduce, and invigorate the boys of Britain.

At that time there was a modest movement of Boys' Brigades, quasi-military units that mixed Christianity, military drill, and social uplift into a rather dour form of character training. Asked in April 1904 to review the brigades, Baden-Powell offered muted praise. The boys looked impressive and seemed proud of what they were doing, he said. But, he added, the movement would have grown faster "if the work really appealed to the boys." And how to make that work more appealing? He suggested scouting, the discipline of nature, woodcraft, military intelligence, and the understanding of the outdoors. He had written about this discipline already in a book entitled *Aids to Scouting for N.C.O.'s and Men,* which he published in 1898. After Mafeking, it became an enormous bestseller.

Baden-Powell wasn't quite sure how to create what he came to call his "Boy Scout Scheme." But he took the first serious step in 1907, when he (with the help of the Boy and two other associates) held a camp for twenty-two boys of all social classes on Brownsea Island off England. Baden-Powell taught the boys camping and scouting skills and regaled them around the campfire with tales of battling Zulus and tracking wild lions. "Eeengonyama—gonyama," the Great Man would sing around the campfire. "Invooboo. Yah bo. Invooboo," they would sing back. It meant, more or less, "He is a lion! Yes! He is better than that; he is a hippopotamus." The boys were organized into patrols, roused each morning by a koodoo horn that Baden-Powell had captured in Africa, and spent their days tracking animals, playing games in the woods, and cooking their own food. In the days before radio, when an adventure might be a picnic in the country or a frolic in a grimy urban park, to camp on an island with the Hero of Mafeking must have been exciting beyond belief.

At the same time, prodded by the newspaper tycoon and promoter C. Arthur Pearson, Baden-Powell was working to adapt his *Aids to Scouting* for boys. The result, *Scouting for Boys,* was a sensation. Pearson, who made most of the money on it, sent Baden-Powell on an extended lecture tour, helped come up with the name "Boy Scouts" (wisely rejecting Baden-Powell's own suggestion of "Imperial Scouts"), and cooked up a weekly newsletter, "The Scout." Unofficial patrols began sprouting immediately.

Pearson, with the instincts of a shark, saw a gold mine in the making. When he realized how many patrols had formed on their own, he helped Baden-Powell put together a formal Scouting organization. Pearson earned nearly all the profits from the book and newsletter; all Baden-Powell got was a one-room office and Pearson's help in getting the organization going, the ability to use "The Scout" to communicate with his boys, and a modest share of royalties, all of which went to getting the Boy Scouts organization off the ground. As a businessman, the Hero of Mafeking was either uninterested or clueless.

Still, if the plan could not have been worse for him financially, it made Scouting an instant sensation. Almost on its own, the movement spread across England, and in 1910 Baden-Powell quit the army to work full time on Scouting. By the end of the year, there were more than 100,000 Scouts in Great Britain.

Exactly what kind of an organization he wanted to create is still the subject of much debate. When he viewed the Boys' Brigades back in 1904, Baden-Powell wrote to recommend Scout training, saying it would help the boys develop their minds by becoming more observant. And he concluded: "The results would not only sharpen the wits of the Boy, but would also make him quick to read character and feelings, and thus help him to be a better sympathiser with his fellow-men."

It was Baden-Powell's first reference to Scout training in boys, and in some ways it got to the heart of an argument that still rages. Was he advocating Scouting as part of a quasi-military scheme, which was devoted to maintaining Britain's social status quo? Or were the humanistic, benign themes of his remarks proof that Scouting was really about helping boys, not just helping to train them to defend the Empire?

Rosenthal, not surprisingly, sees Scouting as thoroughly about the former. As exhibit A, he cites a passage in Baden-Powell's writing entitled "Be a Brick":

> This means you should remember that being one fellow among many others, you are like one brick among many others in the wall of a home. If you are discontented with your place or with your neighbours or if you are a rotten brick, you are no good to the wall. We are all Britons, and it is our duty each to play in his place and help his neighbours. Then we shall remain strong and united, and then there will be no fear of the whole building—namely our great Empire—falling down because of rotten bricks in the wall.

There are other exhibits, particularly a letter Baden-Powell published December 22, 1906, in the *Eton College Chronicle*. Citing the military threats to England, it quite explicitly lays out a plan to form clumps of boys who would be taught patriotism and honor; be trained to scout, aim and shoot miniature rifles, drill, and skirmish; and be prepared to defend England, if necessary.

But Baden-Powell also wrote, "A boy should take his own line rather than be carried along by herd persuasion." In his view, the outdoor life created not just self-sufficient boys, but generous and chivalrous ones—boys who became "gentle men" because of their love of the outdoors. And, as Jeal noted, in many of his lists of the elements that make up an admirable character, intelligence and individuality precede loyalty and self-discipline. Maria Montessori, the advocate of creative education, said Scouting freed children "from the narrow limits to which they had been confined."

Commenting on the Scout uniform, Baden-Powell took pains to say it was an amalgam of practical elements he had observed in his years in the wild and designed to be something that all boys could wear on an equal basis. "There was nothing military about it," he wrote. "It was designed to be the most practical, cheap and comfortable dress for camping and hiking and in no way copied from a soldier's kit." He had little or no use for marching and formal parades, and when a great rally was scheduled in 1911 to show off Baden-Powell's new organization to King George V, the grand moment was not a show of crisp military marching and drill but an inspired bit of boy theater. Baden-Powell, mounted on a great black horse, blew his whistle, and suddenly thirty thousand roaring boys began running toward the king's reviewing area. As one witness described it: "The thirty thousand closed in on the King as a great foaming wave, and it seemed that nothing would stop it; the spectators trembled lest the King should be enveloped. But, at a line, which none but the Scouts knew, the wave stopped dead, as if suddenly frozen—the shouting and the tumult died, and then—silence."

John Hargrave, one of Baden-Powell's most charismatic lieutenants, saw him not as a dour, obedience-engendering bricklayer, but the opposite—a Huck Finn, a backwoods urchin, a "Boy-Poltergeist" allowing thousands of boys to make their escape from "a dreary, half-dead commercialized and deadly dull civilization."

And rather than a cold, quasi-military document, Baden-Powell's *Scouting for Boys* is a rich stew of whimsy and practical advice, patriotism and positive thinking, full of alluring tales from Kipling and Zulu tribesmen, from the Matabele War in

Africa and Scott's last expedition to the South Pole. It begins with the Scout Promise ("On my honour I promise that I will do my best—To do my duty to God, and to Queen, To help other people at all times, To obey the Scout Law") and an early version of the Scout Law, ten items phrased in terms of what a Scout should do, instead of what he should not:

A Scout's honour is to be trusted.

A Scout is loyal to the Queen, his country, his parents, his employers and those under him.

A Scout's duty is to be useful and to help others.

A Scout is a friend to all and a brother to every other Scout.

A Scout is courteous.

A Scout is a friend to animals.

A Scout obeys orders of his parents, Patrol Leader, or Scoutmaster without question.

A Scout smiles and whistles under all difficulties.

A Scout is thrifty.

A Scout is clean in thought, word and deed.

It has short, concise lessons on knot tying, axe handling, and latrine digging, as well as on honor, politeness, and humility. It teaches the right way to breathe (through the nose), cut your nails (square across the top, not rounded), squat (put a piece of wood or sloping stone under your heels), and stalk an animal (always downwind). It tells boys what they should do—smile, be chivalrous to women, be thrifty but generous—and what they should not—accept tips, drink alcohol or smoke cigarettes, masturbate. "Want of laughter means want of health," Baden-Powell tells his charges. "Laugh as much as you can. It does you good."

In fact, it does not take much time reading anything by Baden-Powell to realize how much of the early success of Scouting is a result of the appeal of Baden-Powell himself. On every page of every book, he conveys the jaunty air of an adventurer offering up tales of battlefield derring-do, an analysis of the mountaineering skills of the Ghurkas of northern India, or a tale of woodcraft deduction worthy of Sherlock Holmes. At times, he's a stern lecturer on manly skills: "It is a disgrace to a Scout if, when he is with other people, they see anything big or little, near or far, high or low, that he has not already seen for himself." At others he's just the soul of eccentric Edwardian bloviation, full of charming nonsense from around the globe:

> Montenegro is a small country high up in the mountains on the east side of the Adriatic. The men are splendid great fellows and very patriotic, fond of their country, and although not real soldiers, they all dress in the same uniform, practice rifle shooting, and always go about fully armed with rifle, knives and pistols. Yet they are the most peaceful people, and are the only people I know of who do not know how to steal.

It would be hopelessly naive to think Scouting was simply an exercise in woodcraft fun and games that was divorced from the military and political needs of the British Empire. But to see *Scouting for Boys* and the Boy Scouts as simply a calculated scheme to create loyal, patriotic drones for the Empire, you need to buy a simple, didactic view of Baden-Powell that's wholly at odds with the rich, complicated, conflicted figure he was. And in lots of ways, *Scouting for Boys* is a paradigm for Scouting not in terms of providing one message or one agenda, but in providing many different ones.

So Scouting became a sensation, first in Great Britain, then in the United States, and eventually around much of the world. But it was not wholly admired. Some upper-class types saw Baden-Powell's criticism of snobbery and social caste as almost revolutionary. Some lower-class ones saw the movement as effete and sissified, and a jeer reported during the time went:

"Here come the Brussel Sprouts, The stinking, blinking louts."
A 1912 pamphlet entitled "The Boy Scout Bubble" saw the
movement as trivial and escapist, encouraging boys to engage in
silly, useless adventures. It read in part:

> I refuse to believe that character will ever be built by un-
> settling the minds of the young, by turning their thoughts
> from practical everyday life and the best way to live it, to
> dreams and vision of a life that not one in a hundred will
> ever be called upon to live. So strong is the imagination of
> the youngster that it may be several months before he be-
> gins to ask himself what earthly use the knowledge of how
> to light a damp fire with one match will be to him when he
> answers the advertisement for a junior clerk.

Baden-Powell's Boy Scouts was not his era's only approach
to boy training, only the most successful. In America, the naturalist Ernest Thompson Seton based a movement, the Woodcraft Indians, on an almost mystical attachment to the outdoors
and the values and skills of the American Indians. Daniel Carter
Beard's Sons of Daniel Boone was built on the experience of the
American explorers and woodsmen. In England, on the right,
William Smith's Boys' Brigades flourished in forms as diverse
and unlikely as the Anglican Church Lads' Brigades and the
Jewish Lads' Brigade. Cadet Corps, many tied to public schools,
were even more explicit in serving as training grounds for the
military. Perhaps the oddest and the most direct challenge to the
Boy Scouts came from a group founded by John Hargrave, an
early Boy Scout leader who for a time was thought to be a likely
successor to Baden-Powell. Hargrave yearned for a transforming
wilderness experience, one that would keep "knowledge and
physical training hand in hand and try to breed a race of Intellectual Savages." He came to see the Boy Scouts as infected by
militarism and British imperialism and went on to launch the

Kibbo Kift Kindred, an eccentric blend of woodcraft, utopian economics, and global politics. It espoused outdoors training for boys and girls and an esoteric agenda of economic reform to be disseminated by infiltrating banking and finance, the cinema, the universities, and the other power points of Britain. Boys were to dress in shorts, jerkin, and cowl, accessorizing with a rough ash staff and rucksack. Girls were to wear a one-piece dress to the knee with leather belt and headdress. "The costume of the Kin," Hargrave proclaimed, sounding like the clueless captain of a ship about to hit an iceberg, "releases efficiency, calls for conscious unity of purpose and proclaims a dynamic difference in impressive silence."

Prospective leaders of mass movements will probably not be using Hargrave, whose group finally morphed into an inscrutable organization bent on economic reform called the Green Shirt Movement for Social Credit, for rallying the faithful. Instead, the definitive text for organizations for boys—and the inspiration for the Girl Scouts as well—remains the one Baden-Powell cooked up. Part of Baden-Powell's genius was to steal from everyone, to put together a movement that was nature and militarism, world peace and national preparedness, fun and serious, left and right, an alluring mix of disparate elements—British explorers and Zulu tribesmen, the garish triumphs of Empire and the quiet glories of the woods.

Of course, an organization that can be many things to many people runs the risk of being caught in the middle if different factions or constituencies disagree vehemently on what it should be or how it should evolve. That's probably particularly true for a group dealing with something as emotionally charged as the training of a nation's youths. But it's worth remembering that Baden-Powell succeeded where others failed by building an organization that was inclusive in the broadest sense. It was certainly too regimented for the true wilderness mystics and too frivolous for those intent on training future soldiers. But, in the beginning and for most of its life span, Scouting has prospered by building the broadest possible tent. And it's not hard to draw the conclusion that if the Scouts come to be seen as part of a particular ideology or faction, they do so at their own peril.

6: A Winter Hike on the A.T.

Having survived the raging rivers of the canoe trip and the raging testosterone of the camporee, it was probably time for me to return to what passed for my normal life. I had gone on the first two outings partly to do due diligence—making sure the troop wasn't a cabal of depraved child abusers—and partly to perform some vaguely perceived duty to help Ben integrate into the troop. I'd already done that. Like an unexpected detour off the highway, it was fine for what it was. I was truly grateful that it wasn't worse. But it wasn't a place I expected to hang around.

Still, the next event was something that genuinely sounded like fun—a Troop 1 hike along the Appalachian Trail near the lovely town of Kent, Connecticut, in the foothills of the Berkshires. Ben, of course, was planning to go. It was late fall, getting on winter. There wasn't much on my schedule for the weekend, and I figured I could use the exercise, so I decided to come along on this one too.

Like most Scout activities, it loomed as a mixed experience. My policy was still Hiking = Good, Camping = Bad. This was to be five miles of hiking followed by a night of cabin camping, an interesting compromise. Instead of sleeping in the too-cold, or too-hot, or too-insect-ridden, or too-wet or too-bear-friendly outdoors, we would sleep in the cabins at the Siwanoy Boy

Scout camp nearby. Not the Pierre, but not bleak, freezing wilderness either. It figured to be cold, but not completely miserable. I didn't have hiking boots, but I could always get some. As far as life's challenges went, it seemed manageable.

At the meeting the Wednesday before, Dr. Flank ran through what the kids needed, beginning with a stern lecture on the virtue of wool socks. This was not unexpected. No one had ever found a little red book entitled *The Teachings of Chairman Flank*, but one could imagine a modest volume with Dr. Flank's lectures on the J stroke and the moral virtue of no-trace camping, on the proper way to build a fire and the peril and utter uselessness of the axe. And, if such a volume existed, it is absolutely certain that it would begin with a meditation on wool socks.

"What goes inside your boots?" he asked in his stern, rapid-fire, this-is-a-test classroom voice.

"Wool socks," answered the older kids wearily, like POWs who've been subjected to an interminable indoctrination campaign.

"Right," said Dr. Flank with a look of pleasure far out of proportion to the information being imparted. "Nothing will keep your feet warmer and drier than good, wool socks. And nothing will keep you more comfortable than warm, dry feet. Actually since you'll be hiking, you'll need something else as well. You need a pair of thin liner socks, polypropylene or polyester liner socks. You use them to transfer moisture to the outer layer of socks, so your feet won't get damp and clammy. Then you put the wool socks over that. You want a poncho or rain jacket. You want something for your head, a hat or cap, because the body loses half its heat through the head. You need a good pair of gloves. And you want to dress in layers, so you can peel some off if you get overheated. You, of course, need your hiking boots."

Mr. Toonkel stepped forward brandishing a trail guide that described the hike. "You cross a swampy area on a log here," he said. "You cross the stream by walking across rocks here. You cross a shallow stream to get to the dirt road here. So you should get the idea; it's not going to be a dry trip. If it's cold enough, some of it will be frozen. If it's warm enough, there might be a lot of mud. So what did Dr. Flank tell you? I don't want to see anyone without hiking boots, and I don't want to see anyone who didn't think about what to put over his feet. Do you need a tent? No. We're sleeping inside. You need to bring a lunch, but we'll be cooking the rest. You'll need a mess kit, a cup, dish, bowl, fork, and spoon. I'm not bringing cups for you. You need canteens filled with water. Don't get up there with an empty water bottle and ask where you can fill it. Everything you bring should be in your pack. As far as the hike, you'll need a small day pack to carry your water and any extra clothes, a jacket or sweater you're not going to be wearing when we leave. The guidebook or maps we'll supply. You'll need your compass, canteen, flashlight. You might bring a couple of Band-Aids. I trust you'll all be prepared, gentlemen."

I, of course, wasn't remotely prepared, having no wool socks, no hiking boots, and not much of the rest. So I ventured out to my own bargain-basement version of an outdoors outfitter, a discount emporium on Ninth Avenue in the Garment District in Manhattan where all the employees were Indians, half the signs were in Spanish ("*Se Venta Hoy!*"), and most of the customers were Asian or black. It specialized in huge piles of heavily discounted Levi's, most of them with big waists and small legs or odd-lot dimensions that only fit the characters on *The Simpsons*.

"Fit you good," one of the salesclerks said as he picked up a pair of jeans that two of me could have fit inside.

"No thanks," I replied amiably. "I already have a tent."

He nodded agreeably, apparently satisfied that was the appropriate response, but hovered around expectantly as I moved on to the boot section. I soon spied a sturdy-looking pair of brown Gore-Tex hiking boots marked down to $59.99. Gore-Tex, of course, is the hiker and camper's material of choice for almost anything and a material that costs the same per ounce as platinum. My guess was this was the boot world's answer to the $15 Rolexes that enterprising merchants sold to unwary tourists in Times Square, but they fit just fine, and I figured even if it was faux or semifaux Gore-Tex, that was probably OK for me.

"These any good?" I asked stupidly. Having tried to sell me jeans ample enough to house me and Ben together, the salesclerk was going to tell me to go to Florsheim's for a pair of boots?

He could have just laughed at the idiocy of the question, but instead considered my question gravely and then picked up the right boot and held it up to the light, apparently thinking one evaluated Gore-Tex boots the way one evaluated a bottle of Cabernet. At least he didn't look for the cork and try to smell it.

"Oh, yes," he said, in a lilting Indian accent. "Very good. Very good. You do very fine hiking in those hiking boots."

I figured I might as well let myself feel vaguely comforted by his seal of approval, since these were the only $59.99, more-or-less-Gore-Tex hiking boots I was likely to find. So I took the plunge and found some grayish wool socks to throw in as well. I figured I could make do with what I had for the rest.

On the morning of the outing I threw the usual haphazard collection of couture—jeans, extra socks, extra underwear, fleece, sweater, hideous-looking red sleep shirt—into my backpack, packed up our lunch, and drove off to the usual meeting place. We dithered along at the customary pace, until Mr. Johnson took a look at his watch and then at Dr. Flank.

"Professor, we about ready to roll?"

"Can't see why not. All right, gentlemen," Dr. Flank said. "Let's head out."

The highlight of the drive up came when we passed the group of dank red brick buildings that were the largely deserted remains of the Harlem Valley State Hospital, a state mental institution that loomed off the roadway with memorable, brooding menace. About fifteen minutes later, near the town of New Milford, Connecticut, we pulled off the road and drove over a single-lane covered bridge into a dusty parking lot full of cars and SUVs with kayaks on top and perhaps a half dozen healthy-looking hikers milling outside. We divided into three patrols, studied our contour maps, checked our compasses, and waited for last-minute instructions from Dr. Flank.

It was an awfully big group to be hiking, about twenty kids and six dads. But on Dr. Flank's signal, we began trekking resolutely into the woods like a crack commando force embarking on a precision military operation. We veered away from the river into a dense thicket, past the ruins of an old cottage that had burned down forty years earlier. This was more rustic and obscure than I had expected. Who knew the fabled Appalachian Trail was so dense and wooded and the trail itself so elusive? I tried to imagine walking to Georgia this way. It seemed impossible. Pretty soon there was hardly any trail at all. Like frontier woodsmen, we doggedly pushed on for a minute or so. Before we went too much farther, though, the leaders stopped and huddled together.

"Uh, Bill, what color is the A.T. blaze supposed to be?" asked Mr. Johnson, referring to the tree markings that denote the trail.

"Uh, I don't think it's supposed to be blue," responded Dr. Flank.

Indeed, the A.T.'s characteristic blaze was white, a marking nowhere to be seen. We stopped, and the Big Three hurriedly reviewed our bearings on the hieroglyphiclike topographic map we had brought along. Sure enough, we had begun our hike by charging determinedly in the general direction of downtown Waterbury.

Undeterred, we retraced our steps to the parking lot, where we picked up the white blaze and began our march across a rugged rocky trail winding along the west bank of the Housatonic River. About a half mile later we passed through a gap in a stone wall and then crossed over a 120-foot bridge over the river. We continued along the south bank of Ten Mile River, with the trail unfolding in a gorgeous series of woodland tableaux of mostly bare winter trees, rocky streams, gentle rises, and steep slopes. A little more than a mile into the hike we began an ascent, which varied from moderate to—by my standards, anyway—pretty damn serious, toward the top of Ten Mile Hill, with an elevation of one thousand feet. It left most of us winded and the king-sized kids like Sam 'n Eric gasping for breath and complaining at every incline.

"How far have we gone?" Sam asked about a tenth of a mile into the climb.

"We've just started," said Mr. Toonkel. "Don't start asking how far we've gone."

"How far have we gone?" Sam asked five minutes later.

"I told you not to ask me that," Mr. Toonkel said. "If you're getting tired we'll just leave you here, so the birds will have something to eat."

Sam was quiet for another five minutes, then tried a different approach.

"How much farther do we have to go?" he asked.

Mr. Toonkel was not amused.

"That won't work either. Just keep walking. When we stop it means we're there. If we're still hiking, we're not there yet. Is that clear enough?"

Sam remained quiet as he huffed and puffed for a few more minutes. Then he moved on to more fundamental issues.

"What's the point of the hiking?" he asked when we were ready for our first break. In Scouting, this was one of those ontological questions that got to the nature of reality, like "Is there a God?"

"To hike," said Mr. Toonkel, in a voice as devoid of affect as he could manage. "It's good exercise."

"You hike to hike? That's pretty dumb. What's the point if you're not going anywhere?"

"That's for you to find out," Mr. Toonkel said with finality.

Mr. Toonkel did his best to withdraw from the dialogue, but the thread led to an ongoing discussion between Sam 'n Eric on the pointlessness of the day's events, the unseemly weight of their day packs, the length of the outing, the kind of music they'd rather be listening to, the kind of dirt bikes that would make this trek tolerable, the specific teachers they wished were doing this in their stead, and, most important, how long it was until lunch.

"I call your lunch, in case you die," Tom announced.

"That's not funny," Sam replied.

In fact, Sam lived until lunch, which we ate when we reached the top of the hill, about two miles into the hike. It overlooked a gorgeous vista of wooded glen, above which we perched on rocks like eagles catching the midafternoon sun. Ben and I sat together sharing our sandwiches, Goldfish, granola bars, and sesame sticks. He had a habit of asking me questions I was invariably unable to answer. Do pigs sweat? If you were as rich as Bill Gates, could you buy a fighter plane? Would you rather die painfully without knowing you were going to die or painlessly and slowly but you knowing you were dying? What would life be like if the power source were static electricity? Do things happen to dogs seven times faster because a dog's year equals seven of ours? But sitting here in the wild, neither of us felt much need to talk. And we mostly ate in silence, appreciating the tranquil scene below.

When we resumed our trek, the hardest part was already over. The rest of the hike, which covered 5.4 miles from start to finish, was largely downhill. By the time we got to the cabin it was about three in the afternoon.

Camp Siwanoy turned out to be a seventy-five-year-old, 659-acre preserve that had seen better days. The camp was one of four properties owned by the Westchester–Putnam Council, the local Scouting umbrella group. Unfortunately, the council had the resources for only three, and Siwanoy, which was up for sale, had the frayed and forlorn feel of a place in the process of being abandoned.

Our abode was a rough-hewn cabin sitting on cement blocks with bare pine floors, a pitched roof, a modest front porch, and two main rooms—a living room with a big fireplace and a dormitory-style bedroom with a wood-burning stove and wooden bunks that had the look of the accommodations in prisoner-of-war camps. Off the living room was a kitchen with a stove and refrigerator from the 1950s. On the walls were plaques with the Morning, Noon, and Evening Grace and other variations like the Camp Siwanoy Vespers:

> Now the Day is nearly over
> And the campfire sheds its glow
> Let us stand and sing together
> To old Siwanoy we know
> Camp Siwanoy, to thee forever
> True and Loyal Scouts will be
> And each Scout to one another
> Holding fast to love and memory

Outside was a horrific latrine, with wooden stalls as dank and foreboding as a dungeon and a hideously soiled apple sitting in the middle of a rusted-out urinal. It wasn't clear whether it was there for some pitifully inadequate hygienic purpose or as a bit of Boy Scout conceptual art.

The best part of the camp was a huge fort in the form of a wooden stockade. It had a guard tower about ten feet tall with a ladder leading to the top, a covered area used for storing lumber or stashing prisoners, and enough space for dozens of kids to stage raids, fight wars, toss grenades, and engage in benign, adolescent mayhem. So while the grown-ups retired to the cabin, the kids took to the fort, where they improvised a war game that consisted of dividing up into two opposing sides, throwing rocks and sticks at one another, trying to take and defend the tower, and committing the sorts of low-level acts of violence that once were routine horseplay and now keep personal injury lawyers in brand-new BMWs.

This outing was, in some ways, like our first two outings. But, for both of us, there was a big difference. Ben clearly didn't worry about being an outsider as much as I worried for him. But for the first time, he didn't seem to me like the new kid. The troop was already sorting itself out by age, by big kids and little kids, and he, by dint of being one of eight sixth graders new to the troop, was already just one of the little kids, not the new kid in town. He trotted off with all the others when they played around on the fort or disappeared into the woods in search of wood. He dutifully listened with the others when Dr. Flank was dispensing wisdom on the perfect tomato sauce or Mr. Toonkel was explaining how to tie a square knot or clove hitch. He was part of the appreciative gallery that hung around when Sam 'n Eric embarked on some riff about Dr. Flank's age, or the infirmities of one teacher or another, or the incredibly awesome qualities of this or that paintball gun.

And, as it turned out, the kids he had the most in common with were the Amigos, sixth graders like him, who on further exposure seemed not so bratty after all. Amigo number 1 was Barrett, a relentlessly energetic computer wonk and midget weatherman who obsessively followed the weather channel and various weather Web sites so he could do his own uncannily accurate daily forecasts every day. Jonah had a quietly assertive manner and short blond hair and seemed the most Todd-like of the kids in Ben's grade. He was the keenest naturalist of the younger kids and considered himself a vegetarian, even though his diet consisted largely of McDonald's fries and pepperoni pizza without tomato sauce—the pepperoni and other pork products apparently deemed too far from anything obviously animal-like to count as meat. The third Amigo was Mark, a tall, dark-haired kid with a wry, sardonic bent and a head stuffed full of information on Trident submarines, Civil War battles, and World War II weaponry gleaned from years of watching the History Channel. He wore a T-shirt reading "What if the hokey-pokey really is what it's all about?" which seemed to sum up his sense of humor.

All the kids returned once it began to get dark, with a few cuts and scrapes, but nothing requiring major surgery. The closest anyone came to real injury was when Mr. Toonkel threw a fit when he found Sam 'n Eric in the bunkroom with a box of matches and a tin can, trying to light Sam's farts by trapping them in the can and thrusting a match inside. There was an absolute ban on kids' having matches or other fire-starting implements inside the cabin, and it didn't take a genius to think that a bunch of boys in a rickety old cabin really didn't need to have any matches. Mr. Toonkel confiscated the contraband and stomped out of the dormitory room, leaving Sam 'n Eric with more ammunition for their sense of grievance and victimhood.

Mr. Toonkel marched through the main room to the kitchen, where Dr. Flank and a small group of campers were preparing dinner.

"What is it?" one of the kids asked.

"It's called Edible Surprise," chimed in Mr. Toonkel. "If it's edible, it's a surprise."

In truth, Dr. Flank's cooking was always at least edible, and this turned out to be a perfectly serviceable stew composed of six pounds of Carolina white rice, four pounds of hamburger meat, onions, green pepper, and sundry seasonings, which was prepared by Dr. Flank and a gaggle of kids. Dr. Flank directed the chopping, cooking, Pamming of the skillet, slicing, and dicing while delivering assorted instructional asides ("Searing means you cook the heck out of it. Sautéing means you pay attention to what you're doing.") to the crew, many of whom were using the occasion to work on their cooking merit badge. There was a long picnic table in the living room, and we had the stew, Dole Classic Iceberg Salad with Kraft Free Zesty Italian dressing, sliced onion bread, and Technicolor pitchers of bug juice followed by chocolate chip and oatmeal cookies for dessert.

After dinner, we threw a bunch of logs on the fire from the stout pile just outside the front door.

"All right, gentlemen," said Mr. Johnson. "It's show time at the Rialto."

Show time, such as it was, began with kids doing a few skits. Then Dr. Flank, Mr. Toonkel, and Mr. Johnson each told a story, a traditional part of the Troop 1 canon. Dr. Flank's was a long, elaborate Lenni-Lenape Indian story, essentially a creation myth of how the Lenni-Lenape came to inhabit the Hudson Valley. Sometimes Dr. Flank's stories took hold and sometimes they were a bit abstruse and airy for the members of the Eminem Generation. But this time the kids listened respectfully and attentively.

Mr. Toonkel specialized in horror stories, which were invariably related to the locale of the camp-out. This time his tale was about the depraved denizens of the nearby psychiatric hospital and what he described as numerous unconfirmed, but ominous, reports of missing boys left in their wake. Mr. Toonkel was a great storyteller with a disarmingly sincere affect. He always delivered his frightful tales in an utterly matter-of-fact voice, occasionally shaking his head as if left totally perplexed by the dark mystery of it all, throwing out scary thoughts and then qualifying them with lame, thoroughly unconvincing assurances that all was probably well. He finally concluded with a resigned shrug and a totally unconvincing expression of lukewarm reassurance. "So no one knows what became of the missing boys," he said in his flat, nasal voice, as if passing on a historical oddity from colonial times. "You hear terrible rumors of beheadings and bodies found in distant caves, but you can't really believe everything you hear. They do their best to catch the inmates who escape, but it's not a perfect world, and sometimes they still get out and are never found. I think I read something about one who got out just the other day. Maybe I'm wrong. The odds are it's nothing to worry about. But you may hear a strange sound tonight. It might sound like an owl or a coyote, but, for your own protection, you might want to listen extra carefully, just in case it's someone you don't want around. Like I said, it's probably nothing. I wouldn't let it bother you."

Mr. Johnson spoke with laconic economy and began his story with a succinct preamble about the creation of legends and myths. "This story is a little bit about how legends begin," he said. "Legends begin by people experiencing real events and then passing stories about them along verbally from one generation to another. Legends actually begin with truth. Sometimes they come to symbolize great, momentous things. Tonight we're going to be the first generation to hear a legend about a great chief, the chief known as the Great Leknoot. The chief went with his tribe to the distant reaches of the north country. And he paddled his kayak through the mountains, the rivers, and the lakes. And when he had to go from one lake to the other, he picked up his kayak and put it on his shoulder and carried it across the land until he reached the next body of water."

Some of the older kids seemed to get a titter of recognition, as if they knew exactly what was going on, but everyone else was listening with rapt attention, not knowing where this story was going.

"The great chief, of course, had his tribe with him, and he was a great provider and wanted to provide for all the people. But after the third day of the journey, they had eaten all their food. Leknoot paddled into the shallows of a great lake, and he cast his line out into the shallows. And out from under a log a huge fish with giant jaws came and took Leknoot's feathered lure and dove back under the water. Leknoot knew that his people were hungry, so he jumped into the water and wrestled with this great beast of a fish. And as he wrestled, his people stood along the shoreline by their canoes. Leknoot stood up to his waist in the water, and then he lifted high into the air this great beast of a fish with the giant hooked jaws and proclaimed, 'This evening we will dine.' Leknoot led the troop paddling the rest of the day until they reached an island. There were eight tribesmen and they were all hungry. So they removed the great beast from the water and that night they ate all the pink flesh until there was nothing left but the skeleton and the great jaws. The tribe knew the fish was the favorite food of the black bear, so they had to dispose of it. So they built a great fire, and into the fire they disposed of all that was left of this great fish, the skeleton, the backbone, the jaw. As the tribe sat around with their leader Leknoot telling tales of past exploits, there arose from the flames a great head with a giant hooked jaw. The great beast of the fish sought revenge upon the tribe in the form of a curse. He said whenever the tribe should camp, at some time in the night the great head with the jaws will rise from the fire and devour them all. So tonight, I want you to look into the fire, think of Leknoot and the tribe alone on the island, waiting for the revenge of the great beast, and be careful to look into the fire and see the shape of the great hooked jaws."

It was truly an artful performance. Leknoot, as I realized midway through the tale, was, of course, Toonkel spelled backward, and the tale was one I had heard in different versions before, of the twenty-six-inch brown trout Mr. Toonkel had caught that summer on the High Adventure trip for the older Scouts in the Adirondacks. He had indeed gone into the water with it, and when they finally filleted it, it made three frying pans full of fish, more fish than any of them had eaten in their life. Mr. Johnson's recitation functioned as a tale, as a bit of troop lore, and as a totally credible lesson in the creation of myth, memory, and community.

The differences in storytelling, I realized, were a microcosm of the different styles of the three men. Take any subject: There was a Flank way, a Toonkel way, and a Johnson way. On the hikes, Dr. Flank favored a carved maple walking stick with the Scout seal on it, Mr. Toonkel used a steel photography monopod, and Mr. Johnson just used whatever he picked up in the woods. Dr. Flank drove that sensible, tidy Volvo; Mr. Toonkel drove a big Suburban with assorted crisp, new baseball caps curled up neatly next to the driver's seat; Mr. Johnson drove a modest beat-up Ford Escort wagon with an Elon College bumper sticker on the back. Dr. Flank had an inexhaustible supply of Scouting attire, the most spectacular being an old red wool jacket with patches going back to the 1960s and '70s. Mr. Toonkel showed up in fancy wet suits or camouflage with eccentric headgear, like an elaborate Russian fur hat or a baseball cap reading "Sing Sing Surf Squad." Mr. Johnson wore old flannel shirts and jeans, as if he had just pulled from the closet whatever was appropriate for the day's weather.

The different roles played by the three struck a chord with me. We keep hearing these days about absent dads and failing dads and uninvolved dads. But I grew up with what felt like three dads. Maybe it was because everyone moved from New York City to the same subdivision at the same time, or because all the men were World War II veterans, or because the freshly minted suburban world of new split-levels selling for $29,999 was equally new to all of them, but we at 39 Tanners Road and the Isaacs next door at 35 Tanners and the Biblowitzes next to them at 31 functioned like an extended family. We walked in and out of each others' houses like they were our own. We took vacations together—usually with just one of the other families, but sometimes with both—the kids piled into the back of station wagons so haphazardly that one summer in Lakeville, Massachusetts, we left my brother behind at a grocery store, assuming he was either with the I's or the B's. Sometimes the parents would gather in our den for pizza and beer, and even as a kid their bond struck me as something special. So much for the soulless anomie of suburbia.

I viewed all six parents as expressions of the infinite, mysterious ways that adults effectively or ineptly exerted their will on or imparted wisdom to the young. But most memorable for me were the three men. My father, Jerome Applebome, combined a warm heart, a cranky mind, and a fatalistic soul. You could take all the ineffably descriptive Yiddish words, from *mensch* to *schlemiel,* and they all held a piece of him. Like me, I'm afraid, he had the quality of a Thurber character never quite settled in the world. He was constantly worried about money, trying to keep fenders on old clunkers in place with Fiberglas tape, endlessly fighting losing battles against crab grass or wily raccoons or squirrels intent on stealing the birdseed or balky commodes likely to spray water in all directions or stocks that went down when you bought them and up when you sold them. But he was (and is) utterly devoted to his kids and taught us to do the right thing. If his friend Sol Budd was in the hospital dying, he'd be there to hold his hand and listen to his fevered ramblings before he passed on. He might not have wanted to visit an elderly relative in a nursing home on a sunny Sunday, but he always showed up, the way others went to church. I know we're not as good at those small gestures as he was, but it wasn't for want of a good example to follow.

Jesse Biblowitz was the sweetest man I knew. He was big and lumbering, slightly stooped, with big ears and thick, dark hair. He never seemed rattled the way my father often was, and I can't ever remember him getting even slightly mad. Jesse had some sort of suburban Zen down pat. A bunch of us—kids and grownups—played tennis every Sunday, and even as I got older and clearly was never going to be as good a player as he thought I might become, he'd still treat every failing as a mild, unexpected aberration in my march toward greatness. He spoiled his kids, and, in a way, he spoiled those of us who weren't his kids too. I never doubted that Jesse cared about us almost as much as my own father did.

And Gilbert Isaacs was the smartest man I knew, a man like no one else. Gilbert had zero interest in baseball, basketball, football, or any of the sports that obsessed the rest of us. He did everything his own way. While the other dads tended their lawns, he built a Japanese pebble garden in his backyard with a ten-foot-tall copy of a famous Isamu Noguchi sculpture—he fabricated it himself in his basement. When a storm knocked it down, he painstakingly built another one. He'd never graduated from college, but he knew about everything—orchids, the paintings of Emil Nolde, astronomy, World War II battles. Once he diagnosed his barber's eye infection and thereafter was always greeted with a respectful "Good afternoon, Doc" by the barber, who assumed he was a physician rather than the owner of a jewelry store he ran with his brother. Gilbert didn't share the fashionable leftist politics of the grownups who were regarded as the local intellectuals, but he was the most genuinely intellectual person I've ever known. As he got older he let his white hair grow long, which gave him a presence that was both austere and distinguished. He looked like some nineteenth-century senator from Kentucky or Tennessee. And that imposing presence and his stern, demanding demeanor could be intimidating in the best way. "DON'T MAKE EXCUSES," he would thunder at his daughters. And we would all get the message that you did your best in life, and you didn't blame others for whatever you failed to accomplish. You just tried to do better next time.

Kids can learn from lots of people, I guess, from coaches and teachers and clergymen as well as from grandfathers and fathers and neighbors. But I don't know any people these days who have that same kind of intimate relationship with their neighbors that my parents did with the I's and B's, or any kid who could claim to have three fathers the way I did when I was growing up. I know Ben doesn't. We had a neighbor in Atlanta—an Eagle Scout, it turned out—named Leon, who had some of Gilbert's quiet *über*-competence. But even if we had stayed there, we would never have vacationed with his family, and Ben would never have wandered in and out of his house the way I did with Gilbert.

In the same way, I did not expect Mr. Toonkel, Mr. Johnson, and Dr. Flank to become as big a part of Ben's life as Jerome, Gilbert, and Jesse were of mine. They couldn't be. But, if in some imperfect way, they could play some of the same role— project qualities and skills and competencies that I didn't have— that seemed a remarkable blessing and gift.

We sat watching the fire for a while. Then Dr. Flank invited everyone to get up for the circle. We all linked arms, the grownups and the kids, and everyone quietly waited for Dr. Flank to speak. Troop 1 was about as determinedly free from religion as a Scout troop can be, but Dr. Flank's campfire closings usually took on the air of a benediction, as if this were Baden-Powell's church of the outdoors and he was, if not the priest, at least the guide.

"We had a terrific hike today," he said. "And I was very impressed with your cooking too. I didn't know you knew so much. And I want you to think about our hike today, about the beauty of the woods and the time we were able to share there together. It's almost ten, and we're all tired, so I want you all to get right into bed, so we can get an early start tomorrow. So," and all the kids and all the adults on hand joined in, "May the Great Master of all Scouts be with us until we meet again."

The kids retired to their sleeping bags on the rock-hard cribs in the bunkroom, while the adults and some of the high school kids stayed up watching the fire for another half hour or so, the older kids and the leaders sharing stories of past High Adventure trips. The kids didn't go to sleep right away, but after much stray talk about farts, the movie *Titanic*, the middle school football team, the band Rage Against the Machine, dirt bikes, body odors, and creative ways to make use of the urine-soaked apple, they began to drop off to sleep one by one.

Just before they all went to asleep, a lone voice piped up.

"Is it true that every time the lights flicker someone just got electrocuted at the insane place?" Sam asked.

"Nahhh," said Todd. "Sometimes they're getting electrocuted. Sometimes, it just means the power went out, the locks don't work, the security system failed, the guards don't have a clue what's happening, they can't even get the searchlights to work, and you've got a bunch of murderous loonies running around like lizards in the dark. Go to sleep, Sam."

7: Gear, God, and the Klondike Derby

It was more Joseph McCarthy's vision of stealth Commies in-sidiously infiltrating the country's very core than Japanese planes materializing out of the blue to attack Pearl Harbor, but before long Scouting had begun to insinuate itself into every corner of our life. Not that it was an easy fit. Scouting is based on the premise that there's something in boys' DNA primal enough to outlast changing fashions and mores. Cub Scouts put together miniature cars to race in the Pinewood Derby when Dr. Flank was a kid, and they do it now. Boy Scouts learn their square knots and clove hitches, repeat their oaths, and follow the trail from Tenderfoot to Eagle now much as they did when Scouting began. Try to think of something, anything, in boys' lives—clothes? music? academics? sports?—that looks and feels in the era of palm pilots and e-mail the way it did in the era of fountain pens and Underwood manual typewriters. So as we were drawn further into Scouting it felt like traversing two dis-parate worlds: one, the iconic, timeless world of the Handbook and Dr. Flank's intricately scripted pageant of Scouting activi-ties; the other, the all-enveloping world of pop culture, mass media, and modernity in all its ragged, ever-changing, anti-iconic inconsistency. To the adults, it was at times not entirely clear if we were in the real Scout world or a somewhat loopy modern-day adaptation. But the kids seldom had such qualms. Whatever was encoded in the Scout regimen usually seemed to strike the right chords.

Our immersion into Scouting first manifested itself in the ever-increasing accumulation of gear that began piling up in Ben's room like a version of "The Sorcerer's Apprentice" choreographed by a demented outdoors outfitter. You might think that being a Boy Scout, with its hearty hikes and Spartan summer camp, its ethos of rugged self-reliance, would be a sober counterweight to the heady materialism of our time. You would be wrong. It turns out that for the youth of America, nothing is quite so expensive these days as a simple walk in the woods. Even a hideously expensive activity like skiing, which struck fear into my overextended suburban heart, involved just one equipment outlay for skis, boots, and poles. But hiking and climbing and backpacking is a modern dad's version of the Big Muddy. Once you slog in, there's no way to slog back out without shelling out vast sums of money for things you never knew existed or couldn't imagine mattered.

It was not always thus. The first edition of the Boy Scout Handbook, published in 1911, ends with a catalog of that era's version of Scout Stuff. There's the official Scout axe—"The best axe that money can buy or skill produce"—for 35 cents, a bandana for 10 or 15 cents, $1 breeches, 75-cent knickerbockers, a 10-cent drinking cup, and a 60-cent haversack. For $1.15 you could get a Boy Scout hat. A poncho was $2.50, and mess kits were 50 and 75 cents. The accent was definitely on being simple and utilitarian, so Scouts were advised to make their own tents and find any old footwear for hiking: "Any good shoe that is made up for the purpose of ease and comfort in tromping will serve the Boy Scout's needs. The Boy Scout shoe is convenient, inexpensive and especially designed for scouting." Price $2.50.

This is not quite the way the game is played in the era of Gear Lust as conveyed in the pages of magazines selling hiking gear, climbing gear, adventure gear, camping gear, ab-defining gear, and other accoutrements of today's ruggedly fashionable outdoors lifestyle. You need a tent, of course, like our REI Geomountain three-to-four person, four-season Mountaineering model with dual doors, front and rear vestibules, screen windows, convenient pockets, and enough support, we were told, to stand up under the weight of a blizzard of snow if you happened to be doing particularly out-there winter camping. (That claim, you can be sure, I will never be around to verify.) You need all-weather jackets like Ben's EMS Gore-Tex Downpour shell. You need hiking boots like Ben's Dolomite number, a backpack like his EMS internal-frame Long Trail ST with 4,000-cubic-centimeter capacity, and a sleeping bag like his North Face Thunderhead, guaranteed to keep you comfortable at 20 degrees Fahrenheit. OK, I get that, more or less.

But that's just the start. There's the $12 superabsorbent, lightweight PackTowl ("Soaks up water like a sponge!"), which is apparently needed because plain old towels may have worked well enough for the past century, but only a dolt takes one on a hike now. There's the Guardian Plus Sweetwater portable water purification system, needed to protect us from waterborne viruses such as *E. coli* or cholera and waterborne protozoa like giardia and cryptosporidium. We got a camping stove, a very modest Yellowstone Lite Trail gas stove. Just $28! The cooking set was simple too, a Texsport Stainless Steel, $32.50. There are lots of little things—compass, first-aid kit, carabiners for attaching as many things on your pack as possible, and Nalgene wide-mouth loop-top water bottles. We got a $9.99 tick removal kit, the one extra absolutely invaluable here in Lyme disease country.

There are many midrange things, such as Camelback hiker hydration systems—insulated water bags you strap to your body and sip through a tube to avoid sudden death by dehydration as you're wandering around the A.T. The Outback Oven. Industrial-strength flashlights and tiny high-intensity Mini Maglites and Petzl headlamps suitable for either (a) working in a coal mine or (b) finding a way to the latrine at night. A GCI Outdoors folding chair for short trips or car camping expeditions where you have your gear near at hand, and a lightweight EMS Mountain Chair for those arduous treks into the distant outback somewhere.

To go Dr. Flank one better, in addition to our plain old wool socks, we got two pairs of Trail Runner II outdoor 100-percent super-fine-grade merino wool Smartwool socks. $17.99 a pair! For socks! And I thought Gore-Tex was expensive. To keep our lunch and spare clothes dry on the canoe trips, we got a commodious green rubber SealLine Baja waterproof bag. Tevas! Camping pillows! Mosquito netting! Leatherman multitool set! We got an extra-lightweight tent for hikes when Ben would be alone and our main model would be too heavy to carry. We got an EMS Trekker PL 2600 day pack when the big pack was more than was needed. We got canteens and day packs and canoe pads and stainless steel vacuum-insulated mugs. I say "we," but these were all Ben's purchases. All I bought were my cheapo boots and a copy of Kathleen Meyer's indispensable book *How to Shit in the Woods*. (This is not a joke. Check it out on Amazon.)

I look at the list now and feel faint—*We bought all that??* But built up over time, a purchase made here or there for a birthday or for a trip, it didn't seem like that much. And the other kids were just as bad. Conversation would begin with the ageless query: What would I want to bring if I were hiking to the top of Mount Everest? (This from kids who started whining "Are we almost there?" after the first half-mile or modest incline on every four-mile hike.) And then mumbling stumblebums who heretofore had seemed barely able to string two coherent sentences together would launch into learned disquisitions about North Face Alpenglow Polarguard Delta Sleeping Bags or Patagonia Regulator System shells, the design details of various mummy bags and overbags, goose down versus synthetic insulation, and how much tax you saved by buying at Campmor online instead of getting your dad to take you to the store in New Jersey.

Still, after a while, I got the shakes every time we drove anywhere in the vicinity of Eastern Mountain Sports, Ben's favorite outdoors store, and did my best to rapidly dispose of the Campmor catalogs and EMS flyers and copies of *Backpacker* magazine that arrived in the mail. It was hopeless, of course, and Ben consumed them with religious zeal, sometimes lying in bed with his flashlight after dark, surreptitiously leafing through the Jagged Edge Mountain Gear catalog, sort of J. Crew meets the *Bhagavad Gita*. "The Journey is the Destination," it read. "Follow with Complete sincerity the Path that inspires you most."

While we were accumulating gear, the troop activities were becoming part of our regular schedule. There were the weekly meetings, of course. After the fall hikes, our next event was the annual Christmas tree sale at the Pleasantville First United Methodist Church. So far we had been longer on hiking and camping than on good turns and service. The tree sale was a mixture of service to the church and service to the troop. Each year the church ordered some two thousand trees—balsams and Frazier firs and Douglas firs, which sold for between $14 for tiny desktop models to $75 for the top-of-the-line ten- to twelve-foot-tall balsam premiums perfect for scraping that cathedral ceiling in your brand-new McMansion. The trees were sold by our Scouts, with most kids working a half day each weekend through December. The troop was paid for each hour the kids worked. In the end, it was the church's biggest fundraiser of the year. Half of the troop's proceeds went to our activities, and half went to the council office to support broader Scout activities.

And the kids made tips, which could amount to $10 or $20 a day, not bad for a twelve- or thirteen-year-old.

The trees arrived every year from Canada on the Friday after Thanksgiving, piled fourteen or fifteen high on two huge forty-eight-foot flatbed trucks. Our first job, as we learned when we showed up at eight on a surprisingly balmy November morning, was to unload them all. There were about twenty of us from the troop, plus a handful of men from the church and a dozen or so wrestlers from a nearby high school. The minister of the church soon appeared. He was a big, rugged-looking guy with a full black beard wearing a plain gray sweatshirt and blue jeans. Even the minister was a lumberjack, and he's OK! He gathered us in a circle and led us in a prayer ("Oh, Lord, we thank you for this beautiful day and for this labor we are about to begin. We thank you for giving us this season of peace and love, and we ask that the work goes safely today. May all your blessings be with this group and this church and may this be a joyous season here and around the world. In Christ's name we pray, Amen.").

The troop had more Jewish families—ours included—than Christian ones, but most kids turned out for the sale nonetheless. It struck me that other than the dutiful renderings of the Scout Oath ("On my honor I will do my best to do my duty to God and my country..."), this was the first reference to God in any form we had heard since we joined the troop. The absence of religion was partly a reflection of Dr. Flank's secular, modernist tilt. But just how much religion to inject into Scouting has been a continuing issue. Baden-Powell's version of the Scout Law did not have a single mention of God or religion. He once wrote, "A bad man who believes in a creed is no more religious than the good man who does not." But Scouting in the United States grew out of the tradition of Christian uplift and character-building that gave rise to the Young Men's Christian Association. In fact, when the Boy Scouts of America was getting off the ground, the YMCA did most of the initial organizing. So the B.S.A. stipulated that a Scout is reverent and that a boy cannot become the best sort of man without a grounding in religious faith. But the Scouts were always ambivalent about how much explicit religion needed to be part of the program. The first American version of the Boy Scout Handbook hardly mentions religion. Instead, it precisely mimics Baden-Powell's world view by tying one of its few mentions of God to the duty to do a good turn daily, saying: "It is a practical religion, and a boy honors God best when he helps others most."

Over time, the references to God became much more frequent in the Handbook. The fifth edition of the Handbook, published in 1948 and the best selling of the eleven editions, is expansive in its remarks on God and religion. It notes the importance of worshipping God regularly, and the great religious faith of men like Washington and Lincoln. "Above all you are faithful to Almighty God's Commandments," it advises, and adds: "Sometimes when you look up into the starlit sky on a quiet night, and feel close to Him—thank Him as the Giver of all good things."

The eleventh and latest edition of the Handbook has a broad and somewhat muted sense of religion: "Wonders all around us remind us of our faith in God. We find it in the tiny secrets of creation and in the great mysteries of the universe. It exists in the kindness of people and in the teachings of our families and religious leaders. We show our reverence by living our lives according to the ideals of our beliefs." But while other organizations, the Girl Scouts for example, have explicitly moved away from requiring members to profess their faith in God, the Boy Scouts have chosen to move in the opposite direction, making the requirement an explicit and literal one, leading to controversies in recent years in which Scouts have been expelled for refusing to profess their faith in God.

The tree sale didn't have much to do with faith—especially since it wasn't the faith of most of us anyway—but between the minister's benediction and the air of fraternal comity, it unfolded sort of like a suburban version of a rural barn raising. For our first day's labors, we had all brought sturdy gloves and dispensable old clothes, which were sure to end up caked with pine needles and tree sap. A few of the huskier men and wrestlers climbed a ladder to the top of the trees stacked in the truck bed and began handing them down to the assembled masses below. The men and bigger kids hoisted the trees up on their shoulders, and except for the biggest Douglas firs, lugged them up a wooded slope where signs were set up reading FRAZIER FIR 8-9' $72 or BALSAM PREMIUM 5-6' $29 or BALSAM SELECT 6-8' $41. The kids who couldn't quite manage a tree alone paired off with one another and lugged one between them, eventually heaving it onto the tree pile with a fierce grunt. Then they turned around and marched back for some more. Sam 'n Eric and the bigger kids were in their element, strutting around like construction workers. The church had put out a spread of donuts, bagels, coffee, and hot chocolate, giving the kids the ability to malinger, kibitz, and take long breaks during which they could complain at length about how hard they were working, just like real live grownups did. For a change, none of the three leaders was around. Vince and Robert, the mismatched Italians from the first camp-out, were in charge, giving us the feel of a free-lance one-off operation. By noon we were finished and the kids, for the most part, had done the first day of honest remunerative labor in their lives. The next Saturday we showed up again to build wooden bins, put tags on all the trees, and lug about a third of the trees to fill the bins, leaving the rest waiting in reserve on the piles on the hillside. After that, the real selling began. The message on the church sign read IF WE DON'T HAVE CHRISTMAS IN OUR HEARTS, WE WILL NEVER FIND IT UNDER A

TREE, as if to remind one and all that this was supposed to be about moving hearts and not just about moving product. But the kids were there to sell the trees, not to minister to the shoppers, and they took their duties remarkably seriously.

"This is what you need to know to sell a Christmas tree," one of the men from the church began. He was standing by the sale command post, an old clothes dresser that had been modified for the exigencies of tree selling. The two top drawers were intact and loaded with first-aid gear and spare gloves. The other drawers were missing and replaced with a huge rope spool. The top and sides were bristling with box cutters, price tags, spare gloves, and other essentials. "The Fraziers keep their needles the longest," he continued. "That's going to be particularly important to our early shoppers. The balsams smell the best. The Douglas firs are the fullest and last the longest. Some customers pick one right out. Some want to look at five or six or seven. Just be helpful to them, and they'll find one sooner or later. Your job is to help them pick out the tree and carry it back to the curb. Then you ask them if they want a fresh cut on the trunk. It will keep the tree fresh, particularly if they keep it in water with a little sugar mixed in. If they want the cut, do it with one of the hacksaws. Then cut off enough rope to lash the tree to the top of the car and tie it up securely. If you need it, we're there to help, particularly with cars that don't have a luggage rack on top where you need to run a bowline knot through the car."

He reached into a box and pulled out a dozen green baseball caps with a white Christmas tree and the words CHRISTMAS TREE SALE on the crest above the bill. "Oh, and wear these so they know you work here." We put them on, feeling like we'd made it out of Basic Training. As he talked, you could see the kids' minds working in unison: "Let me get this straight. Box cutters. Hacksaws. Knives. Rope. Donuts. Bagels. Tips. This is work?" The lot was festooned with roping and wreaths and bathed in an aural wash of Christmas chestnuts—"I'm Dreaming of a White Christmas," "Jingle Bells," "I'll Be Home for Christmas," "The Christmas Song." No "Get-Down Hip-Hop Phat Christmas Def Jam Santa Booty Call" or Xmas fantasies with Britney and Christina or anything like that. We might not have been Christians, but we were darn sure going to do Christmas right.

Sam all but pounced on the first couple to show up, sounding as eager as one of the commission salesmen at Circuit City. Ben hung back for a while, but after most of the other kids had latched onto customers, he found himself face-to-face with a slim guy of about fifty-five in a blue satin welders' union jacket and his wife, a husky woman about two inches taller than he wearing a Christmas-tree sweatshirt.

"Hi," he said. "I'm Ben Applebome, and I'll be your Christmas-tree salesman for today." This was a swell icebreaker, and I trailed along as they headed toward the trees, which shimmered in a great green sward.

"Hold this one up, please," the wife said to Ben. He pulled up one of the Fraziers and shook it so its branches, which had been bound tight for shipping, could begin to fall.

"How do you like it?" she asked her husband.

"It's fine. It's nice," he dutifully replied.

"I don't know," she said, circling around it. "I don't quite like the shape. It looks kind of lumpy."

"OK, fine. If it's lumpy, pick out another one that's not lumpy."

"How about this one?" she asked Ben. "That looks nice."

He picked up the new one and held it upright.

"What do you think, Jack?" she asked her husband.

"It's fine. It's nice. It's OK. They're all nice."

"I'm not sure about the color. It looks a little blue to me."

"It's not blue. It's a tree. Trees are green. It's green."

"I don't know. I think it would look funny with the sofa. Ben, put that one down," she said. "It's not right. This one looks nice. Let's try that one."

"It looks like the others. It's good. It's fine," said Jack, before she had a chance to ask him if he liked it. "We don't have all day, Brenda."

"No, it looks a little scrawny when you hold it like that."

And so it went. Too tall. Too short. Too blue. Too green. Too thin. Too full. Bad shape. Bad crest. Looks damaged. Looks dry. A little scrawny. A little puffy. Uneven-looking. Unnatural-looking. Not enough smell. Too much smell. Needles too sharp. Needles too soft. On and on. Finally, after twenty minutes, Brenda reluctantly settled on a seven-to-eight-foot Frazier ("You sure the trunk hasn't been cut on already, and this will last until Christmas? OK, then can you do a nice fresh cut for me, Ben?").

I helped him carry it to the curb. Jack trudged inside the church to pay. Brenda stood over us, looking at the tree suspiciously, as if still looking for the disqualifying feature that was surely there somewhere. Ben sawed off two inches of the trunk, and grabbed a handful of rope. We waited for Jack to pull up in a four-year-old Suburban with a luggage rack on top.

We then came face to face with one of the dirty little secrets of Boy Scouts. You might have the badge, but that doesn't mean you remember how to tie the knots. I, of course, had not forgotten my knots. I had never learned them. But Ben, who should have been our go-to guy in the knot department, having long since made Tenderfoot and nearing Second Class, wasn't much better despite his years of rigorous Scout training. We took to improvising assorted spaghetti-like knots, winding the rope four, five, six times around the luggage rack in various nonsanctioned, unapproved, ad hoc, half-assed maneuvers. The couple looked at our handiwork a bit quizzically but figured their treasure was basically secure. Jack gave Ben two bucks. Ben beamed. They drove off. He went on to customer number 2.

"I'm looking for one that's not too full, has a nice smell, but not an overpowering one, keeps its needles, and won't dry out before Christmas," the woman told Ben. And so it went. Before too long, two things became apparent. The first was that every couple that came in had pretty much the same dynamic. The woman was either mystically or obsessive-compulsively focused on finding the perfect tree with that certain indefinable Yuletide *je ne sais quoi,* and the man was just waiting to get the damn purchase over with so he could go home and watch the Jets or Giants on television. The second was that, in a way that Ben found baffling, I had perfect radar for who was going to tip him. For the most part, it was a simple matter of taking all our social status indicators and turning them upside down. So guys with sweatshirts from Fordham or Long Island University were more likely to tip than guys with shirts from Harvard or Yale. Welders in union jackets driving Chevys were more likely to tip than doctors with MD plates driving a Mercedes wagon. Old cars were better than new, domestic better than foreign. Guys with Noo Yawk accents better than guys with Connecticut lockjaw. Old better than young. Men better than women. Heavy women better than fashionably thin women. You get a fashionably thin doctor's wife with a Yale T-shirt and BMW with a Martha's Vineyard sticker, and she's as likely to tip you as to have Merle Haggard in her CD player. As any parent knows, it is almost impossible to impress your own kids past the age of eleven or twelve, but on this one score, my batting average was so good that finally Ben turned to me and said, "Dad, you're good." My turn to beam. We take our praise where we can get it.

The sale stretched over four weekends. I had periodic panic attacks about the sturdiness of our knots for drivers foolhardy enough to be traveling long distances. In my darker moments I found myself imagining horrid newspaper headlines ("Triborough Bridge Shut for Hours After Christmas Tree Flies Off SUV. Owner Expresses Outrage. Balding Boy Scout Held for Questioning."). But, particularly on the rare days that the temperature dipped below freezing, the whole endeavor became shrouded in the shiny tinsel of seasonal cheer and virtue. Finally, our chance to do a good turn! We'd work for a few hours, take a break for hot chocolate or the big plates of spaghetti and lasagna that the church ladies prepared, talk business with our fellow salesmen, comparing notes on the pace of sales and particularly demanding customers, and then put our gloves and hats back on and wade back into the fray. Bing would be warbling "White Christmas" yet again or we'd be into our fourteenth rendition of "The Christmas Song," but the kids were hustling for business and the dads were pleasantly punch drunk with the seasonal cheer of it all.

It was an unseasonably balmy December for New York, without a trace of snow. On the warmest days, the better-padded kids like Sam 'n Eric showed up in just T-shirts, and the lack of a winter chill gave the undertaking a decidedly off-kilter feel, like the pictures of guys in Santa suits parading down the beach in La Jolla. It was another case of Scouting in the abstract running into the messiness of reality. Instead of the world of Norman Rockwell, it's a half-Jewish bunch of suburban Boy Scouts who've forgotten their knots presiding over a balmy Global Warming Christmas tree sale. Not that we minded; we were all so caught up in the virtuous bonhomie of it all that the warm weather felt as right as anything else. When the sale finally ended the weekend before Christmas with the last scrubby trees marked down and sold cheap, we all wished one another, Christians or not, a Merry Christmas, sorry to see the whole thing end.

The warm weather was just an oddity at the tree sale. But it was an affront to the natural order as our next big activity, the Klondike Derby, beckoned. I really don't know what troops in Florida and Arizona do during January and February. But across the nation's northern tier, Scouts like us were working on building our sleds, practicing our winter skills, and boning up on shelter making, axe management, and first aid in anticipation of the big event. It consisted of two main parts. The first was a series of tests of Scouting skill and fortitude, which were judged by stern and demanding Scouters who were named Mayor of various stations set up around the park. The second was a double-elimination sled race in which Scouts, up to six pulling on a rope in front and one pushing from behind, race across perhaps fifty yards of snow-covered field until one sled team is judged the fastest.

Ben's Falcon patrol convened at Vince's auto repair shop on a Saturday in mid-January to fashion a sturdy-looking sled out of pieces of plywood, a few two-by-fours, and a pair of skis. What a deal! They had the whole cavernous garage to themselves on a Saturday and were able to use Vince's electric drills and detailing paint to cobble together a sled to die for. It had a sleek, aerodynamic design and was painted a fashionable understated gray with blue trim. As the *pièce de résistance,* the kids had cut out the eagles from two Post Office overnight delivery envelopes and pasted them on the sides to serve as fierce-looking surrogate falcons. The result looked like an Alaskan Post Office sled that had taken a wrong turn somewhere around Fairbanks and just kept going, but it still had the aura of a solid, macho sled not to be trifled with—the Derby's version of a Chevy truck. And aside from their construction duties, the kids got to run amok in the garage, riding up and down on the hydraulic lifts and generally having a big old time whether or not the sled was worth a damn.

The other Troop 1 patrols built their own sleds—none, it must be said, quite so imposing as the Post Office Special, but all worthy nonetheless. There were weeks of painting, waxing, replacing perfectly good skis with other indefinably superior skis, designing gallant patrol flags, and making final tinkers to bring the sled to its optimum condition. Finally, at the end of January, the big day dawned clear and bright—too clear and too bright, it turned out. The temperatures had dived into the 20s, giving the day an appropriately Arctic tinge. But when we arrived at Franklin Delano Roosevelt State Park for the Derby, we had everything in place but snow. There had been a minor flurry here or there over the past month, but none of it had amounted to anything and by Derby Day it was all gone. To be sure, a sled race without snow seemed a little like a figure-skating competition without ice. But a Scout is resourceful, and if we had to display our winter skills sans snow, that's what we would do.

When we got there just after 9:00 A.M. a handful of Scouts were pulling sleds of all shapes and sizes out of cars, trucks, SUVs, and vans. Before long the entire lot was filled with more than one hundred Scouts and at least twenty-five sleds, sleds with patrol flags for elks and lions and arrows and antelopes, sleds made from sturdy two-by-fours and sleds that looked like a few pine branches nailed to pieces of wood perched precariously on ancient skis. To be honest, no other sled had the heft, the professional fabrication, the subdued but elegant color scheme, or the fierce faux-heraldic falcons to compare with the Post Office Special. Kids from other troops wandered by admiringly to check it out. But there was not much time for mere milling. The Derby was to begin with inspection and check-in at the Derby starting point, which was designated as Juneau. There the Mayors, equipped with clipboards and scoring sheets, had to make sure that each sled had come equipped with the appropriate patrol equipment. "Before you officially enter the Yukon Territory," our handbook, the Passport, informed us, "you must pass the inspection in order to embark on this extremely hazardous expedition." The list of materials, all of them to be stashed inside the sled, was long and demanding:

Patrol flag
Fire-building materials
1 gallon drinking water
#10 can or pot to boil water in
4 six-foot-long poles
6 ten-foot-long lengths of rope
Tarp
Patrol first-aid kit, including triangular bandages,
    compresses, and splint materials
Blanket or sleeping bag
Backpack stove or equivalent to boil water for lunch
Hot chocolate, Cup-O-Soup, etc. for lunch
Compass
Hand axe
File to sharpen axe
Pencil, paper, and clipboard
Boy Scout Handbook
Garbage bag

I could not tell you what most of that was for and still don't know what a #10 can is, but we had somehow rounded most of it up, scoring eight of a possible ten points. At that point, we began dragging the sled across the frigid grass about two hundred yards away to Station 1, Match Splitting, an exercise in axe handling and fire starting. "The local Indian Tribe has challenged your patrol to a contest," the Passport read. "You must split or light more matches than their braves or lose your scalp." This meant we had to see how many matches we could light by hitting the match head with the hand axe. We ended with a lackluster score of five.

Next was Fire Building. Our Passport informed us that one of the local townspeople needed an operation and we needed to light a fire so the doctor could sterilize his instruments. We had brought plenty of wood, flint, and matches and built one in no time flat. Nine points. Then we went on to Ice Rescue, where a patrol member had fallen through the ice twenty-five feet from the shore. We had to rescue him and treat him for the Scouts' favorite peril, hypothermia. We got nine points again. On to First Aid, where our patrol, we were told, had come upon some injured miners, whom we had to treat for snow blindness, frost-bite, and (perhaps you can guess?) hypothermia.

By this point, we had been dragging a bulky sled through the frigid, snowless park for three hours, and most kids were fading into the "When's Lunch?" zone. As luck would have it, lunch, or Ulcer Gap on our Passport, was next. The idea was to demon-strate our cooking skills, but instead of having to build another fire, we were allowed to use our propane stoves to boil water and cook. Thus prepared, we were able to whip up a welcome repast of hot chocolate, Ramen noodles, assorted soups and sand-wiches, and more of Elliot's famous homemade beef jerky.

"What do Eskimoes eat in the real Klondike, wherever that is?" Louis asked.

"Whale blubber," answered Jimmy.

"Eskimo pies," answered Mark.

"Italian ices," answered Tom.

"Baked Alaska," answered Les.

"Prime rib of husky," answered Bernie.

Clearly, we could have gone in that direction for a while, but we had to move on to Shelter Building. It entailed building a shelter using natural items plus materials the patrol brought along. Once again we were prepared, not just with the assorted sticks, ropes, and tarps in the sled, but more importantly with a copy of Chapter 8, "Shelters," from the *U.S. Army Survival Manual*. *"You cannot ignore your tactical situation or your safety,"* it warned us, and offered hints on concealment from enemy observation and avoiding flash floods and avalanches. We turned to the section on natural shelters, which seemed more promising than the ones that entailed major construction projects. "Do not overlook natural formations that can give you shelter," it said. "Examples are caves, rocky crevices, clumps of bushes, small depressions, large rocks on leeward sides of hills, large trees with low-hanging limbs, and fallen trees with thick branches." Ah-ha! This was more like it. We ended up hanging a tarp from the front of a granite cave about seven feet high that was surrounded by a scrubby copse of pines and maples. We trudged to a few more destinations after that, but by this point there was just one activity left that could really get everyone's attention—the big race.

The Passport announced the race would begin at 2:15, but, of course, at 2:15 only a handful of thuggish-looking kids and scrawny sleds had arrived at the field where the race was to take place. The kids, various Scoutmasters, Mayors, and dads slowly filtered in, but the time crept from 2:30 to 2:45 to 3:00, with the temperatures sinking from the high 20s to the low 20s. Our feet were getting numb in our boots—wool socks or no wool socks. None of the adults would have been sorry to pack it in, but the race was too big a lure for the kids to miss—that and the orgy of Dunkin' Donuts to follow. Finally, after much mayoral conferring and pacing off the exact configuration of the racecourse, which looked to be about fifty yards altogether, a man with an air gun in one hand and a bullhorn in the other strode toward the assembled masses. "Gentlemen," he announced into the bullhorn. "Listen up. I'm only gonna say this once. We're running a double-elimination race. That means you have to lose two heats to be out. You can have a maximum of six Scouts pulling your sled. You can have one Scout pushing your sled from the rear. You can't lift the sled off the ground. The whole sled and all the patrol members have to cross the line to complete the race. You start when the gun sounds. The Judges' decisions will be final. Good luck, gentlemen."

Left unspoken was the minor problem that there was no snow on the ground. What was most striking was not that we went ahead, but that, as far as I could tell, no one seemed to notice. This made complete sense. Scouting, I had come to realize, was largely about the suspension of disbelief, taking advantage of the way kids now, much like kids in Baden-Powell's day, are still capable of the sort of imaginative play that helps them construct their own reality. How else to explain the vestigial axemanship (when will kids possibly need to strike a match with an axe handle?), the feral shelter building? For all our worries, kids, even in a place like Chappaqua, still seemed to be able to be kids. It was nice to know that in the continuing tug of war between mythic Scout reality and the modern world, the Scout reality could still hold its own.

As we milled around, at least two things were clear. The first was that the Post Office Special was still by far the most solid-looking and artfully decorated sled of them all. The second was that while our kids were mostly sixth and seventh graders—and not particularly imposing ones at that—some of the other patrols were filled with high school jocks. They took off coats to flex bulging biceps, practiced running sprints to warm up, and engaged in all sorts of macho grunting and chest butting to get their juices going.

Before long, the man with the bullhorn called out the names of the patrols in the first heat: "Bears. Arrows. Panthers. Bulldogs. Jackals. To the starting line, gentlemen." (Scoutmasters cannot refer to their charges as "gentlemen" often enough, as if merely using the word will somehow transform ungainly adolescents into suave James Bond clones.) The pullers took up pieces of the rope and wrapped it around their wrists. The pusher got ready to shove off from behind. And at the sound of the horn, they began sprinting forward. Well, some of them began sprinting forward. The Bears, with a benign Yogi Bear–like figure on their patrol flag, began by tripping over one another's feet and pretty much going nowhere. But the rest took off, arms flailing, legs pumping, occasionally slipping and then scrambling to get going again. Two of the patrols with the bigger kids raced forward as if the sleds were greased. They raced along neck and neck until the Bulldog sled pulled away and won easily. It was the most modest-looking sled out there, two diagonal bars of pine limbs on a frame over the skis.

Finally we were called, and we headed toward the starting line. Jimmy, the World's Biggest Scout, was behind. Ben, Mark, Jack, and Sam were in front, plus Elliot, no doubt as a reward for bringing along his famous jerky. Our team got into a runner's half crouch and waited for the horn. HHHOOONNKKKK. They were off. Sort of. Well, they were off, but they were off in slow motion. It soon became painfully clear that while the Post Office Special had the virtue of being the most solid and substantial sled out there, that also made it the heaviest and bulkiest sled out there. And while the Egrets raced along in their ratty little bare-bones sled, dragging the Post Office Special across the grass was like trying to drag the *Queen Mary* across Franklin D. Roosevelt State Park. And had there actually been snow, making traction that much harder to come by, it would have been that much worse. We did our best, but we were about halfway across the field when the Egrets crossed the finish line. There was a second heat, but we had no more chance than we did in the first. We stuck around to watch a bunch of beasts from one of the tougher towns near New York City compete in the finals, then lugged the Post Office Special up the hill to the check-in area, where the Mayors were all warming their feet by a hearty fire and twenty or so boxes of Dunkin' Donuts were laid out as a final reward for the Klondikers. We ate our fill of Boston creams, glazed and apple donuts, and petite donut holes, then lugged the grass-stained sled for a final time to Victor's van, its fierce falcon/eagle now looking suspiciously like an albatross. We bid it good riddance until next year, cranked up the heat to high, and got the hell out of the Yukon.

8: The Church of the Woods

The weekly meetings were just one of the places where Troop 1 passed on its values and traditions. Another was the ceremonial Courts of Honor, held three times a year, where merit badges and Eagles were awarded. A third place was camp each summer. But the main transmission came through the camp-outs and hikes. This would have come as a great comfort to Ernest Thompson Seton and Daniel Carter Beard. It seems both utterly remarkable and highly unlikely that a British war hero could have founded a movement that has come to be perceived as so quintessentially American. But Scouting in America has two other fathers, Seton and Beard, who began boy movements even earlier than Baden-Powell. Both formed movements that were grounded in the most fundamental kinds of American images, one the American Indian, the other the American frontiersman. Both, along with Baden-Powell, are reminders that Scouting's origins were diverse and complex, far more interesting than the bland stereotypes Scouting is shrouded in today. And both raise the same question: How much relevance can Scouting have for kids in the twenty-first century if it drew all its inspiration from three eccentric dreamers whose goal was to keep the virtues and values of the nineteenth century alive in the twentieth? Indeed, the more I got involved with the troop, the more Scouting seemed an uncertain jumble of distant past and murky present. Sometimes the disparate parts meshed; sometimes they did not. And even our excursions into the woods almost always ended up being mediations between the two worlds.

Ernest Thompson Seton, born three years after Baden-Powell, created the most compelling and perhaps the most influential alternative universe to the one created by Baden-Powell. Both had similar concerns—what they saw as the moral and physical decline of youth and the threat that that posed to national welfare. But while Baden-Powell's worldview was wildly eclectic, Seton's was so focused as to be almost a manifesto. "This is a time when the whole nation is turning toward the outdoor life, seeking in it the physical regeneration so needful for continued national existence," Seton proclaimed on the first page of his handbook, *The Birch-bark Roll of the Woodcraft Indians,* published in 1906. According to Seton there was an evil afoot in the land, urbanism and the bustle and "grind of the over-busy world." And there was also a cure: the slower, natural world of the woods and the teachings of the American Indians. One of the most affecting pieces of writing in the Boy Scout canon is the introduction Seton wrote for the first Scout Handbook. It revisits a theme he came back to over and over in his writing, but it does it with an urgency and passion that takes your breath away:

There was once a boy who lived in a region of rough farms. He was wild with the love of the great outdoors—the trees, the tree-top singers, the wood-herbs and the live things that left their nightly tracks in the mud by his spring well. He wished so much to know them and learn about them, he would have given almost any price in his gift to know the name of this or that wonderful bird or brilliant flower; he used to tremble with excitement and intensity of interest when some new bird was seen, or when some strange song came from the trees to thrill him with its power or vex him with its mystery, and he had a sad sense of lost opportunity when it flew away leaving him dark as ever.

He continued: "Young Scouts of America, that boy is writing to you now. He thought himself peculiar in those days. He knows now he was simply a normal boy with the interests and desires of all normal boys, some of them a little deeper rooted and more lasting perhaps—and all the things that he loved and wished to learn have now part in the big broad work we call Scouting." In the most narrow sense, Seton was extolling the virtues of the Handbook, "the book that I so longed for in those far-off days when I wandered heart hungry in the woods." But what he was really talking about was his dream for Scouting and what it could offer to boys.

The psychological currents running through Seton were even more complex than the ones that made up Baden-Powell. Seton was an esteemed naturalist and wildlife artist, a celebrated lecturer and a man with aspirations to lead his nation's youth much like Baden-Powell's. But as much as he was animated by his love of the outdoors, he was also animated by his hatred for three people: St. Paul the Apostle, General George Custer, and his own father. He hated St. Paul for the role he played in establishing the doctrine that Woman was created to serve Man—a doctrine, he decided, that forced his mother to submit to the will of his despotic father. He hated Custer as the symbol of the White Man's reign of terror against the Sioux, the Cheyenne, and all of America's Indians. And his father? Seton, the eighth of ten brothers, wrote in his memoirs that his father was "a worthless loafer, a petty swindler, a wife-beater, and a child-murderer . . . the most selfish person I ever heard of in history or in fiction."

His judgment of his father baffled his brothers, who did not see the monster that Ernest did. But the elder Seton was a rigid fundamentalist, who meted out frequent beatings and wanted his children inside reading religious literature, not playing outside. When Ernest turned twenty-one, his father handed him a bill for $537.50, the money he calculated it took to raise his son, right down to the cost of the midwife's service at his birth. But however much his sense of grievance was based in fact and however much in paranoia, Seton from a young age identified utterly with life's victims, both human, like the Indians, and animal, like the wolves and hares destined to live their lives as man's prey. As a boy, he regularly found refuge in the wild and fantasized about being an Indian brave. The single most revelatory moment of his life happened years later, on a train ride in the middle of a ferocious blizzard. Just outside Winnipeg, he saw outside his window a lone wolf ringed by dogs, successfully fighting them all off. ". . . chop, chop, chop," he later wrote, "went those fearful jaws, no other sound from the lonely warrior; but a death yelp from more than one of his foes, as those that were able sprang back, and left him statuesque as before, untamed, unmaimed and contemptuous of them all."

Seton came to identify utterly with that wolf. He too, he decided, could be "untamed, unmaimed and contemptuous of them all," and he came to see the wilderness as the ultimate teaching tool. His friends took to calling him "Wolf." He signed his letters with a paw print, and seldom took a bath or cut his hair. For Seton, woodcraft was not the wily, practical military scouting that appealed to Baden-Powell but was akin to religion.

Seton's passion for the outdoors animated a remarkably productive and accomplished life. He all but invented a form of wilderness narrative in which he wrote about animals not as cute anthropomorphic figures, but as heroic, doomed individuals. He was a brilliant illustrator, admired in both popular and professional circles, and an amazingly acute observer of nature. He saw the outdoors as the cure for disease and a balm to the spirit. But, he added, it was not enough to go outdoors. He told the tale of a benevolent rich man who chartered a steamer and sent hundreds of slum boys to the Catskills, where they disappeared and were soon found in groups under the bushes, smoking cigarettes, shooting craps, and playing cards. "Thus," he wrote, "the well-meaning rich man learned that it is not enough to take men out of doors. We must also teach them how to enjoy it. The purpose of this Roll is to show how Outdoor Life may be followed to advantage."

He began promulgating his vision of woodcraft as a national movement in 1902 in, of all places, the *Ladies' Home Journal,* which published seven articles outlining his idea for tribes of Seton Indians. Boys would be grouped in bands of fifteen to thirty, loosely supervised by an adult medicine man. They wore headdresses and won feathers for specific achievements. Each band was identified by a particular totem, and boys won noncompetitive badges for achieving particular goals in the form of wampum medals made from shells engraved with the symbol or deed the boy had accomplished. The organization had a strict code of conduct each boy swore by, and a vow that each boy took upon joining: "I solemnly promise that I will obey the chief and council of my tribe, and if I fail in my duty, I will surrender to them my weapons and submit without murmuring to their decision."

In 1906 when a collection of his work, *The Birch-bark Roll of the Woodcraft Indians,* was finally put in book form, Seton sent a copy to Baden-Powell in England. Baden-Powell, who was struggling to determine precisely how to organize his own movement, read the book with great eagerness. He was particularly taken with the games that Seton used to keep the boys engaged in the wild and the noncompetitive framework for advancement. Seton saw a potential ally for bringing his scheme to England. The two met shortly afterward, and before long Baden-Powell published his *Scouting for Boys* and unveiled his Boy Scout scheme.

Baden-Powell was frank in saying his organization borrowed from many sources, but he never fully conceded how much of his book and movement, its patrols, merit badges, and system of noncompetitive merit-badge advancement, were influenced by Seton. Seton was deeply hurt when Baden-Powell failed to credit some obvious borrowings, including five of Seton's outdoor games, in the first edition of *Scouting for Boys*. Things got worse when Seton decided that Baden-Powell had reneged on an agreement to help promote the Woodcraft Indians in Great Britain. They reconciled somewhat a few years later, and when the Boy Scouts of America was founded in 1910 as the American form of the movement Baden-Powell had started in England, Seton came aboard. He was named Chief Scout and was main author of the original *Handbook of the Boy Scouts of America*. But Seton never really made his peace with Baden-Powell's vision. Seton and the Boy Scouts soon had a falling out, and he went to his grave thinking Baden-Powell had stolen Scouting from him. He was wrong. Baden-Powell borrowed from many people, including Seton, but Seton's idea in the end was doomed by the almost mystical purity of his belief in the outdoors and the narrow focus of being so closely allied to the imagery of the American Indian—particularly at a time people were more likely to think of Indians as drunken savages than as heroic woodsmen. Baden-Powell's was a much richer and more fanciful mix of disparate elements. But Seton remains a true visionary, one of the pioneers of American environmentalism and the source of the passion for the wilderness that is one of the richest threads woven through Scouting in the United States.

Daniel Carter Beard, the founder of the Sons of Daniel Boone, was not quite as complex as Baden-Powell or Seton. But he became more of an icon and role model to the first generations of American Scouts than either of them, a colorful, beloved figure known as "Uncle Dan" who consciously turned himself into the embodiment of the disappearing frontier. Beard, a folksy bear of a man, was in many ways yin to Seton's yang. Outdoorsmen and illustrators, both were attracted to training boys and using the outdoors as their teaching laboratory, but that's where the similarities ended. Raised in Kentucky, Beard saw himself as the last link to the world of Daniel Boone and the personification of American nationalism and the pioneer scout. While Seton evinced an almost spiritual sense of unity with the wilderness and its vulnerable creatures, Beard saw the wild as a laboratory for cultivating rugged frontier virtues that conveyed to him the essence of the American experience. Seton's totem and inspiration was the lonely, untamed wolf; Beard's was the endangered buffalo of the American frontier. In the foreword to his best-known book *The American Boys' Handy Book,* he cites heroes like Daniel Boone, Kit Carson, Davy Crockett, Johnny Appleseed, and Abraham Lincoln. He says:

> Men of this description are not the product of an over-refined civilization. At times they might be and, indeed, are called barbarians. They are essentially boyish; like boys, they have restless minds and are noisy, energetic, fun-loving creatures ... One of the principal purposes in forming and carrying on the Society of the Sons of Daniel Boone was to awaken in the boy of today admiration for the old-fashioned virtues of American Knights in Buckskin and a desire to emulate them.

Beard propounded a sort of hypermasculine, hyper-American brand of Scouting, and he became its folksy image, given to

Crockettlike aphorisms ("This was a good country in the past. It is a good country today. It will be a good country tomorrow unless we fail it."). In his organizational scheme, eight boys made up a stockade and four stockades made a fort. He had his boys dress in homemade pioneer costumes, talked of an organization that would promote "wholesome manliness," environmental awareness, and "admiration for the old-fashioned virtues of American Knights in Buckskin." Beard had the soul of a tinkerer and inventor, and his books, *The American Boys' Handy Book, Shelters, Shacks and Shanties,* and *What to Do and How to Do It,* are an eccentric cavalcade of instruction on how to do almost everything—build a pushmobile, rig a house-wagon, celebrate Johnny Appleseed's Day, handle a gun, decorate and paper the inside of a shack, throw a tomahawk, make a swimming hole, make snowshoes, build a pioneer bob and a cheap bobsled, make an attic gym. So what if we no longer know what half those things are? And so what if he could get carried away with his pedagogical duties, making throwing a tomahawk ("Take aim, as in Fig. 233, bring the tomahawk back over the shoulder, as in Figs. 234 and 235, then bring your hand quickly down, following the line A B, Fig. 233, and swinging the body forward, let fly the tomahawk as in Fig. 236.") sound like AP calculus? For all his frontier machismo, Beard was also an admirer of utopian political movements like the Single Tax Movement, inspired by Henry George's 1879 book *Progress and Poverty,* and a cantankerous radical critic of big business, big money, and industrial plutocrats. He lived to the age of ninety-one and his every utterance and reminiscence made him sound like a character out of Mark Twain, for whom he did the illustrations for the first edition of *A Connecticut Yankee at King Arthur's Court.*

Beard was more a charismatic figure than an organizer, and he promoted his ideas mostly through magazine pieces in periodicals that he inevitably ended up feuding with and/or suing.

Unlike the Woodcraft Indians, the Sons of Daniel Boone never really developed a full program. In fact, for all their celebrity, neither founder knew how to build a real organization, and it is doubtful either group had more than two thousand members. But as Seton and Beard would stress as time went by, both groups were American-born versions of Scouting that existed before Baden-Powell got the English version going. Both were rooted in the romance of the outdoors. And all three were rooted in an alarmism, bordering on panic, about the state of the young.

Indeed, if there's one way that the instincts that drove Baden-Powell, Seton, and Beard seem entirely relevant now, a century later, it's the way boys are seen as imperiled creatures in need of both moral uplift and wholesome activities designed to steer them away from sin. The imminent moral decline of youth—particularly boys—appears to be a constant refrain in modern life. American boys, it seems, have always been on the verge of being swept up by some sinister threat. At the beginning of the century it was smoking, spectator sports, and urban life. They were imperiled by comic books, juvenile delinquency, and rock 'n' roll in the 1950s; then drugs, long hair, and psychedelic rock in the 1960s and '70s; MTV, video games, and heavy-metal, headbanger music in the 1980s; and computer games, the perils of affluence, and gangsta rap since then. Now, depending on which school of pop psychology appeals to you, boyhood itself is under assault from two entirely different directions. One side, in what might be called the neo-Beardian worldview, says that boys are either being feminized or shackled by a culture that is so tame, wussified, and politically correct that it would take Huck Finn and label him a learning-disabled underachiever who needs Ritalin and weekly counseling. A normal, rambunctious boyhood is diagnosed as a disability. The other, with a large dose of Seton in it, says that we demand so much of boys as to turn them by elementary school into competitive fighting machines, unable to tap into the gentler, more eloquent instincts they're so desperate to touch. They don't need to get harder and tougher; they need to have the same kind of transcendent experiences—in the wild or elsewhere—that Seton had as a boy in the woods.

Most of this discussion says more about adults than kids. One comforting thing about Troop 1 was just how normal, in their own ragged ways, the kids seemed. The kids I saw around me did not square with the overheated accounts of the crisis facing America's youth. Yes, these were privileged kids, but the literature of adolescent despair—not to mention the most graphic examples of it, like the shootings at Columbine High School—is often centered around privileged kids. Still, if overblown, there is an element of truth in the two scenarios of boyhood in crisis, and Scouting at its best, I was beginning to think, addresses both of them. It is usually associated with the Neo-Beard school. No wusses here! Toughen 'em up, teach them their knots, let them survive in the woods. But Ben's attraction to Scouting seemed to me all Seton and little Beard. Ben did seem to find something magical in the outdoors. He dreamed of hiking the whole Appalachian Trail, not as a test of physical endurance, but as a wondrous journey. He looked forward to each camp-out or hike the way I used to look forward to the Jets games my father took me to at Shea Stadium when I was a kid. Kids do face unholy pressure these days—I knew we were in trouble when my daughter, Emma, came back from third grade one day and announced that she'd heard that Yale was a good place to go to college. Ben seemed most insulated from those pressures when he was in the woods with his friends in Troop 1.

One Saturday in early April, when we were just about safe from one last freeze, we had our first camp-out of the spring at the Clear Lake Scout Reservation adjacent to Fahnestock State Park. The core of the park was once the estate of Major

Clarence Fahnestock, a Manhattan physician who purchased a rugged swath of abandoned farmland and former iron mine in 1915 as a gentleman's farm and shooting preserve and then died three years later in France during the influenza epidemic.

We parked at the edge of Canopus Lake and got out of our cars. The air was heavy and damp. It had rained overnight and looked like it could drizzle again, but the temperature was already in the high 50s, and it felt like a propitious day to take a hike. "OK, everyone, listen up," Mr. Toonkel barked, as about twenty kids and five dads were gathered around him. Mr. Toonkel, as always, was a sight. He had on his Sing Sing Surf Squad cap and camouflage pants. In his hands was his steel hiking monopod. He handed out topographic maps, with squiggles that brought back vivid, unwelcome memories of my least favorite course of all time, Geology 101. He broke us into groups of seven or eight, pointed out some landmarks we could expect to find, and said the hike would cover only about three miles, so if we were still hiking late in the day we were hopelessly lost.

Next, Mr. Toonkel took out a roll of paper towels and gave two sheets to each kid and adult. Then he tore one into a little shred and held it aloft. "What happens on High Adventure is that if you ask for a paper towel, Dr. Flank gives you a little piece like this. This is your paper towel. Now I'm going to give you each two sheets. Two whole sheets! Put it away. Use it sparingly. Use it for KP to clean your dish and pot, blow your nose, wipe your bottom. It's plenty, believe me."

Various predictably disgusting scenarios immediately began to play across my mind and the dirty little minds of my fellow Scouts. Mr. Toonkel went on as if reading our minds: "What we're trying to teach you is respect for nature and a recognition of how wasteful we are at home. At home you'd use a roll of paper towels in a few days and think nothing of it. Throw it in the trash. Not our problem. But, of course, it has to be someone's problem in someone's landfill. It doesn't just disappear. So here, we want you to be aware that you can get by with so much less if you just think about it a little."

We all strapped on our packs, crossed the two-lane road, and headed for the trail, which was soft and moist after the evening rain. I fell in somewhere in the middle of the pack, right behind Jack, our patrol leader; two Amigos, Mark and Jonah; and a trim dad with a modest mustache and a fly rod poking out of his backpack. Ben and I walked together for a while until he hooked up with the Amigos. I knew enough, by this point, to make sure my pack was snug and my hip belt was carrying the bulk of the weight, rather than having the pack's weight borne by my shoulders. I had on my new Gore-Tex boots, now reasonably broken in, and various layers of plain old clothes, none of them the catalog gear of Ben's dreams, but working fine for me. And while most of the trek was relatively flat, I welcomed the occasional inclines and felt some small macho pride that, despite my advancing years, I was certainly as fit and prepared as most of these little twerps.

We hiked for a half hour or so, took a short break for water and rest, and then resumed. Before long, Mr. Johnson pointed toward a gentle rise to our right. "Anyone know what that is?" he asked. No one did. "Believe it or not, it used to be a railroad," he said. It could have fooled me. "This area used to be full of iron mines, and they built a narrow-gauge railroad to cart out the ore."

Indeed, long before Clarence Fahnestock was around, the area was host to the Sunk Mine and the Canada Mine, part of the Reading Prong formation, which stretched from Pennsylvania to the Berkshires. The formation was rich in magnetite, an iron ore, which was mined as early as the days of the Revolution. First, the ore was smelted and used locally. Later, it was hauled about five miles to the West Point Foundry in Cold Spring, now a spruced-up and tourist-friendly village on the Hudson River, where it was used to make the Parrott gun, a rifled cannon used in the Civil War. The railroad consisted of the track and mule-drawn cars, which carried the ore to horse-drawn wagons for the trip to Cold Spring. But it never became economical to transport the ore for broader commercial purposes, and the mines closed in 1876. Thomas Alva Edison tried to reopen them in 1890, but failed. You can still find old entrances if you root around through the brush.

Our comfortable suburban world was a few light years from the region of rough farms where Seton had stalked the woods. But the kids were hardly immune to the backwoods adventure and romance that captivated Seton, and the story of the abandoned mine struck even me as appealingly spooky, making the place a perfect site for one of the Hardy Boys mysteries (there doesn't seem to be *The Secret of the Lost Mine,* but there should be). You could tell that the kids found something intriguing in this ambitious, low-tech enterprise that flourished fitfully for a time in what were then distant, unforgiving environs that now lay lost and forgotten in this wooded glade a half hour's drive from their own world.

That did not turn out to be the only lesson of the day. The park is laced with old hemlock groves and large areas of second-growth hardwood forest, which have grown up since the rocky farmland was abandoned around the turn of the century. The most conspicuous greenery is vast strands of mountain laurel, which have survived because the deer, which are all over the place, won't eat them. There are swamps and bogs and numerous streams that are small enough to cross on rocks, downed tree limbs, or makeshift tree-stump bridges. Mr. Johnson, it turned out, knew every tree, bird, and rock formation in the park. Without being too didactic about it, he managed to turn the hike into a naturalist's tour of the woods.

"See this," he said at one point, pointing to a tubular plant growing by the side of the trail. "This is called horsetail. The Indians used to use it as a scouring brush. Inside it is a mineral called silica. You take this stuff and break it up, and it works like steel wool. The Indians used it to clean dishes and pots with. This particular one is called *Equisutum hyemale.* You often see it growing around railroad tracks. This was a very valuable commodity back then. Here's another thing. See this little thing on the plants. It's called an insect gall. Who can tell me what a gall is?"

"A seed?" one of the kids guessed.

"Well, sometime it's an egg and sometime it's an insect," Mr. Johnson said. "It doesn't always contain the egg. Sometimes what happens is the insect gets inside the plant and the plant would form this around it. It was kind of like locking him up in jail."

He pointed out Christmas ferns and tulip trees, and what the difference in acidity between Clear Lake and Sperling Pond meant for the fish that could survive there. A little later, we stopped by a mammoth boulder seemingly resting against two modest-sized oak trees. "Gentlemen," Mr. Johnson said. "Aside from the fact that there was a big guy around, how did that get there?"

"A glacier," several kids answered. (That one was easy. It was already a private joke among Ben and the Amigos that anything that was ever moved—earth, boulder, mobile home—was always moved by a glacier.)

"Notice how it's sitting on a smaller rock and how it was pushed there and deposited. What kind of rock?"

"Granite?"

"No, it doesn't look like it. It looks fairly uniform. It's probably a metamorphic rock called gneiss. See the injections in there? What's doing this? It's called frost wedging. The water gets in it, it freezes, and it expands and starts to crack it. See this side? This little flat section? The piece that comes off here? Have you guys talked about exfoliation yet? It heats. It cools. It heats. It cools. And the top layer breaks off. You now know what a glacial erratic looks like. Amaze your friends."

There was a clump of lichen on the rock, and Larry, the dad who had flown in from Georgia for the hike and was wearing a ball cap that read MARKETING MANIAC, asked them what lichen is a combination of. No one knew.

"Fungus and algae," he said. "Freddy Fungus and Alice Algae took a lichen to each other. It's dumb, but you'll never forget it."

We stopped for lunch around 12:30. In the past, Ben and I had found a rock to eat at together. But Barrett, the little weatherman, had pretty much dropped out from the troop, and Ben was spending most of his time with the two remaining Amigos as if he were slipping neatly into Barrett's vacated spot. So they all ate and talked about video games and advanced weapons systems while I sat down with the guy with the fly rod, who put us to shame with a grilled portobello mushroom, roasted pepper, Italian ham, and mozzarella cheese sandwich on a big slab of Italian bread with mustard and crushed jalapeños. He had driven up in a van with a FLY GUY license plate and immediately started talking about his favorite subject.

I had seen *A River Runs Through It,* but other than that I had less than zero interest in the cult of fly fishing. Still, I found Fly Guy's enthusiasm rather charming. Clearly, he was another guy with a thwarted version of the Seton gene. The father of George, who was a year younger than Ben and a blur of adolescent energy, Fly Guy was an attorney for some big investment firm, who worked like a banshee all week. Fly fishing—and the outdoors in general—was his refuge from all that, and he seemed to look forward to the Scout outings more than the kids did. He talked about his law school professor who made the hopelessly boring course in agency and suretyship tolerable by injecting fly-fishing lore and analogies throughout the course, so that any miscreant who committed fraud and fled, for example, would inevitably be found bonefishing in the Bahamas or some such thing. I'm not sure it worked for everyone in the class, but it definitely worked for him. He talked about the days B.C.—before children—when he did a lot of camping and fishing on the Salmon River, where you woke up to the sound of eagles' wings flapping over the water. I had never heard of John Gierach's *Sex, Death and Fly Fishing,* but Fly Guy made it almost sound like it would be worth reading even for a non–Fly Guy like me.

No one was in any great hurry to get going, but after a while Mr. Toonkel passed out his lollipops and then we all saddled up and got back on the trail. After a while it changed from the soft, beaten-down trail we'd been on to a clamber across huge chunks of rock until finally we reached our destination: a rocky hilltop overlooking Clear Lake that is part of the Clear Lake Scout Reservation. Everyone scrambled to lay claim to whatever scarce patches of relatively flat, rock-free territory they could find, with the biggest piece of turf claimed by a group that had carried with them a four-man tent the size of a modest condominium. We had a new tent of our own, an orange REI Mountaineering model that was a gift to Ben from his Uncle Walter, a doctor in Louisiana and an Eagle Scout himself, who actually knew what he was doing. Now, it seemed, Ben did too. Between our first trip and this one, Ben had become completely proficient at putting it up. I looked on or helped pound in stakes. We dragged our packs into the front vestibule, taking care to remove our food, which we then placed in a bear bag, which, as any idiot knows, is a bag that you hang from a tree so bears can't get into any food you've brought along. Then we wandered around to see what our confederates were up to.

From the condominium-sized tent came much merriment over someone's choice of food storage containers—"Look, everyone, Tupperware! We're having a Tupperware party in our tent!" From another came a conversation about the correct way to prepare chicken teriyaki. From a third, Allen, the chef and musical expert, was leading a spirited group rendition of "Old Man River"—context unknown.

Doug and Elliot sat on a rock discussing their favorite subject, the computer game Starcraft. Like the Koran or the Bible for the devout, it seemed to them a text of infinite richness. And those who were most versed in its dark mysteries, like Doug and Elliot, could spend hours in the wild discussing the fine points, attack strategies, and metaphysical depths of its infinite permutations. Starcraft was based on three species warring with each other somewhere in a dark future following a nuclear war and the rise and fall of one hideous order after another. Terrans are human beings. Zergs are disgusting, alien, buglike monsters. Protoss are telepathic aliens who don't like the Zergs. On and on they went, analyzing the various weapons—Protoss Zealots and Archons; Zerg Hydralisks, Multilisks, and Ultralisks; Terran Wraiths, Vultures, and Arclite Siege Tanks—then parsing strategy, like grandmasters playing out chess games in their head. How could they remember all this? It was apparent that Doug in particular, one of the smartest kids in the troop, even dreamed in a different language than I did. On one trip he had relayed a dream about the battle between two groups—one evil humans, the other a benign group of tadpoles, or maybe mudskippers. It was so baroque and layered it left me feeling like a caveman. It was hard enough for adults and adolescents to communicate when they spoke the same language, but their Starcraft talk might as well have been in Urdu. I wanted to ask them what they were doing here in the woods, if their heads were still most at home on their computer screens, the place where today's scouts and explorers apprehend new and strange worlds. But clearly, they were quite used to swinging from one world, one screen, one century, one mindset to another, so it was at least possible for Seton and Beard to coexist with Hydralisks and Wraiths. And really nothing on the trip was neatly situated in either the present or the past; it was all a combination of the two.

When we returned to the campsite, some of the Scouts were clearly ready to practice the manly arts of cooking and camping in the spirit of their primordial ancestors in the woods. As they gathered in little conspiratorial clusters, a red Swiss army knife surfaced here, a Bic lighter there (even for them, eating like a caveman didn't mean rubbing two pieces of wood together). And the more enterprising started to gather firewood, breaking up brittle old oak branches and stray twigs.

"What are you guys doing?" snapped Mr. Toonkel, as he spotted Bernie and Hal comparing knives. They looked up, embarrassed, and mumbled something. It was fairly easy to feel embarrassed by Mr. Toonkel. If Dr. Flank, by dint of his age, experience, and role as Scoutmaster, had a sort of unimpeachable moral authority in the troop, Mr. Toonkel had the no-nonsense air of the keeper of the practical virtues. Dr. Flank could be stern as hell when riled, but he was sort of philosophically tolerant, so he put up with a fair amount. Mr. Johnson was truly affable by nature, and I'm not sure I ever saw him genuinely angry at the kids. Of the triumverate, Mr. T was the easiest to annoy and had the shortest fuse with the kids who got on his nerves.

"Look around you," Mr. Toonkel said, with mild irritation. "There's really not that much usable wood, is there? This place gets used a lot, and each troop that comes through takes away its own little piece. So the days of using the knife as a survival tool or pioneering instrument are pretty much over. That's why people are going more and more to those Leatherman-type tools. They're more appropriate for an industrialized society, when you come down to it. We bring stoves with us and cook on Coleman propane stoves, not on campfires. We bring prefabricated tents, not something we fashion out of the elements. So what do we need a knife for? Rather than having to cut something, we'd get more use of a pair of pliers to bend the metal of a tin back or close a loop or screw something back together. What we mostly want is something to help us cook our meals. So I'm not going to keep you from bringing a knife, although you better not bring it to school. But we really don't need knives. And we certainly don't need axes. An axe is an accident waiting to happen. And we don't need to be tearing up much of the wood you'll be finding here. So, why don't you relax, and get your dinners ready, and we'll get the stoves going."

Indeed, in a few minutes, four propane Coleman stoves were hissing away, their domesticated blue flames boiling water for suppers great and small. Kids and grownups emerged from tents carrying dinners, all of which came from Column A or Column B. Column A, call it the traditionalist fare, consisted of one-pot stews, the foundation of the Scout culinary regimen. They contained various elements, but most of them were built around the following holy quartet: ramen noodles, precooked chicken or beef, rice, and Birds Eye frozen vegetables. There were endless possible variations: a little adobo seasoning, some fresh mushrooms or corn, some Worcestershire sauce, a Cheez Doodle or Pringle thrown in for seasoning or comic effect. But most of the kids played it relatively straight, their ingredients transported in various saggy baggies and soon dumped in pots great and small and boiled till dead.

More common, on this trip at least, was Plan B, the no-work-at-all idiot-proof, buy-it-in-a-bag-add-water-and-eat approach, the outdoors' answer to astronaut's food. There was just-add-water fettucini alfredo and chili, spaghetti with meat sauce, beef stew and beef stroganoff. Squarely in the Troop 1 mainstream, we had brought along fettucini alfredo, which after our long day on the trail seemed awfully inviting.

We waited for Mr. Johnson to finish his cooking and then sprang into action. First, I whipped out my own red Swiss army knife and cut the bag open, decisively proving that a knife can be a survival tool even in these advanced times. Inside was what appeared to be a mixture of sawdust and stomped-on popcorn. Expertly following directions, we poured water from our Nalgene jar into the two pots we'd brought along that were part of Ben's spiffy Texsport cooking kit. Sure enough, in our capable hands, the water soon reached an insouciant boil. With a chef's intuitive sense of timing, we waited until the most propitious moment, poured the water into the bag with a Gallic flourish, and sealed it shut. We waited the requisite three minutes, like expectant fathers, fighting off the urge to peek too early. Before long, voilà, it was time to dig in. And if our fare was not quite worthy of Le Cirque, it really wasn't bad. It definitely had that ineffable Tang/astronaut/*Rosemary's Baby*/what-the-hell-is-this quality. But somehow it tasted more like food than like faux food, though after a hard day of camping maybe I couldn't tell the difference. We still had our Sprites and some of our sesame sticks. And for dessert, we had brought a four-pack of little tins of peaches and pears that I thought added a healthy grace note to the meal. We tore through the packaging, peeled back the lids, and scooped out the watery fruit swimming in its syrupy ooze.

Mr. Toonkel had been watching us with a vaguely disapproving eye and finally felt moved to speak. "Do you really want to bring that much junk that you'll just have to carry back out with you?" he asked, with a slightly less mild note of irritation in his voice. Indeed, I belatedly realized that no one else had brought anything with the elaborate, environmentally suspect packaging of the tins of peaches and pears. They had all used one pot—or none at all—to the two we'd used just to pour water in the bag. Most had used their cup for both eating and drinking, or eaten their astronaut glop from the bag. We'd used the two plates and two cups. In the land of the one-pot stew and leave-no-trace camping, we were the Ugly Americans. Troop 1 may have been a bunch of comfortable suburbanites, but the troop ethos had a bit of Earth First environmental zealotry in it. None of the adults ever killed a bug if they could help it, and Todd was constantly rescuing caterpillars and ladybugs trapped in someone's tent and releasing them into the wild. The men took "leave-no-trace" incredibly seriously—if they were at a site where they did gather up wood for a fire, they would disperse everything that was left over at the end, flinging it into a facsimile of the natural order they had encountered. And woe unto the kid who kicked at a rotting tree stump or broke a tree limb for no good purpose. Chances are some animals and bugs were safe and warm in the rotting stump, and the Zen of the limb didn't need to be disrupted by some heedless youth with aggression issues.

Still, at least one traditional camp-out accoutrement lived on almost unchanged: After giving the kids a hard time for gathering firewood, Mr. T later dispatched everyone after dinner to gather enough for the night's campfire. The kids, working with respectful quiet and dispatch, built a properly pyramidal Boy Scout campfire, which soon bloomed into a compact blazing pyre. It was almost dark. A luminous band of sunset orange hung over the lake like the day's final exclamation point. Soon everyone gravitated toward the fire. Some kids sat or squatted on the ground. Everyone else got their camping chairs or stools.

Sitting there watching the light slowly fade, I found my thoughts awash in male trios—Seton, Beard, and Baden-Powell; Flank, Toonkel, and Johnson; Zergs, Protoss, and Terrans; Jerome, Jesse, and Gilbert (Father, Son, and Holy Ghost?). Not for nothing were triangles and threesomes constants in rites and religions around the world since ancient times. Flank, Toonkel, and Johnson weren't Seton, Beard, and Baden-Powell, but they had pieces of all three. In a very rough way, you could say that Dr. Flank had much of Baden-Powell's almost spiritual sensibility about boys and their possibilities, Mr. Johnson's knowledge of nature was our answer to Seton, and Mr. Toonkel had a lot of Dan Beard's practical wisdom and skills. It wasn't that simple, of course. Dr. Flank, for example, certainly had Seton's fascination with the American Indian and his love of nature, Mr. J was pretty good on the Beard elements, and Mr. T, in his own gruff way, had some of B-P's leadership skills and Seton's love for the outdoors. If Scouting often felt irrelevant in the abstract, sitting here by the campfire on this night, under these stars, it seemed entirely rich and alive.

Dr. Flank, who had missed the hike but joined us for the dinner and campfire, loved the ceremonial aspects of Scouting and his role as Troop 1 paterfamilias. So when he addressed the kids at a campfire, there was nothing casual about his delivery. He spoke slowly and deliberately like a minister addressing a congregation, allowing long pauses to punctuate what he had to say. "Listen up, please," he said, as the crackling of the wood provided the evening's ambient noise. "For those of you who have not been with us, here are a few rules to understand. The campfire is a sacred thing, an entity unto itself. It goes back to the beginning of man. They gathered around the campfire because that's how they sustained their lives. But in addition to keeping them warm, the campfire also brought them together, as a tribe, a people, a community. We now gather around the campfire in much the same way, not that we need it to survive, though it does feel nice and warm and toasty tonight, but as a social gathering, a way to bring us together and to reflect on the things we did today and what it meant to us. Throughout history, the campfire has been looked on as something almost mystical, a kind of religious experience, something that touches an important part of us in ways we might not completely understand sometimes. So here are some rules. Turn your flashlights off and put them in your pockets. You don't need them here. The focus should be on the campfire. Second, there is normally one person talking, whoever is telling a story or performing a skit. That should be the only one voice you hear. You need to respect that as part of the way we respect one another. Finally, you need to pay attention. This is an important part of being a member of the troop, and I want your attention here at all times. All that clear? Good. Anyone want to start with a skit?"

Well, there were a few, with the tone set by the first, a ramble through the woods that turned up an unexpected treasure trove of delicious M&Ms. Or were they Skittles? Or Tootsie Rolls? They tasted a tad odd, so it was hard to be certain. Turns out they were rabbit droppings. It wasn't much better in the performance than the précis.

Dr. Flank told one of his Lenni-Lenape tales. "All cultures have myths about the Great Flood," he began. "It's one way very different cultures see the world in similar ways. This is one tale the Lenni-Lenape told. After the Mysterious One made the earth, he put far above it a roof which was sometimes blue and sometimes black. This angered the spirit of the waters, because he was afraid the rain would no longer be able to reach the earth, the earth would become parched and dry, and the people would have no water to drink. So the Mysterious One brought the clouds under the roof. He gathered the dark clouds together and caused the lightning to flash across the sky. Each time the lightning flashed he spoke in deep tones, telling the clouds to shed their water on the earth. The clouds poured out their water until only the highest mountain peaks could be seen above the water. Now the spirit of the water was sorry he had become so angry because he worried the flood would bury all the animals and people. So the Mysterious One caused it to stop raining. He took away the clouds and put a rainbow in their place. Since then the Lenni-Lenape have always been glad to see the rainbow, because it tells them that the great spirits are no longer angry and there will always be life after the waters recede."

Then it was Mr. Johnson's turn. He continued the journey of Chief Leknoot. It seemed the Chief had taken his band of braves to the Mountain of the Great Hunter. Probably by coincidence, the troop just that previous fall had taken a trip to Hunter Mountain. There, he said, they hunted and hunted for what was said to be the great fire that would keep them warm all through the long winter. They had many adventures, at one point scaling the tower of the Eagle to look down over the hills and valleys below. In the end, they returned to the valley and made their campfire, though they never did find the great fire of legend and lore. "They sat around their campfire," he concluded. "And they looked to the left and looked to the right and saw their brothers around them. And all the people realized that there was no need to find the great fire. The great fire burned within them and they were warm."

Finally, Mr. Toonkel stood up. The kids listened respectfully to Dr. Flank's Indian tales, but in truth they could get a little too symphonic for thirteen- and fourteen-year-olds, who were a little old to be into Indians and a little too young to be into myth. Mr. Johnson's Leknoot tales were increasingly popular, but they played out like a nice brisk scherzo, pleasing but fleeting. Mr. Toonkel's dark horror tales, the Grand Guignol of the woods, were clearly the kids' favorites. Everyone sat utterly still as he got up and started pacing around, as if troubled by something and unsure whether he wanted to talk about it. "I don't know if you guys noticed the signs saying 'Posted. Keep Out,' this afternoon," he began in a hesitant voice. "They didn't use to be there, and then they put them up a few years back, not that long ago.

I'll tell you how they got there. Remember when we were walking by the path along the lake? Remember how there was a hollowed-out area just off the trail? It was sheltered and protected. You could sleep there if you wanted to. And that's what happened in the past. Kids would come here and sleep right under there, right where we were today. But in the morning, no one was there. It was quite a mystery. I only bring this up because it became a matter of serious concern, a while back, maybe seven, eight years ago. First, they just chalked it up to inexperience. They figured the kids must have wandered off from the troop. Clear Lake is a large glacial lake, so it's very deep and people figured maybe the kids wandered off, went skinny-dipping, got in too deep on a beautiful warm night, and didn't come out. So they dragged the lake, but they didn't find anything. They had planes fly overhead with searchlights. Still nothing. Back in the old days perhaps parents could dispose of their children more easily than now, but the kids kept disappearing and it was getting very distressing. So they had to close the place down, and the fact that they never found any traces of them made it that much worse. Then a few years ago, Todd Davis can probably remember hearing about this back then, another strange thing happened. A troop was camping on an unnaturally quiet night, a night much like tonight, come to think of it. Everyone had retired to their tents. And when they woke up one of the tents was missing. Father and son and tent, gone. Everyone figured they must have left early and gone to their car, but when everyone got to the parking lot the car was still there, and the father and son were missing. Then about four or five years ago, they were thinking of selling this place and they hired a geologist to come in and do a survey. They found these caves formed over millions of years by glacial action folding layers of earth and rock onto each other. When they went in they could feel a strange, unearthly chill. And what they saw floored them.

There were bags and gear from all different eras, modern stuff like you have and ancient stuff from the '20s and '30s. They went farther into the cave and they found tents. Then they found corpses, not just corpses with regular bones, but corpses that seemed to have been gnawed on and broken apart. This was a rather unsettling experience for these young men. They came out and called the police and the police got the FBI involved and a number of other agencies, but they really came up with nothing. There were theories about a crazy person or a cult of some kind, but no one really knows. It just seems that every four or five years, something like this happens. Anyway, I don't want you to think about it. The last one was four or five years ago, so we might be a little overdue, but it's probably not something to worry about. So when we're through just go back to your tents and go to sleep. And don't think about it. And, if it turns out it is your time to go, just go quietly and don't disturb the rest."

9: Terra Incognita

I'm having a very strange dream.

In my dream, I'm at some corporate training building near Westchester County Airport. On the walls are posters and spreadsheets and corporate exhortations about team building and creativity and thinking outside the box. It's a drab, gray low-slung building, the kind of place that breeds in endless profusion in places like Atlanta and Scottsdale, but this feels like an early incarnation with worn carpeting and water stains on the ceiling tiles. It has the sense of being in some fundamental way behind the times. Still, the place is ordinary enough except for the fact that instead of aspiring junior managers, it's full of men in Boy Scout uniforms. It's winter, and the men—and a handful of large, serious-looking women—come in from the cold in heavy coats and parkas carrying sheafs of paper with the front page reading *Curtis S. Read Scout Reservation Troop Leaders' Guide.* Many of the men are in Scout shirts full of patches and badges and a tooled leather belt with Scout buckles. The rest are in business attire minus the tie or in winter casual dress—old flannel shirts or heavy sweaters. Many of the men seem to know one another. They talk knowingly of Waubeeka and Buckskin, High Cope and Low Cope, Zip Lines and Dragon Wagons—words that mean nothing to me but seem to be fraught with significance for them. One of them, a huge man with cropped hair whose knees barely bend, like Frankenstein, seems very important indeed, because most of the others come by as if to pay their respects. He is there with a smaller, heavy-set man, who seems like his aide-de-camp. I think of him as Igor.

We are in a large room, filled with perhaps sixty of us in plastic chairs. The atmosphere is partly cheery bonhomie and partly dead-serious negotiating for various, only vaguely apparent perks having to do with things like access to tickets for the shotgun range or adequate supplies of bologna and salami at lunch. "Let's make sure we know we're all on the same page here," says the man at the front of the room, who has been identified as the Director of Support Services. "We all want the same thing—the best summer at Camp Read we've ever had." It dawns on me that this is no dream. This is real. My casual descent into Scouting has taken me to a still-more-distant stretch of terra incognita—a meeting of parents prepared to spend a week or two of their summer living in mosquito-infested tents; doing their business in smelly latrines; eating French toast, mashed potatoes, and turkey loaf prepared by thirteen-year-olds; and bringing some semblance of order to adolescent chaos. At forty-nine, I was preparing for my first summer at Scout camp.

I still was not entirely sure how I got to this point. At one of the first meetings of the year, Dr. Flank said that enough boys had expressed an interest in camp that this year we planned to go for two weeks rather than the one we had done in recent years. The only hitch was that we needed enough dads—a minimum of three per week—able to take time off from work to participate. The statement had a buy-this-magazine-or-we'll-shoot-this-dog quality. With Dr. Flank scheduled for the first week, that meant we needed just five dads out of some twenty-five active kids. This hardly sounded like much, but the ranks of volunteers remained meager. Some dads had vacation plans.

They were bug-phobic, too busy, too old, too heavy, or too camping-averse. As it turned out, I was at a Wednesday night meeting where Dr. Flank raised the subject again. My vacation plans remained in flux, and I was too slow to lie, so I told Dr. Flank I'd think about it. I might as well have signed on the dotted line then and there.

The meeting I found myself in now was one of two held by the Westchester–Putnam Council to brief prospective Scoutmasters and their assistants on what to expect this summer at the Curtis S. Read Boy Scout Reservation at Brant Lake in the Adirondacks. We were told about bus schedules and camp orientation, medical forms and swim checks. We were reminded that Camp Buckskin was a mess-hall camp, with all the kids fed three times a day, and Camp Waubeeka was a patrol-cooking camp, meaning the kids prepared food for themselves at their campsites three times a day. There were questions about bringing cell phones (forget it), how to accommodate the number of kids who wanted to do shotgun and rifle shooting, and whether the wilderness survival staff was up to snuff. There were lots of rules delivered with Old Testament sternness. No matches! No lighters! No sheath knifes! No aerosol bug spray! No fireworks! No chainsaws! No blowguns! No computers! No alcohol! No drugs!

For the first time, I realized, I was stepping outside the familiar, comfortable, rather idiosyncratic world of Troop 1 and into the musty maw of the national organization, the Boy Scouts of America. I felt like I was going from Dr. Flank's version of Scouting to Norman Rockwell's. Like all great crusades, the B.S.A. began with a great metaphor. In this case it was The Good Turn in the Fog, which, as a friend and Eagle Scout says, is to Scouting what Saul's conversion on the road to Damascus is to Christianity. In 1909, as Scouting was beginning to spread throughout the British Empire and across Europe, a Chicago publisher named William Boyce was lost one night in a London pea-soup fog. As the tale has been told over the years, a boy materialized like an apparition out of the fog. He saluted smartly and offered to guide Boyce to his destination. When they arrived, Boyce offered the boy a reward of a shilling, but the boy turned him down, saying he was a Scout and Scouts never accept money for doing a good turn. Then the Unknown Scout, as he has come to be known, disappeared into the fog, never to be identified.

Impressed by what he had seen, Boyce decided to start a similar organization back home. It was incorporated on February 8, 1910, in the District of Columbia, but Scouting was becoming such a phenomenon that Boyce soon realized that the idea was bigger than he was. Baden-Powell himself came to the United States to talk up Scouting's virtues, President William Howard Taft was named honorary president of the organization, and Theodore Roosevelt became honorary vice president and chief Scout citizen. The nation's most eminent youth leaders, as well as giants of industry and commerce, signed up to support this wholesome crusade for national renewal. From the start, American Scouting began with audaciously lofty goals. Not only would Scouting restore the moral fiber of the nation's youth, its organizers said; in the process it would create an idealistic movement that would restore the moral fiber of the nation.

Who would head it? Baden-Powell was the image of British Scouting, but he could not serve that function here. YMCA leaders helped get it off the ground, but they were not charismatic figures. So American Scouting began with a delicate and almost certainly doomed balancing act: It needed Seton and Beard to give an inspirational face to the new movement, but instead of designating either as the sole American Baden-Powell, it gave both prominent positions without real authority, naming Seton Chief Scout and Beard National Scout Commissioner.

In the end, though, a third figure was more influential than either Seton or Beard. Executive director James E. West was a lawyer who had grown up lonely in an orphanage and was partially crippled by a deformed foot. He had great energy, flinty will, little charm, much insecurity, and a mania for efficiency. He, more than anyone, made the B.S.A. into the force in American life it would become. And his limitations became the B.S.A.'s limitations as well.

Baden-Powell wanted an organization that was loose knit, decentralized, intuitive, and flexible. West, as things turned out, wanted one that was just the opposite. He wanted Scouting to be orderly, centralized, and run like a business; he soon attracted many of the biggest names in American capitalism as advisors and supporters. He wanted a uniform program so that a troop in Colorado would follow the same program as one in Alabama. Rather than depending on the camp followers and volunteers Baden-Powell had surrounded himself with, West wanted to hire paid staff members ready to provide guidance on everything from the amount of equipment to be taken on outings to the exact ratio of adult supervision.

From the start, an organization dedicated to teaching wholesome, cooperative values to youths developed in an atmosphere of internecine warfare and feuds among adults. Both Seton and Beard never got over their resentment of Baden-Powell, and, though suspicious of the B.S.A., saw it as their vehicle for getting their proper due. Seton almost immediately became convinced that West, like Baden-Powell, had in mind an organization with the covert aim of training soldiers rather than helping boys become honorable men. Seton prepared a first edition of the Scout Handbook, which was two-thirds his own *The Birch-bark Roll* and one-third Baden-Powell's *Scouting for Boys*. Published in 1910 it named Ernest Thompson Seton as its author. You can still go to a Scout shop and buy what's billed as a reprint of the first version of the Scout Handbook, but it's not the one Seton prepared. Seton's attempt to function as the voice of the B.S.A. was immediately overruled—one year later the book was rewritten, newly titled *The Official Handbook for Boys,* and Seton's name was taken off the cover. West and Seton soon were feuding, with Seton demanding more say in running the organization and threatening to resign. West remained firmly in control, but attempted for a time to avoid an ugly public spat that would make the B.S.A. look like it was turning on its best-known public spokesman. Finally, when World War I broke out, the feud went public. Seton, who was still a British citizen even though he had lived in the United States for eighteen years, publicly offered his services to the British crown in any way that might help in the war effort. West made it clear it was inappropriate for the B.S.A. to be headed by someone with allegiances to a foreign power. Then Theodore Roosevelt, West's friend, advisor, and ally, wrote West a public letter, citing "wicked and degrading pacifist agitation" by certain Boy Scout leaders, that all but called Seton a traitor.

Furious, Seton demanded that West accept his resignation and then called a press conference to vent his displeasure. He summed up his version of Scouting's history with epigramatic succinctness: "Seton started it; Baden-Powell boomed it; West killed it." And he dismissed West as someone with "no point of contact with boys, and who, I might almost say, has never seen the blue sky in his life."

With that, Seton was gone. The Scouting magazine *Boys' Life* wrote off his departure as a trifling matter, saying that even his contributions to the handbook were minor and that the "comparatively small number of pages of material" he had written could "be easily replaced in future editions by eminent American citizens"—a cheap-shot reference to Seton's British citizenship.

Beard had watched this with great interest. He and Seton had shared a rivalry with Baden-Powell and a deep suspicion of West, so they were natural allies. As Beard put it, Scouting was being pulled by two factions, the dreamers and the clerks. But even the dreamers had their Machiavellian qualities. Beard had also plotted against Seton, claiming no foreign-born person could head the Scouts and that Seton was insufficiently patriotic. He figured to be the biggest beneficiary when Seton was ousted, and stayed on hoping at last to become Scouting's acknowledged leader. He injected the organization with a solid jolt of patriotism—even some of his peers considered his jingoism a bit excessive. He chafed too at West's power, writing him in one letter that when the Scouts ran off the last of the dreamers, "then the movement will have lost its soul and become a machine which only runs from the momentum of its original impulse." Unlike Seton, Beard never quit. But it soon became clear to him that only one man ran the Boy Scouts—and that man was James E. West.

Seton and Beard's experience carried with it two main lessons. First, Scouting may have been advertised as fun for boys, but it was serious business for the men behind it. Second, within Scouting, one strayed from the most conventional notions of what the organization was about at one's peril. It was hardly the last time that lesson would be taught.

Scouting in the United States developed over the next century with a methodical, relentless sense of manifest destiny. Indeed, it was as if the notion of Scouting—however ill-formed and malleable—had immediately tapped into some primal impulse in American life. West, like any ambitious corporate manager of his era, focused at first on securing his franchise and striving for monopoly. William Randolph Hearst, the publisher and promoter, was trying to create a rival scouting organization, the American Boy Scouts, which dressed its boys in quasi-military garb and trained them in military drill. Using his high-powered business and political connections, West lobbied Congress to designate the B.S.A. as the nation's official scouting organization, succeeding in 1916 when Congress granted a federal charter to the B.S.A. as the rightful owner of the term "Boy Scouts." Congress authorized a Boy Scout uniform, similar to the U.S. Army, Navy, or Marine uniform, and the B.S.A. set about enforcing its copyright. Since 1911, it had already grown from 61,495 Scouts and Scouters to 245,183. Who knows if it was really 245,183 or 245,182—or 230,000 or 240,000, for that matter—but Scouting went about methodically documenting and publicizing its achievements and growth from year to year as if each new membership by itself was testament to the success and worth of the entire organization.

Even now, Boy Scout literature spells out in excruciating detail and quasi exactitude Scouting's long march to greatness. In 1917 Scouting's full resources were placed at the service of the government under the slogan "Help Win the War"; membership was 363,837. In 1918 it adopted a new slogan, "The War Is Over, but Our Work Is Not." Scouts rendered nationwide service in the influenza epidemic, and membership was 418,984. In 1932 Scouting set a goal of enrolling one of every four twelve-year-old boys and keeping them in Scouting for four years. In 1936, the silver jubilee year, membership passed one million for the first time. In 1937 the first national Scout Jamboree was held in Washington, with 27,232 in attendance; membership was 1,129,841. When the second Jamboree was held in Valley Forge, Pennsylvania, in 1950, 47,163 Scouts and leaders ("from every state and territory in the U.S.!") were on hand. Membership was 2,795,222.

From the start, there was something suspect about the accent on numbers, as if the whole enterprise were like a corporation relentlessly focused on getting its profits to meet Wall

Street expectations. And as early as the 1920s, there were minor scandals in which Scout organizations were accused of inflating their numbers. One widely reported case in Cleveland in the 1950s led to the firing of a local Scout executive. For all the bluster, Scouting failed to succeed on its own quasi-corporate terms. The plan in 1932 to recruit one in four twelve-year-old boys was Scouting's first great challenge to itself. But it failed miserably, and the B.S.A. did its best to bury the results rather than face up to its shortcomings.

The numbers game goes on unabated, with local council and district executives knowing that their performance is graded on how many Scouts they can keep moving through the pipeline. In 2000 the B.S.A. celebrated its ninetieth anniversary and the addition of its 100-millionth youth member—said to be twelve-year-old Mario Castro from Brooklyn, New York. According to the 2000 Annual Report, 4.9 million youths participated in B.S.A. programs, both conventional Scouting and an in-school educational program called Learning for Life, over the past year—thanks to the efforts of 1.4 million adult volunteers. More than 40,000 Scouts made Eagle, and 234 Scouts and Scouters earned awards for lifesaving and meritorious actions. The Scouting magazine, *Boys' Life*—which, we're told, has published more than a billion copies—served more than 3.4 million youths. There's a bit of sleight of hand in those numbers. The difference between the 4.9 million youths in B.S.A. programs and the 3.4 million who gets *Boys' Life* is 1.5 million youths who are not Scouts at all, but participants in Learning for Life classroom programs, which began in 1991 as a way for the B.S.A. to contract with school districts to teach values and character development. That program has prospered while membership in Scouting itself has declined. The whole saga of growth and success is delivered in the kind of language West would have understood and Seton and Beard would be baffled by: "Future growth of the Boy Scouts of America is dependent on how we are perceived by our customer groups. The goal of our marketing message is to build awareness and solidify the fact that the Scouting program supports physical, mental, and spiritual development needs of young people and their families."

Much, of course, changes. The original handclasp, in which the little finger was separated from the other three on the right hand, was changed to the normal handclasp—only given with the left hand, the hand closer to your heart. The uniform began with a doughboy look in which the whole thing, including knickers and hat, cost about $4. In 1929 the neckerchief, tied with a square knot and secured with a neckerchief slide, made its debut. By the 1940s, Bermuda shorts had replaced jodhpurs, giving Scout socks an unfortunate prominence that came to define the Scoutmaster as dork. The 1950s saw the broad-brimmed campaign hats of earlier times replaced by a field cap like the ones the GIs wore in *Sergeant Bilko*. In the 1960s the old cotton uniforms gave way to—what else?—polyester, and the whole thing took a lurch toward the disco era in the '80s with epaulets on the shirt, utility pockets on the shorts, and an absurd red beret, which thankfully didn't last long. The epaulets are still around, but the almost intractable problem of finding appropriate headgear has been solved by replacing the ridiculous beret with the same baseball cap that has replaced virtually all other forms of headgear.

And you definitely can't buy the whole uniform for $4. You can't even buy the neckerchief for $4. These days a long-sleeve Scout shirt goes for $28.70. Trousers run from $36.50 to $50.35. A cap is $11.50 or $12.50. Even the little things add up: $4.40 for Scout socks, $4.95 for a neckerchief, $1.65 for a shoulder loop, $1.20 for a flag emblem, $5.15 for a merit badge sash, $7.95 for the handbook, $19.95 for the fieldbook. It can get pretty expensive even before you get to the serious gear.

Merit badges have also changed to fit the times. Since Scouting's beginning there have been 221 different merit badges. There were 57 in the 1911 handbook, and there are 119 now, 27 of which remain from the 1911 list. However, you can no longer get a merit badge in bee farming or blacksmithing, automobiling or mining, nut culture or first aid to animals. Handicapped awareness, phased out in 1984, had the ring of being too un-PC before anyone knew what PC was. World brotherhood sounds nice, but the badge ended in 1972. We're no longer an ag culture, so farewell to badges in cotton farming, legumes and forage crops, and rabbit raising. There's still plenty of cement work and skiing, but the badges died in 1952 and 1999. Given all the sexual innuendo, the Scouts did themselves a huge favor by phasing out their stalking badge in 1952. Now, lots of badges are Boy Scout staples like camping, first aid, swimming, or lifesaving. But you can also get badges in atomic energy, crime prevention, dog care, golf, plumbing, music and bugling, sculpture, and space exploration.

And the Handbook itself, with more than 37 million copies in print—almost certainly more than any English-language book other than the Bible—is a window onto the changes in American life. The first thing the newest version, the eleventh edition, offers is a twenty-one-page pamphlet on avoiding child abuse in the troop and elsewhere. Along with warning them about the perils of the wilderness, it counsels Scouts to "treat all blood as if it were contaminated with blood-borne viruses." It is the first version of the Handbook to deal with dangers lurking on the Internet: "Don't respond to messages or Web sites that make you feel uncomfortable or that you know are meant only for adults." And it warns Scouts not to forsake their map and compass for the false gods of high-tech seductions like the Global Positioning Systems their dads have in their SUVs. It broadens the options for that one-pot stew to include tofu and espouses a brand of no-trace camping that feels like something out of the Green movement.

And yet, as Paul Fussell put it, "The pliability and adaptability of the scout movement explains its remarkable longevity, its capacity to flourish in a world dramatically different from its founders. Like the Roman Catholic Church, the scout movement knows the difference between cosmetic and real change, and it happily embraces the one to avoid any truck with the other."

The comparison with the Catholic Church these days is more unfortunate than Fussell intended. But if one were to leaf through Handbooks published over almost a century, from the presidency of William Howard Taft to the presidency of William Jefferson Clinton, at least as striking as what has changed is what has not. It's not just the practical lessons on knots, splints, tarp tents, camping gear, compass reading, water rescues, ice rescues, and first aid. What's most consistent is the voice— calm, clear, tolerant, sensible, more than a bit square maybe, given to simple words, common wisdom, and a quiet sort of spirituality. Try to pick the years of the following passages:

> [A scout] should never look down upon anyone who may be poorer than himself, or envy anyone richer than himself. A scout's self respect will cause him to value his own standing and make him sympathetic toward others who may be, on the one hand, worse off, or, on the other hand, better off as far as wealth is concerned. Scouts know neither a lower nor a higher class, for a scout is one who is a comrade to all and who is ready to share that which he has with others.

> A scout is a friend to all. He is a brother to other scouts. He offers his friendship to people of all races and nations, and

respects them even if their beliefs and customs are different from his own. Friendship is a mirror. When you have a smile on your face as you greet someone, you will probably receive a smile in return. If you are willing to be a good friend, you will find friendship reflected back to you.

Reverence toward God is a whole lot more than going to church. It is shown in the way you act every day. You take care of your body. You live by the moral code and worship God in the way taught by your own religion. There are many different religious beliefs in the world. Some are like your own. Others are very different. The men who founded the United States of America believed in the right of all men to worship God in their own way. This is a great heritage they have given us. Scouts can strengthen it by their actions.

The passages come from, in order, first edition, 1911; eleventh edition, 1998; eighth edition, 1972. But the passages are virtually indistinguishable in tone and message. All of them could have slipped comfortably into any other year. And the remarkable continuity in terms of programs and philosophy, combined with a selective and often shaky instinct for change, has shaped the balance between the timeless and the ephemeral that has allowed Scouting to keep its core while redefining itself around the edges.

Scouting never reached its most ambitious goals, but it was certainly in synch with the cultural life and values of the nation through the 1950s and early 1960s. The Norman Rockwell paintings of eager Scouts, helpful dads, and kindly Scoutmasters tending the campfire felt like they were channeling the essence of the country. But when the culture changed in the 1960s, Scouting, for the first time, suddenly found itself out of step with much that was going on in American life. In the culture wars of the

Vietnam era, all the vivid iconic imagery built up around Scouting suddenly evoked bad connotations as well as good ones. If Scouts were still trustworthy, loyal, helpful, and friendly, to some they were also militaristic, uptight, sexist, and irrelevant. As racial unrest shook the nation and minorities became an ever-more conspicuous part of American life, Scouting was stuck with the image of being of, by, and for white folks. And finally, West had succeeded in making Scouting run like a business, but it started to feel like one of those corporate dinosaurs about to have its lunch eaten by a more nimble competitor. By the mid-1970s, the B.S.A. was a bureaucratic behemoth that spent more than $100 million a year, owned 453,000 acres of land worth $233 million, and had 4,600 paid employees.

And when the culture changed, Scouting's grand spiral of eternal growth finally petered out and year-to-year membership began falling for the first time. Even by the Scouts' own count, the total number of Scouts and adult volunteers fell from 6.52 million in 1972 to 6.40 million in 1973. The next year it took a real plunge—to 5.80 million. Now it's down to 4.5 million. Some of the falling membership was a function of demographics and the dwindling pool of youths following the baby boom that peaked in the late 1960s and early 1970s. But the B.S.A. knew its problems extended beyond just demographics.

The drop in membership sparked a major fundraising and recruitment drive called Boypower 76, aimed at raising $65 million and recruiting two million new Scouts, a third of them minorities, by 1976. But, once again, the high-pressure push to meet quotas and goals backfired. In 1974, after a four-month investigation, the *Chicago Tribune* reported that the Scouts had padded their membership rolls with nonexistent minority children or troops left on the rolls long after they became defunct— all in the interest of keeping the numbers up and securing charitable funding from groups like the United Way.

Boypower 76 was soon abandoned, but Scouting's problems in recruiting continued. In the mid-1970s, for example, our local council, the Westchester–Putnam Council, put out a piece of recruiting literature with copy reading: "Parents. What do you want for your son?" Below it were two pictures of a cherubic-looking kid with floppy bangs. One was a police mug shot; the other was the kid in his Scout uniform. Even the most socially conservative parent—not the norm in Westchester County—might have been somewhat skeptical of the notion that their choice was a kid in a Scout uniform or a kid in prison overalls. And selling Scouting as a substitute for packing the kid off to some cold military academy didn't make it sound like much fun. At times, Scouting had the look of an organization that was getting a bit desperate and tone deaf. "This tight financial condition will become even more pressing over the next five years unless significantly better progress is made in raising revenues than has been the case during the past five years," wrote Warren B. Coburn, the council president at the time, in a letter sent out in 1978. "In fact, extraordinary efforts will be required just to keep the Council operating at present levels of service, let alone the new higher levels recommended by the Long Range Planning Committee."

The Scouts deserve credit for trying to attract minority youths (though whether that happened out of a sense of mission or one of self-preservation is a more complicated question). The program was altered in the 1970s to put more of an emphasis on urban Scouting and less on swimming and wilderness activities. And Scout publications like the Handbook, once full of white faces, suddenly began to look like brochures for an interracial church advertising its inclusiveness. In fact, it's hard to find a picture of a group of boys in any recent Scout publication that doesn't include black and brown faces. But after three decades of trying to diversify, the results remain spotty at best. And the scandal of inflated rolls keeps recurring. In 2000 Todd Bensman of the *Dallas Morning News* reported on a federal investigation of allegations that the Circle 10 Council, a twelve-county B.S.A. council in the backyard of the national headquarters, had inflated membership rosters by up to 30 percent and treated inactive troops as if they still existed. The chairman of one district was able to verify only fifty-four of ninety-one listed Scout troops. One man listed as a Scoutmaster said his troop had disbanded twelve years before. Three of the six Scouts listed as members of one troop were said to be living at an apartment complex that was bulldozed four years earlier. Scout officials said they were pressured to keep ghost units, particularly inner-city ones, on the rolls to justify funding requests.

Similar incidents were reported in Los Angeles in 1991 and Jackson, Mississippi, in 1994. In 1999 a study by the University of North Florida said the Scouts had exaggerated the growth and success of a Scouting program targeted at inner-city youths in public housing projects. It found that Scouting was almost nonexistent in thirteen of the seventeen apartment complexes where it was said to be flourishing.

Local officials who have blown the whistle on abuses in their own areas say the problem is not a few rogue officials, but something much more systemic. "The name of the game is money," Ardis Russell, a Mississippi accountant who pointed out the fraud there in 1994, told the *Morning News*. "It's always, 'Get the names and get the money.' It's a national problem and the Boy Scouts of America knows it." No one knows just how widespread the problems are, as no one outside the B.S.A. is responsible for checking its membership figures. At the very least, the continuing incidents are an indication that Scouting still has a long way to go in recruiting minorities. At the most, they raise questions about the vitality of Scouting overall.

Back in Scouting's heady beginnings, Dan Beard gave a speech in his distinctive, folksy voice that had summed up his era's view of Scouting as an integral part of the nation's life and the training of its boys and young men:

> There is nothing on God's earth as great as this true training for the boys, and as for we men, we don't amount to shucks, although we pretend we do, but we act as engineers on that train, that is all—engineers and brakemen—and carry this train of boys on toward their future, which is going to be greater and grander than any future we have ever dreamed of.

But by the time he died in 1941, ten days before his ninety-first birthday, even Uncle Dan was disillusioned with Scouting's direction. And as the years have gone by, the notion that Beard's "true training for boys" is the inevitable path for raising boys into men has no longer seemed so certain, not even to the men serving as the engineers and brakemen on the train.

10: Summer Camp 1: The Zen of Scout Socks

The weeks leading up to my departure for camp took on an odd, charged quality—part low-level dread, part expectant glow, as if I were a nervous pilgrim getting ready to embark on a portentous spiritual journey. Ben, of course, used the time to add to his cache of provisions and gear, trooping off to EMS and a Scout supply store to get new mosquito netting, industrial-strength insect repellent, and redundant reinforcements of T-shirts and shorts. I bought nothing, but I prepared nonetheless. First, I went to the doctor for my required camp physical. She was, it turned out, an engaging young woman a few years out of Brown University Medical School.

"Anything you need to tell me about your health?" she asked with an air of solicitous sincerity.

"Well," I said, "I'm going to summer camp in two weeks, and they need to be sure I won't keel over and fall face first into the kids' mashed potatoes."

For some reason, she didn't seem sure what to make of that but replied with the requisite expressions of reassurance.

"Oh, I don't think we need to worry about that, but let's see," she said sweetly. At that point two thoughts occurred to me: First, she was young enough to be my daughter. Second, even if I had been single, I was now too old to date my doctor.

I had my Boy Scouts physical form for her to fill out, a matter of CODE 1 total urgency, I had been repeatedly told, because without it, I wouldn't be able to serve as a Scoutmaster at camp. This warning merited a full five exclamation points in my troop leaders' guide in case anyone had missed its urgency.

"Well," the doctor said pleasantly, as she filled it out, "you seem to be in excellent shape for your age." (See: "too old to date my doctor.")

The deadly kicker—"for your age"—would have stung at any time, but this happened to be the week before I hit the doleful monument of fifty, a number whose import had become an insistent backdrop to daily life. I began casually perusing the obituaries, feeling a sudden urge to check out the various checkout times of the honorably deceased. I hung around the local Borders scanning books on health and nutrition and resolving to eat more garlic, broccoli, green tea, tofu, oatmeal, salmon, and other foods I didn't much like but were allegedly good for me. I took pride in the fact I was in better shape than most of the squirts in Troop 1, but was plagued by the nagging thought that it said more about them than about me.

On the other hand, I took pains to make sure this halfway-to-one-hundred (yikes!) navel gazing didn't get out of hand. I had once written a book with a very famous motivational speaker, who had an uplifting aphorism ("Don't find fault, find a solution," "If you say you can or you say you can't, you're right") for any situation. To my surprise, the turn-lemons-into-lemonade worldview more or less stayed with me. And rather than lament my impending geezerhood or dread my imminent departure into a horrid world of mosquitoes, latrines, and mornings without the *New York Times*, I did my best to put what we in the motivational world call a positive frame around the two unfortunate events. So as geezerhood and camperhood loomed simultaneously, I found myself conflating the two into an opportunity, rather than a burden. At my advanced age, I was preparing for something entirely new. I was not finding fault. I was finding a solution.

Fortified with that patently delusional self-spin, I did the rest of my preparation, such as it was. Ben, who was going for two weeks, took off on the Scout bus a week before I was scheduled to depart. I was counting on him for all flashlights, bug spray, mosquito netting, camping gear, and whatever else we needed from his vast survival arsenal. My packing was more rudimentary. I threw T-shirts, shorts, and underwear, a fleece for cool nights, assorted toiletries, and whatever else seemed vaguely appropriate into a travel bag. I picked out a couple of books and some old Scout handbooks to read. I conferred with my fellow Scoutmasters-to-be on a plan of action, and awaited the big day.

The plan was this: We were to meet with commando-like precision at 6:00 A.M. at Rocky's, a justly famous twenty-four-hour-a-day deli, near the entrance to the Taconic Parkway. Fortified with whatever donuts, bagels, or coffee we deemed appropriate, we would head north in a caravan, communicating via cell phone in the event of enemy attack, geezer bladder, or other problems. We figured to arrive there about ten, in time to get settled and unpack our gear before all heading off for a forty-minute drive to historic Fort Ticonderoga followed by a gala afternoon of doing our laundry and eating dinner we didn't have to cook ourselves.

I got up in the dark, threw my bag plus Ben's discarded sleeping bag and a pillow in the car, and headed toward Rocky's. My watch read 5:49. Sure enough, right there at six were my two compatriots Harry and Dennis, whom I had first met at the Paul Bunyan Camporee. Like Flank and Vanderbilt, they were another odd couple. Harry was the child of Holocaust survivors, organized, businesslike, and totally committed to Scouting. He had his own public relations firm and the orderly, composed personality of the guy at the head of the table at every business meeting. Dennis was a quiet, deferential Southern Baptist from Mississippi with a visceral love for the outdoors. He worked in market research and had an appealingly open, unaffected quality. He was the only person I've ever met whose jaw literally dropped and eyes bugged out when he was surprised by something. Harry was in a spotless new champagne-colored Infinity QX4 SUV. Dennis was in an old Volvo that was even creakier than mine. Harry had a books-on-tape version of Bill Gates's *Business at the Speed of Thought* in his tape deck. Dennis had Eric Hanson's *Stranger in the Forest,* an account of a trek through Borneo. They joked about using semaphore as a backup system in case the cell phones didn't work, a joke I only vaguely shared because I wasn't sure what semaphore was.

We flew past Albany and soon reached the foothills of the Adirondacks. We drove though the village of Brant Lake, whose main features were a tiny beach, Daby's General Store, and the Horicon Free Library, a cobblestone library the size of a phone booth. We passed the main expanse of lake, then came to a dirt road with a sign reading CURTIS S. READ SCOUT RESERVATION, WESTCHESTER–PUTNAM COUNCIL. We turned right and followed the road past the camp garage and the camp ranger's house until we reached a well-worn grassy area with cars parked around its edges. Up a hill was a nondescript brown frame cabin that turned out to be the Camp Waubeeka office, from which one could pick up the sounds of an electric guitar and bass stumbling through the most rudimentary version possible of "Sunshine of Your Love."

On the way up I had realized that the week Ben had been away in camp was the longest time I had been away from him since he'd been born, so I felt a surge of paternal longing as I waited for him to appear. A few minutes after we pulled up, I spotted him walking toward us down the rocky rise in front of the camp office. It was apparent something was not quite right. He appeared to be walking with one shoulder scrunched up, his shoelaces were untied, and from a distance his face looked kind of dirty, even by the standards of Scout camp. But as he got closer it was clear his face wasn't dirty. Instead, there was a vast purple swelling in the general vicinity of his right eye, which was nowhere to be seen but presumably hiding somewhere behind the swollen mass of facial tissue, which was the color of a slab of calf's liver. And his scrunched-up walk, it turned out, was his best Quasimodo imitation, a theatrical effort that was the subject of much merriment within the troop, especially when accompanied by a creaky "Come. There is much to see in the bell tower."

"WHAT HAPPENED TO YOU?" I shouted, thankful only that his mother was not around to witness the sight.

"Hey," he said, as if his feelings were hurt. "What kind of greeting is that?"

"WHAT HAPPENED TO YOU?" I repeated, not at all mollified by his apparent good cheer.

"Well," he began. "There's this game we play called tarp ball . . ." And he proceeded to describe a game that consisted of two players throwing a hardball back and forth over the steeply pitched tarp that hung over the cooking area. The most enthusiastic player was Jack, the tenth grader who was serving as Senior Patrol Leader during camp. The day before he had unfortunately missed the tarp entirely and sent the ball flying in the precise direction of Ben, who was innocently walking nearby. After his fellow Scouts picked him off the ground, they used their Scout training to realize they'd better have someone take a look at him. At the camp infirmary, the head man, a paramedic named Russ Fleer, decided it was indeed your basic, heavy-duty black eye and gave Ben some ice to put on it. Since then Ben had been something of a camp celebrity, tarp ball had been suspended until further notice (which never came), and life had gone on.

The fact that the guilty party was supposed to be the mature, responsible kid in the troop did not provide great comfort, but Jack seemed genuinely contrite and we could spend only so much time gawking in horror at Ben's hideous shiner. The kids helped us unload our gear and led us past the office and commissary, down a rocky path, across a rudimentary footbridge over a shallow, rocky creek, around a bend, and finally down to the Wolfjaw campsite, Troop 1's home base for as long as anyone could remember.

I'm not quite sure what I expected, but Wolfjaw, unfortunately, came close. It was about two acres of second-growth hemlock, maple, birch, and ash trees that sloped down from the north end to the south. Scattered around were granite outcroppings and boulders. Its most impressive structure was a five-year-old lean-to. It served as Dr. Flank's domicile and office during the first week and was decked out like an officer's barracks, with uniforms neatly hanging from nails and paperwork, flashlights, and lanterns neatly arrayed on a plastic folding table that took up most of the available space. Everyone else bunked in ancient green military surplus tents that were mounted on wooden platforms a few inches off the ground. There were three cooking sites. Each had a wooden picnic table and two wooden benches and a rudimentary pantry called a monster box, stuffed with yellow cooking oil, pink dish soap, breakfast cereal, peanut butter, jelly, napkins, plastic utensils, bread, and whatever else had been saved from previous meals. Cooking was done on sheepherder and half-barrel stoves at each site. In the middle of the site was a bulletin board, which had various announcements, safety messages, a copy of the camp newsletter, "The Waubeeka World News," and the riddle of the day: "How far can a dog run into the forest?" (Answer: Halfway before he starts running out.) Near the upper cooking site was an area for chopping wood, called the axe yard, even though Dr. Flank forbade us from having axes around. At the north end of the site was a long metal basin used for washing, with a pipe above it that dispensed water through four holes that dripped noisily into the basin.

About ten yards from that was my own vision of the heart of darkness, the plywood edifice that housed the Wolfjaw latrine. Sam had already given it the appellation of "the deucer"—meaning the place where one deposited solid waste or, in the gentle lexicon of the troop, dropped a deuce. It had a molded plastic receptacle one urinated into with a pipe underneath it leading into some hellish space underground. There were two toilets with unsteady metal seats above the revolting devil's brew below. Luckily, posted on the wall were explicit instructions about latrine hygiene and information on sweeping the floor, scrubbing the toilets with pine solution, and pouring a chloro solution ($^1/_2$ cup of chloro and water) down the latrine. Unluckily, it still stank like holy hell.

For tonight, at least, I was planning to share a tent with Ben, and we had to move my stuff in before we left for the day's outing. The tent was already a mess, full of gear, dirty towels and T-shirts, Coke cans, and books. The latter were either humor (Dave Barry, Dilbert, The Onion) or macho variations on the Tom Clancy canon, all of them, it seemed, with names using some variation of the words Fear, Steel, Fatal, Phoenix, and Shadow. Was it *The Shadow of the Phoenix* or *Shadows of Steel*? *Fatal Terrain* or *Fatal Phoenix*? *The Sum of All Fears* or *The Shadow of All Steel*? I couldn't keep them straight. But Ben seemed to bridge the gap between the whimsical/ironic and the cold/paramilitary by periodically tossing off stray quotes from the Clancy books ("Gratitude is a disease of dogs") as if he were auditioning for the Sean Connery role in some upcoming thriller. I picked my way through the mess to my cot, which had a mattress that looked like it dated back to the Punic Wars resting on top of a skeletal frame. I put down my sleeping bag and pillow, tied a mosquito net to the post, and figured I'd make the best of it.

The day's activity was a trip to Fort Ticonderoga, a massive stone fortress on a dramatic rise overlooking Lake Champlain, followed by a festive afternoon of doing laundry. The fort, built in 1755 and still a thing of brooding wonder, allowed the kids to drool over ancient weapons—espignoles, halberds, and matchlock muskets—in a reminder that times change but man's lust for mayhem does not. Then we descended, laundry bags on our backs, on the tiny town of Ticonderoga like a parody remake of *The Wild Ones* with Boy Scouts instead of bikers taking over a quiet burg. For most of the kids it was their first time to do their own laundry ("Dude, you pour the white stuff in, turn it on, and it all comes out." "Awesome."). They seemed quite happy to shovel muck-infested shirts, shorts, socks, uniforms, and underwear into the machines, comparing aromas the way the French compare wines. On the way back, the sun was beginning to set and a hint of a chill had crept into the air. We passed a bunch of tepees set up incongruously on a golf course under a pink pillow of puffy stratocumulus clouds. By the side of the road were brilliant patches of orange day lilies. For the first time, I felt that not only were the kids at camp, but I was too, and when we got back, Ben and I and Mark and Jonah sat at the upper picnic table, talking a little and listening to the night sounds of the woods before going to bed.

The next morning we had nowhere to go and no provisions to make breakfast with. Instead, we were supposed to go over to Camp Buckskin, the other camp mentioned at the precamp meeting, where the kids ate their meals cafeteria style, a development Dr. Flank viewed with unveiled contempt. "What we do is real camping," he told the kids. "What they have over there is a hotel."

In fact, Newtown Hall, Buckskin's two-year-old dining and meeting hall, made our dilapidated Waubeeka facilities seem like slums. It had a concrete slab floor and a gleaming laminated pine interior that gave the place the feel of a chapel as much as a cafeteria. On the walls inside were the Scout prayers for the three meals.

We were ushered into a room full of kids in their orange Camp Buckskin T-shirts, and motioned toward a table where we recited the morning grace with the others and waited expectantly for our turn to eat. When one of the counselors finally came by our table and announced, "OK, your turn to go," we filed into the serving area. There, prepared to ladle food onto our plastic trays, was an alarmingly cheerful group of the camp's junior staff and kitchen help. Either they were utterly imbued with the Boy Scout spirit or they had a sense of humor about the cuisine, because in one meal—and a breakfast meal at that— we were about to experience all the major food groups of the average American diet. First came bagels representing the increasingly important food-with-a-hole-in-the-middle group. Then came some colorful sort of hash representing the don't-ask, don't-tell group. Then a little egg, more or less scrambled, from the cholesterol food group. A moist clump of oatmeal representing the Wilfred Brimley/kids-could-care-less group. A sweet roll and a sticky dab of macaroni and cheese representing the dominant carbohydrate group. A touch of quiche for the sophisticates among us. Then over to Old Italia for the traditional breakfast meatball and ziti in breakfast spaghetti sauce. Next up, for the real risk takers in the group, was a little chicken salad. And then finally, for the health conscious among us, a soupy vegetable medley of cooked carrots, peas, and green beans. All were plopped down on the plates in discrete clumps like Balkanized countries sharing a dysfunctional culinary continent. On the table outside were individual servings of various cold cereals, with an accent on the Technicolor varieties like Froot Loops and Lucky Charms. We sat back down and the kids began engaging in a bit of commodity trading—say, a meatball for a sweet roll. Needless to say some objects, particularly the vegetables and oatmeal, were of limited trading value while others, particularly the sweet rolls, consistently traded at the top of their range.

After breakfast Dr. Flank, who planned to leave that day, gave us a brief history tour. First, he showed us a plaque embedded in stone marking a bridge built in the memory of Don Vanderbilt. Then he presided over an impromptu groundbreaking for a new shower building to be built in honor of Todd Frohmann, who had put three kids through the troop and had died of a heart attack the previous year. It wasn't clear how much this meant to the current Troop 1 members, but the observances were incredibly ill timed for Stu Hillman, the camp superintendent. Stu had a problem. Waubeeka, he had realized early Sunday morning, had more troops than space, or at least more than the space that was available. And our troop was down from twenty kids the first week to eleven the second, which left things pretty sparse at a campsite with three cooking sites. Stu, a tall, thin earnest fellow in his early thirties, ambled into Wolfjaw with a modest proposal for Dr. Flank. He hated to do this, he began, but with just eleven kids, Troop 1 didn't have enough kids to make use of the three patrol sites at Wolfjaw. What he'd like to do is move us to a smaller site, so one of the bigger troops could use Wolfjaw. Dr. Flank listened silently, his face stony, his eyes narrowing. Did not young Mr. Hillman realize, he asked, that Troop 1 always camped at Wolfjaw and that we were settled in, having already spent our first week there? Well, yes, Mr. Hillman replied evenly, but the camp policy clearly stated that a troop had to be able to take up a specified percentage of the campsite, and our troop for the second week did not meet the standard. Soon, they were going at it like $500-an-hour litigators, arguing both the letter and the spirit of the camp regulations.

"Bill, I respect where you're coming from, but the policy still says, if I'm reading it right, that a troop must take up 75 percent of the site."

"Yes, but the policy doesn't cover this, a troop that's already settled in a site."

"I understand that, but if you put yourself in their shoes, the other troops, there's a very persuasive case."

"Well, I don't want to move a sitting troop. You don't come to camp and then be told you have to move. That's not right, and I don't think it's something we want to do."

On and on they went, neither budging in a characteristically mulelike male discourse that, to be sure, was better than pistols at ten paces or something else definitive. Finally Harry, in his role as Dr. Flank's heir apparent as top dog for the second week, stepped in to try to mediate.

"We're all trying to be reasonable adults here," he said. "In your opinion, Bill, what are the options?"

They went at it some more, but the obvious fact was that Dr. Flank wasn't budging. Particularly after contemplating Don Vanderbilt's plaque and Todd Frohmann's legacy, this was about something more than a piece of turf or a place to sleep at night. The closest thing we came to a compromise was allowing another troop, which turned out to be Greenwich Troop 35, from the tony town in Connecticut, to expand toward our southern border by taking over the vacant cooking site that was closest to their campsite at neighboring Sunrise.

That battle won, Dr. Flank prepared to take off for home. Dr. Flank's usual drill was to stay the first week only, and he had been packing up since early morning, so the kids knew he was preparing to leave. But it still felt like a big deal, both to the kids who on some level appreciated having him around as an undisputed authority figure and to those who felt that once the boss man was gone they could really run amok. So it was important to send out the right signal that order would be maintained and fully deputized adults would be in charge even if Dr. Flank were not around. For better or worse, that meant Harry, Dennis, and me.

"It is my pleasure to turn this motley crew called Chappaqua Troop 1 over to you, and Mr. Applebome and Mr. Walker," Dr. Flank announced, looking directly at Harry. "I'm sure you will have a great week."

"It is my pleasure," said Harry, "and we'll do our best to maintain your standards."

Both Dennis and I were thrilled to see Harry officially in charge. Not that there was much question. Harry had been active in Scouting in Brooklyn for many years as a young man, even working for a time as a paid Scouting district staff member. He was the only one of us who had shown up in uniform, with neatly pressed khaki shorts and high Scout socks pulled up to his knees. And he had the take-charge personality both of us lacked.

We loaded up Dr. Flank's Volvo, watched him drive off, and then contemplated our first major management issue—a proper Scout hike, or a wild jaunt into Lake George? Harry, responsibly, leaned toward doing what Dr. Flank would have done—the hike. But Dennis and I, the irresponsibility caucus, figured the kids deserved a break before embarking on the rigors of week two. Democracy won out, and before long we were all heading toward Lake George, a teeming menagerie of video-game arcades, ice-cream shops, pizza parlors, hot-dog stands, fast-food franchises, souvenir shops, and wax museums. The kids paraded around like sailors on leave. Sam 'n Eric and Tom took the occasion to flirt with various girls, most of them four years older and at best amused by, at worst utterly indifferent to, these preening little jokers in their Boy Scout uniforms. "There's something about a man in uniform," Sam said, intuiting a far more welcoming response from a passing blond in a tight halter top than was readily apparent. "Yeah," added Mark. "There's something about a man in an ape costume too, but it's not necessarily good." Then it was back to camp for the assembly at the parade grounds, the gala barbecue, and the merit badge sign-up that would begin the second week of camp.

In our brief absence, the camp had become a different place. We had been almost alone in Waubeeka when we arrived, but while we were gone, other troops had streamed in. They were busy setting up camp in Sunrise, Polaris, Cascade, Haystack, and Avalanche, the other campsites at Waubeeka. We could see kids lugging in their gear, throwing a football around the parade grounds, and wandering up and down the rocky road to the office and commissary. When we got back to Wolfjaw, Harry and I took over the two cots in the lean-to, clearly the power position in the campsite. Harry was already established as the week's adult leader, but my status as a lean-to dweller gave me an illusory air of authority as well. I did my best to adopt a stern, don't-mess-with-me demeanor as Harry called all the kids together to prepare for the night's festivities.

The barbecue was our first official gathering of the tribes, and instantly one got a sense of the troops as utterly distinct little pods. Sitting next to us was Troop 4 Bronxville with their purple ball caps and matching neckerchiefs, each kid decked out in matching full uniform. Their hulking leader looked vaguely familiar until I remembered he was the large fellow with the stiff-kneed walk who had been treated with such deference at the precamp meeting the previous winter. Troop 285 Bellmore from Long Island had the rowdy look of an Italian wedding without the bride and bridesmaids, and featured a handful of fierce-looking Mohawks that one of the dads, a barber, fashioned each year for willing victims. Troop 68 from Wappinger Falls in Dutchess County upstate had fringed red neckerchiefs and something of the quality of 4 Bronxville, though without quite the same cocky spit and polish. Other troops were from Rye, Scarsdale, and Greenwich, though I soon found out that it was common for troops to have the name of a ritzy town but really be made up largely of kids from the less high-powered town nearby. We all waited at long picnic tables until called to line up for hot dogs, hamburgers, potato salad, macaroni, and coleslaw, all of them doled out by staff members who were mostly just a few years older than the kids.

Then we all lined up at the parade grounds, where we were addressed by the camp director, Tom Logan. He stood on a rocky outcrop on the hill in front of the office, with his whole staff lined up obediently behind him. In the usual call and response, he made sure we felt real good, that we could always yell louder than the yell before, and that we had a positive mental attitude.

Next was merit badge sign-up, which felt like precomputerized college registration as orchestrated by the Marx Brothers. Most of the kids had come equipped with a list of the four or five merit badges they wanted to earn out of the thirty-five offered at Waubeeka. But, for those still waffling, the staff acted like carnival barkers advertising their wares.

"Come to the econ lodge, where a real man handles snakes and reptiles and learns astronomy, bird study, insect study, and mammal study," announced one teenaged counselor in his finest manly man baritone.

"Come to the econ lodge, if you want to turn into a pathetic sniveling wuss of a girly girl," announced another in the identical voice. "Come to Scoutcraft and learn camping, hiking, orienteering, and pioneering—Scouting the way the Good Lord meant it to be. And Scoutcraft is fun, not school in disguise."

"Scoutcraft is for dorks, and dorks are for Scoutcraft," the first kid yelled back.

Before long a third chimed in—not very credibly—for the manly man-ness of the handicraft shelter, where rugged Scouts could take basketry, leatherwork, and woodcarving, Scout camp's version of rocks for jocks. Before long there was a cacophony of mock baritones improvising together like a Scout camp's version of a free jazz ensemble. The only ones who didn't try to sell their wares were the counselors from the shotgun and rifle range, since it took no prodding to get almost every kid in camp interested in doing both sooner or later. The kids eventually filled up their calendars and lost interest in the show. By now, it was almost dark and time for the evening's final event—the campfire.

We gathered in a little natural amphitheater by the banks of Waubeeka's lake. The amphitheater was ringed by a shimmering crescent of trees and had logs for seats arranged in a semicircle. In the middle of the clearing was an impressive pyramid of logs, branches, kindling twigs, and debris that was set afire as soon as we were all seated, immediately billowing into a flickering orange tongue.

Tom, the camp director, led us in various time-worn Waubeeka cheers, yells, and fight songs—though it was hard to figure out whom we would be fighting against. The prissy hotel dwellers in Buckskin? The girls' camp we had passed along Brant Lake, with dozens of long-limbed girls running around on a perfectly manicured soccer field? The kids against the grownups? No one knew, but the kids got into the spirit nonetheless, urged on by the straight arrows from Bronxville 4, who jumped up, waved their arms wildly, and urged on all the laggards. We were supposed to make up in spirit and voltage what we lacked in eloquence, and the simplest yell was the most effective of all. It went: "Waaaaaahhh-Beeka. Waaaaaahhh-Beeka. Waaaaaahhh-Beeka. Camp. Camp. CAMP." The idea was to shout it out, cut the last word off as if with a knife, and listen to the echo roll over the water. We tried it once and got a modest but unacceptable—at least to Tom—echo. But then we did it a second and third and fourth time, each time a bit louder and producing a clearer and more expansive echo that lingered with a ghostly staying power over the dark waters of the lake.

Finally, the songs and cheers and skits were over, and Tom was standing alone in front of the bonfire.

"We come here to enjoy the true beauty that surrounds us," Tom said, the bonfire crackling and dancing madly around him. "Take only pictures and leave only footsteps. Maybe you've heard that. Maybe you haven't. It's all part of the spirit of Scouting. I want you to think about that as you go back to your cabins. File out quietly, and we'll see you in the morning."

We went back, finding our way along the path by flashlight, visiting the wash basin and the latrine and then crawling into our sleeping bags. In my head, as I drifted off to sleep, I could still hear the echoes of the echoes of the echoes—Waaaaaaahhh-Beeka, Waaaaaaahhh-Beeka, Waaaaaaahhh-Beeka. Camp. Camp. CAMP.

I woke up the next morning in time to see boys trudging into camp with brown plastic garbage cans strapped to their back. It looked like a scene out of a bad Dickens Boy Scout novel.

This, I soon learned, was not a dour form of punishment, but our food delivery system. Each morning at 6:45, one or two kids from each patrol strapped on an empty brown plastic trash can attached to a harness like a backpack and trekked up the trail to the commissary, where a sallow-faced trio of junior staff members loaded it with eggs and cheese, milk and cereal, toast and butter, pancake batter and syrup, and whatever other goodies like bacon or sausage were on the morning menu. They threw in the one mimeographed page of the "Waubeeka World News" plus whatever cups, plates, napkins, or plastic utensils or toilet paper were needed. Then the Scouts trekked back down to Wolfjaw, where the morning psychodrama was already in progress.

A friend who worked at a hospital emergency room once told me that arriving patients were informally, if cruelly, sorted by the staff into two classes of humans. There were citizens—regular folk who chopped off digits with power saws, or fell off ladders, or brought in children who had been bitten by the family dog. And there were dirtballs—essentially denizens of the night who shot, stabbed, stuck, or stomped one another with enough frequency to guarantee business in perpetuity for the ER staff. The level of mayhem at Waubeeka hardly approached the ER level, and "goofball" rather than "dirtball" seemed about the worst label one would care to stick on a thirteen-year-old Scout. But, particularly when there were chores to be done, it was immediately clear that we had our own informal typology at camp—performing and nonperforming assets. And for an enterprising Patrol Leader, the secret to getting meals cooked, latrines cleaned, or litter picked up was to find a way to get some work out of the laggards while not relying overly much on the kids who were willing to work but did not expect to do everyone else's chores as well.

So as our bleary-eyed crew prepared for their first day of activities at seven in the morning, the Scouts were already sorting themselves into tasks like a somewhat dysfunctional ant farm. Clearly of use were the two mules, Tom, now thirteen going on eighteen, and Mark, who had trudged back with the supplies and were now gaily unpacking them and stacking plastic apple juice cups, single-serving boxes of Lucky Charms, Froot Loops, and Apple Jacks, and milk cartons into neat but rickety towers perfectly positioned for someone else to knock over. Ben wouldn't have earned many merit badges for room-cleaning or chore-doing at home, but he and his Amigo Jonah were already up getting wood and helping to make the fire. At the other extreme were Les and Rick, who despite their obvious lack of interest had been talked into giving Scout camp a try. During the first week, Dr. Flank had told us, Les and Rick had tended to huddle together for comfort. They shared a tent. They did the same activities, which usually took place in the relative safety of the handicrafts lodge. And they shared a common distaste for camp chores—and to be honest, for camp altogether. Les was a round-faced twelve-year-old with red hair and a perpetually stricken look in his eyes. He spent most of the day simply pacing, back and forth, back and forth—around the cooking site, around the campsite, toward the latrine and back. Rick was a year older, a good bit taller and heavier, good at math, computers, and drawing nature sketches. But he had no interest in any of the troop activities, particularly those that involved mere chores. So as the others hustled in varying degrees to get breakfast going, Les and Rick wandered dolefully around the campsite and its environs in listless pursuit of firewood, or fire twigs, to be more accurate. They would roam for a few minutes, pick up a desultory twig or two from some distant cover of the site, trudge back to the cooksite, and ostentatiously place their booty on the firewood pile. Then they wandered off again.

In the middle of the performance/nonperformance scale at the upper campsite was Bernie, who had not been particularly active in the troop during the year, but gained a measure of camp-wide acclaim the first week by downing a five-gallon container of fruit punch in one sitting, a feat that won him about the only citation Troop 1 had earned the first week. Bernie specialized in accents and imitations—Fred Flintstone, Homer Simpson, some idiot proclaiming "You can do it," pronounced "you ca do eeet," apparently a particularly memorable phrase from the stupid Adam Sandler movie *The Waterboy*—so he tended toward jobs that involved social interaction more than vigorous initiative. He was quite happy to do his accents, eat, and tend the fire, throwing in kindling wood or discarded packaging with a few of his fellow pyros who were thrilled to keep the fire going. So, by a process of elimination, most of the first day's cooking was really produced and directed by Jack, the Senior Patrol Leader. He did get Bernie to break sixteen eggs and dump the remains in an orange plastic bowl, bidding each a fond farewell in his Homer Simpson voice. But after that, Jonah greased the cooking top with butter, poured messy globs of eggs onto the grill, and mixed them around with a wooden spoon. Then he slathered some more butter onto the grill and went back to work. Within ten minutes he had a dozen pieces of toast, about the same number of strips of bacon, and enough eggs to totally clog the arteries of a previously healthy Olympic marathoner.

The eating was characterized by the same imbalanced effort as the preparation had been. Les and Rick between them ate not much more than the marshmallow pieces they picked out of their Lucky Charms cereal. Les said he was too cold. Upon consideration, Rick decided he was too cold too. Bernie, on the other hand, ate two bowls of Froot Loops, three pieces of toast, three pieces of bacon, and a big clump of eggs that was piled up like a heap of mashed potatoes. The others did their parts in varying degrees. What they didn't finish, Bernie did, which helped the cleanup process immensely. At nine, the kids all fanned out across the camp to go to their activities. For the first time since we'd met at Rocky's, the three adults were alone to compare notes and plot strategy. Harry took the lead. He was decked out in his Scout uniform, shirt, shorts, and socks—no neckerchief—and had with him the troop's schedule for the week, which he had printed out at home before he left. The activities included a visit to the dry and wet caves, the latter a spooky cavern in which one had to dip underwater at various points. One day we had the low COPE course, the kind of team-building they do these days at corporate retreats, with teams helping one another across boards or forming human chains to retrieve a ball. There was a visit to the Zip Line, a trolley on a metal wire that Scouts rode halfway into the lake, hanging on by one or both hands and then letting go and dropping into the water. And one day we were scheduled to leave camp to go white-water rafting forty minutes away in Lake Luzerne.

"I thought the transition when Bill left went well," Harry said. "I think we're in good shape for the week. What issues do you guys see as needing our attention?"

There were a few. The site was a mess. There were pods of dissidents, the Sam 'n Eric faction in particular, intent on asserting their tribal hegemony in the lower part of the camp, which I came to see as The Underworld. Les and Rick and one or two others definitely needed some kind of a jump start. But, in addition to them, there was the issue of us. Just what did we *do,* Dennis asked.

This was a subject that had occurred to me prior to arriving, and uncharacteristically, I had followed Boy Scout protocol and was prepared. We, of course, had models from our own troop of effective leadership—Dr. Flank's patience and wisdom, Mr. Johnson's wry forbearance and ability to teach, Mr. Toonkel's cranky air of authority and competence. But I figured I'd scour some Scout literature for more explicit instruction on just what it was we were there for.

The Scoutmaster's Handbook was updated over the years just as the Scout Handbook was, but it spoke in a remarkably consistent, and, I thought, sensible voice about Scouting and Scouters. So, for example, the 1972 Handbook seemed not a bit outdated in its introductory passages on what it took to be a Scoutmaster:

> What qualities should you possess to be a good Scout-master? One could make a very long list, but that wouldn't help. Basically, you need to be an open person—one who speaks honestly and listens intently. You need a sense of humor. Not the ability to tell funny stories, but the ability to smile at yourself and at life. You need to understand the place of the outdoor program in Scouting and your part in it. And then—and this is quite important—you ought to like boys.

OK, the last phrase these days is hard to read without a hint of the wink-wink, nudge-nudge of sexual innuendo that has become Scouting's cross to bear. But the rest of the agenda—make it fun, make it educational, there should be a purpose behind each activity, never do for a boy what he can do for himself—was hard to argue with. I had also found two eccentric accounts of the Scoutmaster's lot, one from the 1930s, one from the 1950s. They were a reminder that despite the B.S.A.'s strenuous efforts to mold Scouting into a one-size-fits-all operation, the troops invariably took on the personality of their Scoutmaster.

Take A. Lewis Oswald. Please. Mr. Oswald, author of *Troop One Marches On!* published by the Rotherwood Press of Hutchinson, Kansas, in 1934, peers out from the back cover of his slender little book with a truly maniacal gleam in his dark little eyes. He's wearing a rounded, flat-brim, World War I–era military-style hat strapped tightly around his chin. Across his uniform, which is festooned with medals and patches, is a sash, presumably his Eagle sash, full of badges. If Rosenthal accuses Baden-Powell of putting together a character factory, Ozzie, as the boys call him, was darn proud of it. He writes: "I have no apology for saying to each lad on his twelfth birthday before he takes his oath, 'It is better not to join Troop One than to join and not be an Eagle.'" Yikes. If my friend Dan felt his Scouting experience was a bit harsh, he's lucky he avoided life with the hyena and rattlesnake patrols in Hutchinson Troop 1. Ozzie's obsessive account of life with his boys couldn't be much more creepy. He wrote of a favored class of Eagles:

> They say I gave them Scouting. They are wrong; they taught me the great game. When they outgrew their uniforms, I had a feeling that my heart would never again feel the thrill which was mine when I watched the one and only Charles Grimes Colladay, Eagle Number One of Troop Number One. He and Jerry and Jimmie were the pillars. After all, the test of success is not the make of the family's car; it's the boy, the heir-apparent!

Ozzie's zeal for molding his boys made him, like Machiavelli and Attila the Hun, before him a model for management theory. The Ozzie way of knowledge revolved around two principles, the primacy of the patrol system and the importance of troop ranking—"two of the golden keys, which unlock our secret shrine." So not only were boys organized into patrols, but within the troop Ozzie ranked every boy—Senior Patrol Leader Sidlinger, already an Eagle, at the top, on down to lowly Tenderfeet Leach, Stuckey, and Hamilton at numbers 23, 24, and 25 at the bottom. "Thus the position of every Scout in Troop One is known," he wrote. "By delivering the goods, he moves up. If he falters, others will pass him . . . If he dallies too much with the precious hour in front of him, he is tossed out, on the same principle that the dead wood is removed from the apple tree and for the same purpose, too." As for the older kids, not long after they made Eagle they were told to hit the road to make way for new blood: "It's hard and it's a trifle bitter, but Troop One must March On!" he concludes.

Oh, well. Ozzie was a product of his time and his locale. A more familiar voice is the narrator of *Be Prepared! The Life and*

Illusions of a Scoutmaster, by R. E. Cochran, published in 1952. In a less totalitarian way, Cochran too, sees himself as part of an enterprise dedicated to molding boys back in the days when Scouting was still considered an irony-free zone. "I felt," he says, at the beginning of his tenure, "rather like Toscanini arriving to conduct a rehearsal or Knute Rockne looking over a green squad he would soon mold into a championship team." Ozzie sees himself as a benevolent puppeteer helping to mold the heirs apparent. Cochran wisely sees himself a partner in a mysterious, osmotic process between the boys and their alleged leaders. "A Scout troop," he said, in a phrase he wouldn't dare use these days, "is more effective than a nagging wife in getting a man to do something about his shortcomings."

Cochran's narrative is good-natured and likably earnest. He notes approvingly that during two wars, Scouting never taught military techniques or hatred of the enemy, stressing instead "physical fitness, mental resourcefulness and war service chores." And mostly what he sees in Scouting is a largely respectful community of men and boys. He and his Scouts discuss Walt Whitman, survive pleasant and miserable outings in the woods, navigate the line between chaos and order at their meetings the way we do now, and coexist in a process that benefits both sides. He concludes:

> While it is true that Scouting builds character, it is especially true with reference to the Scoutmaster's character. Almost willy-nilly, he acquires cleanliness, strength, cheerfulness and other virtues listed in the Scout Law. As I slowly became aware, a Scoutmaster's troop is more or less a reflection of himself. The more time he spends with it, the more he finds his own personality mirrored and magnified in it.

Oswald and Cochran hardly covered all the bases of troop management, but they defined its two poles: Robert Duvall in

Apocalypse Now and Ward Cleaver. And in their own ways, their approaches raised at least two of the fundamental questions at the heart of the Scouting enterprise. First, were they training boys (*the heirs apparent!*) for the combat and competition— hopefully in peace, not war—that they'll likely face in life, or were they helping to mold character in a broader, less Darwinian sense? And, second, how much were they ringmasters and how much were they part of the circus?

Cochran had described a Boy Scout summer camp as "a remote, mysterious place to which visitors seldom penetrated and from which campers return speaking in cryptic jargon. Usually, it is entrenched in the farthest shore of some lake or river behind a mountain barrier." This wasn't a bad description of Waubeeka. The Curtis S. Read Scout Reservation, named for an Eagle Scout, assistant Scoutmaster, and naval aviator who died in 1918 in World War I, sprawls over one thousand acres of land not far from the site of the first Boy Scout camp that Seton presided over in 1910. Waubeeka's sliver of the Adirondacks was organized around activity areas that harkened back in a surprisingly literal fashion to Scouting's past. Just before the footbridge, on the way to the lake, was the Scoutcraft compound, surrounded by elaborately lashed-together limbs and planks that gave it the air of a forest fortress. At its heart was the Dan Beard area. There campers learned the basic knots and skills, and counselors laid out the requirements needed to reach Tenderfoot, Second Class, and First Class, the first three ranks on the advancement ladder. Back at the camp office, the walls were covered with quotations from Baden-Powell ("The Patrol is the character school of the individual"), all accompanied by archaic-looking drawings and the simple citation "B-P." It was hard to be sure how many kids even knew who Baden-Powell was, but his presence gave at least the appearance of purpose to the place.

Not surprisingly, there was no formal recognition of Seton, but he too seemed to be there at the Tom and Sonya Hays Memorial Nature Center. The center, a very modest open-air structure built in 1981, was presided over by a fiercely intelligent, bearlike college student named Ted Watson, who had a properly Setonian know-it-all air and a polymath's ability to sound like he knew what he was talking about whether he was spouting off about calculus, astronomy, insect study, geology, or computers. His assistant was Frankie Stanton, the Scout who made the carnival barker's pitch for nature study at the merit-badge sign-up.

I walked down to the shooting area, where kids were happily blasting away with shotguns and rifles. At the handicraft area they were weaving their baskets and carving neckerchief slides out of wood. I walked down to the waterfront, briefly considered taking my swimming test, and then figured it would be too embarrassing if I failed, so I decided to skip it and restrict my aquatic activities to the shower located adjacent to Wolfjaw, where campers and Scoutmasters followed a strict schedule that made sure adults and campers never used the shower at the same time. It occurred to me that, after all the urgent red-alert directives about how crucial it was to get my medical form in, no one had even asked for it. Apparently they did ask for it at the lake, but if you didn't sign up for swimming you could have a medical form saying you had high blood pressure, tuberculosis, or leprosy and were about to drop dead at any second, and no one would ever know.

Before I knew it, it was lunchtime. The commissary had given each patrol two pounds of salami, some American cheese, an industrial-size loaf of white bread, a few heads of iceberg lettuce plus tomatoes, oranges and apples, a big bag of potato chips, and two boxes of chocolate chip cookies. I ate down in The Underworld with Sam 'n Eric and their merry men. They made sandwiches with the salami, cheese, and potato chips; hurled the lettuce, tomatoes, oranges, and apples into the woods; and then downed all the cookies and vast quantities of cherry punch.

After lunch and siesta, during which kids napped, played cards, worked on their merit badges, or read, the kids trekked off again and Dennis and Harry went to the waterfront, where they took and passed their swimming test. I wandered back to the nature shack. It was an inspired blend of Setonian love of nature and contemporary love of wonkdom. The shack consisted of a back room enclosed on three sides full of books; computers; insect, rock, and flora specimens; knives, pins, and other gear. There were books on calculus, butterflies, and chemistry, many versions of the Scout Handbook, nature guides like *The Simon & Schuster Guide to Plants and Animals, The National Audubon Society Field Guide to North American Rocks and Minerals,* and *Birds of North America.* There was also, I was delighted to see, Seton's *Wild Animals I Have Known.* Downloaded on the computer were all sorts of iconic songs and sounds, from Sinatra's "New York, New York" to Weird Al Yankovich's "Barney's on Fire" ("Oh boy, Barney's on fire. It's what we've always desired.").

Ted Watson definitely had a show-off quality, like the camp's version of the Shell Answer Man. He was teaching calculus to a bunch of kids from Scarsdale, answering some kid's question about the likelihood of spontaneous combustion, and extolling the virtues of mica, all at the same time. Some of his schtick was his version of Science Guy stand-up comedy:

KID: "Ted, do you think there are aliens out there?"
TED: "Have you ever met a taxi driver in New York?"

The rest was random displays of knowledge, esoterica, or whimsy. Ted was too intense to keep an assistant for more than a year. But he and Frankie were a perfect pair. One took himself too seriously; the other didn't take anything seriously. One was all full of abstract knowledge; the other was more likely to be out hunting for snakes or talking about *Star Wars* characters than stars when teaching the astronomy merit badge. And the econ lodge—it was officially the ecology lodge, but "ecol" didn't have the right ring—had the feel of a node of Scouting that had evolved the way God intended it—boys teaching boys, techy and fun, respectful of nature and respectful of the boys. Ted had already achieved a top rank nationally in the Order of the Arrow, the national Scouting honorary society. But he was surprisingly unreflective about Scouting—Did it reach enough kids? Did he worry about Scouting being seen as uncool and behind the times? Does the uniform still serve a positive purpose? When I asked, he looked at me as if mildly annoyed. "If you say it's not what the modern Westchester boy does, and it's uncool, you haven't been much of a devil's advocate, because you're not saying anything," he said. "If you say it's uncool, fine. But if you check with the kids who are Scouts, no one really cares about that. Scouting's not much different than it ever was. The goal is to develop character, foster citizenship, and teach fitness. And I think kids get that, without being hit over the head with it."

I headed back toward Wolfjaw. As I approached, I heard the faint strains of a song that sounded a bit like the call of a stricken animal. It was an ancient camp song known to generations of campers hither and yon:

> Scout socks.
> They never get dirty.
> The longer you wear them,
> The stronger they get.
> Sometimes I think I should launder them.
> Something keeps telling me
> No no not yet.

For Troop 1, though, the song had taken on a quality that was one part totemic and one part sadistic. During the first week,

Sam 'n Eric had made it their personal calling card. They gave it a straight manly Scouts reading, a Whitney Houston soulful reading, a Celine Dionne bombastic reading, and a particularly weaponized *La Traviata* operatic reading. They sang it loud and they sang it louder and loudest. Their rendition had made them instantly famous in camp—over-the-top obnoxiousness always being the quickest route to notoriety for adolescent boys. And their vocal skills had immediately become an enormous sore point for our nearest neighbors, the Scout troop from Greenwich. When I reached camp I learned that Sam 'n Eric had been singing it for perhaps twenty minutes, and every time they resumed their oratorio, screams of pain and anguish could be heard from our friends from Greenwich. One little boy in particular would run to the rise overlooking our site, a stricken look on his face, reminiscent of Munch's *The Scream*. Each time the singing resumed, his eyes would bug out, he'd put his hands over his ears, and he'd yell, "Shut up, shut up" at the top of his lungs. But, of course, the more he complained and hollered, the more Sam 'n Eric were encouraged to sing, often pausing just long enough to lull the Greenwichites into thinking they were finally through, only to crank it up con molto brio once again.

Antagonizing the kids from Greenwich had particular appeal. Greenwich 35 did not have quite the well-drilled hauteur of Bronxville 4, but it soon became apparent that our relationship with them was somewhat like that between the John Belushi frat and the straight-arrow frat in *Animal House*. They stood silently before meals, bowed their heads, and said their vespers, while we didn't do so much as a "Rub a dub dub, thanks for the grub." Their kids showed up in neatly pressed and tended uniforms. Their Scoutmasters were all trim, friendly, and unfailingly polite, except when they were complaining that we weren't pulling our weight in cleaning the latrine we now were sharing. The Greenwich site went dark and quiet right after

"Taps" was played at ten—we pictured them drinking warm milk and kneeling by their cots in their jammies to say their prayers at night. Their one excess was building humongous bonfires every night that they stoked up to hadeslike intensity, as if allowing all their sublimated energies to play out in each evening's pyre. Still, whether walking to the shower with their monogrammed towels or coming back from the handicrafts shed with that perfect piece of lanyard or the wicker basket done just so, both the Scouts and Scouters of Greenwich 35 had enough of that air of WASPy Connecticut virtue to stir the darker sauces of our guys, particularly the crew down at our lower site, where Louis may have been Patrol Leader but Sam 'n Eric were the true capos.

We made our dinner—chicken patties in marinara sauce, salad, Italian bread, bug juice, oatmeal cookies—and cleaned up quickly. Harry had made it clear he wanted everyone to be on time for all the retreats, which took place at 6:45 each evening, so our guys straggled over to the lean-to by 6:30, and we all trekked up to the parade grounds. We lined up next to Bronxville 4. Each of their kids was in an impeccable uniform right down to a neckerchief perfectly positioned in its slide. Their Senior Patrol Leader inspected their lineup with a cold, unforgiving gaze, like a Marine Corps Drill Instructor, straightening a kid's neckerchief or moving the line another six inches to keep it perfectly straight. All our kids had their Scout shirts on, but otherwise we looked like we'd been outfitted at one of those *ropa usada* places in South Texas where people buy mix-and-match clothes by the pound.

Before long, Tom Logan strode out from the camp headquarters and took his position on the hill above us.

"Camp Waubeeka, attention!" he hollered.

Bronxville 4 turned to ramrods. Greenwich 35 stood erect like perfect toy soldiers. We slouched a bit less than usual.

"Parade rest," he continued. Then he ordered a bugler to sound the retreat. The flag was taken down and folded, we were ordered at ease, and he paced on the rocky rise above us with a sheet of paper in his hands.

"Gentlemen, we had a great day today. I saw a lot of Scout spirit. I saw a lot of hard work. I saw a lot of fun. Gentlemen, if you've been here before, this is something you already know. If you haven't, it's something you need to know. Every week one troop is awarded a special honor."

He held up a large, yellow wooden "W," with names scrawled all over it. "This, gentlemen, is the Waubeeka Award. Each week troops are graded on their daily site inspection, on competitions like the staff hunt, the water carnival, or knot-tying competitions between the SPLs. At the end, the troop with the most points is awarded the Waubeeka Award at the final campfire, and every Scout and adult leader gets to sign his name on it. In that context, I have the results of today's inspections. Remember that nothing counts more than your inspection—how well you keep up your campsite and cooking sites each day. And today, we had three perfect scores—thirty-six of thirty-six. When I call your names, will the SPLs for each troop come forward to receive your inspection report. First, the perfect scores. 'Bronxville 4.' (Big surprise.) 'Greenwich 35.' (Ditto.) 'Scarsdale 2.'" Three perfectly outfitted SPLs briskly marched forward, accepted the report, and returned to their troop. I thought I detected something of a self-satisfied smirk on the faces of the older Bronxville kids. Then the rest were called: 285 Bellmore, where the SPL looked like a linebacker for the Jets. 313 North Bellmore. 68 Wappinger Falls. 2 Rye. 1 Chappaqua. Jack accepted the report, brought it back, and took a peek.

"How'd we do?" asked Bernie.

"You don't want to know," Jack replied, then relented. "Eighteen."

"D'oh," Bernie replied in his best Homer Simpson. "You bat .500 in baseball, you make the Hall of Fame."

"I don't think that's something we need to worry about," Jack replied.

As soon as the retreat finished up, the kids went to the camp store at the rear of the commissary to get ice creams or Cokes. The big shots in camp were readily apparent. Some were the more conspicuous staff members, like Ted Watson or Frankie Stanton. Others were the most intimidating SPLs, who were figures of unimaginable stature to the smaller kids. And then there were those who just became instant camp characters, a group exemplified by Sam 'n Eric. They strode into the store like Belushi and Ackroyd in *The Blues Brothers,* twice the size of most of the kids and all confidence and bravado. I wasn't quite sure how their fame had spread so quickly, but it was clear that the kids at Waubeeka already knew all about Sam 'n Eric.

There were fraternal "yos" to greet the older kids in Bronxville 4 and Scarsdale 2; informed gossip about who might be interested in dating Rita, a lifeguard who was one of a half dozen female staff members; advice to younger Scouts on which merit badge counselors were least likely to bust your chops, and whispered conversations about Sam 'n Eric's favorite topic—life in Staff City, the collection of tents and huts down the hill from the main office where staff members, it was said, got to stay up all night, play guitars, smoke cigarettes, play Nintendo 64 or Play Station video games, and do cool and scandalous things too fabulous to even contemplate.

Still, there was one personage at Waubeeka who loomed above all the others. If anyone missed the point, there at the flagpole was a plaque with his name: "Dedicated to Lester Allen Rattner. Eagle 1958. Silver Beaver 1990. 27 year Scouter Troop 4, Bronxville. Dedicated July 4, 1994." It was, of course, the big guy from Bronxville 4. Lester Rattner spoke in a deep, raspy growl of a voice, sort of like what Johnny Cash might have sounded like if he'd grown up in Yonkers, New York, instead of Dyess Colony, Arkansas. At Waubeeka, Lester seemed to be everywhere, badgering his kids to straighten their neckerchiefs as they walked to retreat, getting on the commissary about the quantity of salami they were giving out for lunch, or just hanging out on the front porch of the Waubeeka office. Which was where I found him midmorning on the third day. Lester, I soon learned, had a troop philosophy as deeply embedded as anything by Kant and an opinion on all things having anything to do with Scouting. "The slogan of our troop is 'Scouting the way it used to be,' and, parenthetically, we say 'Scouting the way it ought to be.' We wear the full uniform, and we wear it correctly," he said, as he sat on one of the wooden benches that ran around the front porch. He was at least six foot three with a crew cut and had the appearance of a Scouting Zeus dispatched to the Waubeeka porch to check out the mortals. "I joined the troop in 1955 at the age of eleven, and I never left, so by now I should know what I'm doing. At the Scoutmaster meeting the other day, someone said, 'Lester is so rigid, he always wants to do things the same way.' And I said to him, 'I'm not rigid. I'm just not flexible.' There's a rumor that's always going around camp that I'm an ex-Marine. Well, the truth is my entire military training was growing up at a Boy Scout camp."

Like most traditionalists, Lester seemed obsessed with what was no longer so traditional, and the troop motto summed up his view of Scouting as an institution under siege. The assailants came from all corners: the national headquarters in distant Texas, nervous meddling moms, predatory lawyers, feminists intent on turning boys into wusses.

"The biggest problem with Boy Scouts today is that the guys making up the policies sit down in a room in Texas and don't know what the heck is going on in the field," he said. "They don't know how to deal with boys. It's strictly a corporate thing. They're concerned with their careers and with raising money. That's about it. The chief scout executive makes about $400,000 a year. Like a lot of nonprofits, the people there make a hell of a profit. The other big problem is their excessive concern with liability. They've gotten so uptight about everything because they think someone's going to sue them. We used to build signal towers and bridges across streams made out of rope. Now they're all worried someone might fall and cut themselves. Boys aren't supposed to run in camp anymore. They can't climb trees. The raft in the lake used to be twice as far from the dock. You know why? They're afraid of getting sued, so each year kids have to swim less and less to get there. You can't tell ghost stories anymore. Boys might lose sleep. Most of the old songs, if they mention alcohol or gambling or liquor, they're no longer any good. I used to have a guy come to the campfire dressed as a girl with balloons in his blouse. Can't do that. It's sexist. What's the big deal if a couple of guys dress up like girls? It doesn't make them homosexuals. At the water carnival, we used to have a watermelon fight. You greased a watermelon and greased the boys' bodies and you had two teams trying to grab these greased watermelons and push them over to the other team's goal line to score. It's been a tradition at Boy Scout camps since the '40s. But now they think it's too rough, so at the aquatic carnival last week they had an event where they put a watermelon in the water and had the boys get in a line and pass it under their legs to one another. What American boy wants to pass a watermelon under his legs? We've got a girl running our waterfront who plays rugby in college. The girls are playing rugby and the guys are passing watermelons under their legs. Where are we headed in this country?"

The litany of Lester's complaints went on. Kids started too young in the Tiger Cub program, which enrolled boys younger than the Cub Scout minimum age of seven, and left them burned out on Scouting before they finished middle school. Scouting had fouled up the badges in an attempt to save money by using fewer colors in them. There was, he was sure, a slow, relentless move toward integrating girls into Boy Scouts, beginning with what were called Explorer units for older kids. "Sooner or later they're just going to call it Scouting USA and do away with Boy Scouts altogether." Over the past fifteen years, there had been more focus on sports and merit badges for competitive sports like basketball. "If you want to play baseball, you don't join the Boy Scouts. You join Little League."

I was completely respectful of Lester's mastery of the Scouting Way of Knowledge and fully aware of my deficient knowledge base. But Scouting didn't seem quite so bloodless to me. Maybe Troop 1 was so far outside the mainstream that in some ways it was Chappaqua 1, not Bronxville 4, that was Scouting the Way It Used to Be. Troop 1's problem, it seemed to me, was less the kids as docile wimps but the opposite. So when I wandered back down to Wolfjaw after listening to Lester, what I found did not entirely comport with the new dessicated, Politically Correct Scouting environment he seemed to see. Bernie was mincing around the site like a two-bit hooker wearing two big water pitchers inside his shirt, and beckoning to his fellow Scouts with a come-hither voice as he showed off his new Pamela Lee–style chest. "Oh, boys, boys. Over here, boys," he cooed in his best falsetto. Jack, our not-so-strict SPL, was chasing Mark and Jonah around the site carrying two pots full of water as part of an escalating water fight. Running around a rock-strewn site did not seem like the smartest idea to me, but I let it go for a while at least.

While these sideshows were going on, Sam trudged into Wolfjaw holding his head and looking a little dazed.

"You OK?" I asked him.

"I think so, but my head hurts," he replied. Indeed, there was a healthy knot on his forehead.

"What have you been doing?"

"Well, I was over at the shotgun range, and Grissom dared me to break three of the clay pigeons against my head," he said, Grissom being one of the counselors in training, or CITs, at the range—yet another responsible authority figure.

"And?"

"Well, I figured I should at least try. I did three OK. But the second three hurt."

"You mean you broke six clay pigeons against your head?"

"Well, no. I broke four, but the other two just bounced off and didn't break."

Harry and Dennis were returning from their afternoon swim, so I filled them in on what was going on and decided to take Sam to the infirmary for observation. It was a frame house at Buckskin, which had Russ Fleer's Jeep Wagoneer out front and eight empty cots inside. Russ listened to Sam's tale with the mixture of amused familiarity and dutiful disapprobation common to large state prisons and Scout camps. He checked Sam's eyes and the lump on his head and decided the patient would live to sing "Scout Socks" again. He gave him some ice to keep down the swelling and some Tylenol, but said otherwise he was fine.

"I hope you learned a lesson beyond the fact that it's not a good idea to break skeets against your head."

"I guess I did," Sam replied.

"And what might that be?"

"Don't do something stupid because someone tells you to?"

"That's close enough. That and the fact that when you do something that puts you or others at risk, you're all responsible for whatever happens. I don't know who's more to blame, you or Grissom, but you both should know better. In the future, use your head in more productive ways, OK?"

"Yes, sir."

We drove back, Sam temporarily chastened and looking like a twelve-year-old knucklehead rather than an aspiring big shot. We got out of the car and walked down to Wolfjaw. It was quickly apparent it was not a happy scene. Most of the kids were sitting around glumly. It was the middle of the dinner hour, but at least one of the patrols did not seem to have any food prepared. The site was still a mess, with random candy wrappers and bits of foil scattered here and there. Harry was talking with Bernie, whose eyes were downcast and shoulders slumped, like a POW stuck in an interrogation session.

Sam peeled off to huddle with the others. Harry motioned me over. He asked me about Sam's condition and then filled me in on the afternoon's events, which began with the water fight soaking one patrol's monster box and continued through the other patrol forgetting to schedule someone to pick up the food for the evening meal. Harry did not find this funny. He was also not amused when he learned from one of the kids that one reason everyone enjoyed an afternoon rafting outing outside camp so much was that Bernie had entertained the troops on the way back by pulling down his pants and mooning passing cars from the window of the official Curtis S. Read Scout Reservation van. (Only a bunch of fiftyish dads could have thought the kids were so entranced by oldies radio.) Hence the heart-to-heart I'd walked in on.

Like Lester, Harry took Scouting seriously. As a kid growing up on Coney Island with little talent for athletics, the one chosen sixteenth of sixteen, he'd found a home in Scouting. When his troop went to Staten Island to camp, it was his first experience of the outdoors. He got to follow the advancement trail to Life Scout, the step before Eagle, and was elected to the Scouting honorary society, the Order of the Arrow. After college in 1976, he got his first real job as a Scouting professional, working seven days a week for $7,500 a year in a job that was charged with forming units, fundraising, and keeping Scouting alive in an area rapidly going from white to black and Hispanic.

He still has a well-stuffed box at home of his Scouting memorabilia—his 65 ¢ Order of the Arrow Handbook from 1968, old badges and neckerchiefs, the natural fox neckerchief slide he used to wear, his Order of the Arrow sash. Most prized of all are the black-and-white patches, neckerchiefs, and T-shirts reading "Sheepshead Community Scouting Experience Nov. 4–5 1978." The gathering, billed as a tent-o-ral, which is like a camporee only hyphenated, was staged in the area between Brighton Beach and Coney Island. Four blocks from the original Nathan's Famous hot-dog stand, in Asser Levy Seaside Park, close enough to the beach to see the boardwalk and hear the D train rattling by, he organized a jamboree in the heart of Brooklyn that took a half year of planning to pull off. The Army Corps of Engineers supplied water-tank trucks. The Parks Department helped build a midway, and the phone company installed temporary phone booths. The Scouts put up the booths and signs and manned stations exhibiting first aid, map, and compass skills, the Pinewood Derby, and—what else?—knot tying. In the end, six hundred kids camped out in the heart of Coney Island as if it were the Poconos or the Adirondacks. The event got played up on all the local television news shows, and Scouting got more visibility in Brooklyn than it had in years. "Scouting is more alive and viable than ever," Harry told the *Brooklyn Times*. It may have been more a statement of faith than objective reportage. But the event was a big success as something for the kids to enjoy and as a way to fly Scouting's flag and remind people what they were about. It was the coup of his career.

Other moments were not so easy. One troop had a rigorous numerical ranking to choose its Scout of the Year. Its outstanding Scout one year was a hard-working young kid named Evan.

And when the scores were toted up, Evan, to no one's surprise, was the clear winner. The plaque with his name was prepared, and the award ceremony was scheduled. But before it happened, Evan just snapped at home one day. No one really knows why, but the model Scout stabbed his mother to death in her bed. He was sent off to reform school and came back a few years later, showing up at a troop meeting like an unexpected apparition, his plaque still stashed away in a closet at the school where the troop met.

So Harry was acutely aware that Scouting came with no guarantees. It was essentially a volunteer operation. If you had good volunteers you had a good program (unless it got screwed up anyway), and if you had bad ones you probably had a crappy one. And while Harry had complete respect for Dr. Flank, he wasn't in complete accord with the way he ran the troop. He thought the meetings needed more structure and variety; the loosey-goosey, post-'60s ethos of the troop worked fine for Todd Davis but not for a lot of the others. And after half a week at Waubeeka, he was pretty well disgusted with Troop 1's half-assed brand of Zen/*South Park*/Homer Simpson/Scouting Lite. Dennis and I felt if the kids didn't burn down Waubeeka or do irrevocable harm to themselves or each other, we had done our jobs. Harry had much higher expectations. He figured if he could pull off the Brooklyn Jamboree for inner-city kids, he should be able to have a respectable week of camp with a bunch of privileged suburban brats.

"Tonight's the Staff Hunt," Harry said to me, referring to the popular exercise in retribution in which kids got to roam through the woods searching for hiding counselors and staff members and then escort them to the waterfront for a ceremonial dunking. "I'm going to tell them we're missing that, and we're going to have our own meeting instead. They won't like it, but they have to know this is important. I know this is the second week of camp, and they're getting restless. But I don't want to finish the week like this."

Dennis and I nodded and muttered words of support. It was almost time for the evening retreat. Harry called the kids over to the lean-to and told them the plan—that he was not happy with the way things were going, and we were going to have our own meeting and miss the staff hunt. There were assorted groans and whines, but it was clear Harry's mind was made up, so we made the desultory trek up toward the parade grounds. Someone with a sharp pair of ears could have picked up repeated uses of the word *asshole*. As the other troops got ready for the staff hunt, we marched back down to the campsite. Some of the kids stood. The others sat on the benches by the picnic table.

"Everyone present and accounted for?" Harry said evenly. "Good. Let's begin. First of all, I want you to know this is not punitive. You're not here to be punished. But I thought we should all get together to talk about the week so far, how it's gone, what we can do better."

With that relatively neutral introduction, he began enumerating some of the week's greatest hits. The monster boxes no one had bothered to stock with essentials like dish soap, plastic utensils, and paper plates. The trash strewn around the site. The meals barely cooked. The times kids had sat down to eat without bothering to wait for the others or the time they were so late the visiting staff members had to leave before they were fed. Louis so frustrated at not being obeyed that he had started crying. Yes, we had a great white-water rafting trip, but Bernie didn't do much for the camp's image by dropping his pants and mooning passing cars from the Camp Read van. (Luckily, none of us knew about one other highlight, a Scout who will remain nameless pissing into an empty water jug as a joke.)

"Can any of you tell me what Scouting is supposed to be about, why we're here?"

There was only a slight pause before various kids came up with answers.

"To learn discipline."

"To have fun."

"To become a team."

"To work together around common goals."

"To develop leadership skills."

Some of it was strained and dutiful, but mostly kids seemed to be taking the question seriously.

"Those are all good answers," Harry continued. "Scouting is not set up as an organization where the adults show up and tell the kids what to do and run the Scout units themselves. Baden-Powell based his idea of Scouting around something called the patrol method, the idea of boys leading boys. And the patrol system was set up as a way for Scouting to foster all those things, discipline, fun, teamwork, leadership, that you just talked about. For now, Louis and Jimmy are the Patrol Leaders and Jack is the Senior Patrol Leader. Tomorrow it might be Sam or Elliot or Tom. But the point is we need to show respect for the leaders and we need to work together as a team to get things done. Because right now we're not working together, we're not exhibiting leadership, we're not completing tasks, we're not having fun. So everything you guys told me before that's part of Scouting doesn't happen when the leadership and the patrol method breaks down. I'm not trying to lecture you, but I really wanted you to be able to sit down and think about what's going on, so we can figure out ways to make this thing work better."

It was hard to tell how much of what ensued was genuine and how much was the kids doing their best Eddie Haskell, but almost everyone had something to say. Eric said the patrol method was fine in theory, but it didn't work when Patrol Leaders issued arbitrary demands and didn't do their share of the work. Sam and Tom seconded the motion. Doug said maybe kids were jealous that they weren't leaders, but there was no excuse not to do the jobs you were supposed to do. One suggestion was to recognize a quartermaster for each patrol to keep the monster box stocked. Someone said it was simple respect to keep the site clean. Someone else said if it wasn't a specific person's job, it would not get done.

My usually brilliant son complained about missing the staff hunt. "No one really wants to sit around and talk about this stuff when other kids are running around yelling, screaming, pushing the staff in the water, finding the counselor you really despise and dunking him in the lake. You could have done it later and still made your point."

Harry heard him out, but said he felt things had gone so far downhill it was important to make the point while the memory was clear rather than having everyone run off and have fun as if nothing had happened. None of the kids seemed convinced.

No fingers were pointed. No edicts were handed down. The kids remained unhappy with the session and with Harry, who had now fully inherited Dr. Flank's status as The Man. But it seemed to make a difference. When we finished, some kids on their own started picking up stray candy wrappers. Singing of "Scout Socks" was curtailed for the evening. The overall tone of the language, at least for a night, improved. Ben and Dennis and I walked up to the parade grounds, where Ted Watson was leading a stargazing class. It was a brilliant, clear night, and Ted was pointing out Mercury and Vega and the North Star, the stars that make up Leo and the Little Dipper, expounding on binary systems with two suns and the death of our solar system. "Scientists disagree on many things, but there's one thing that every scientist on the planet agrees on, which is that eventually our sun will grow cold and die," Ted proclaimed in his best Mr. Wizard voice as we lay on our backs staring mutely into the inky darkness. "When that happens, Einstein and Aristophanes and

Marilyn Monroe and all the rest, all the existence we know of, will be for nothing unless we go to the stars and find a place to begin anew." This seemed an appropriately big thought with which to conclude our evening of introspection.

Maybe it was that cheery thought, or maybe it was the aftermath of Harry's address to the troops, or maybe it was that camp's end was only two days away, but from then on things took a surprisingly benevolent turn. Our performances in the Waubeeka rankings remained dismal, and our absence from the staff hunt guaranteed us yet another last-place finish. But we did keep the site a little cleaner. The meals tended to get done on time, the pantries stayed full, the level of griping and vile language stayed within a reasonable range. With the end nearing, the kids were more focused on piling up merit badges than acting out. And even the adults started to get a little sentimental about the impending end of our Waubeeka experience. So on Thursday morning, while the kids were at their activities, Harry, Dennis, and I decided to embark on our own little adventure, a climb to the top of First Brother, the peak at the Summit Base at the far end of camp. Many of the kids had been there already for their wilderness survival badge, which involved climbing to the top at dusk, building a shelter out of limbs and leaves, and sleeping outdoors without a blanket or sleeping bag while getting bitten to death by mosquitoes. I was perfectly happy not to include that in my Scouting experience.

We set off equipped with water bottles, insect spray, and plastic containers for picking blueberries, said to exist in great profusion at the top of the hill. About ten minutes into our journey, Harry, who was not in the best of shape, found himself totally winded. Opting for discretion rather than valor, he turned around and headed back to camp. But Dennis and I pushed on and with only two stops for water completed the forty-five-minute hike to the top. There we were rewarded with both a majestic view and luxuriant tufts of blue and purple blueberries poking out from rocks and patches of greenery almost everywhere you looked. For a few minutes we sat silently, swatting off mosquitoes and looking out over the lakes, hills, and valleys of Camp Read and the surrounding wilderness. Then we grabbed our berry containers and wandered here and there in a blissful daze. Finally, after we had filled two big containers, we sat on a hard outcrop of exposed rock, eating our berries and talking about our sons. This in itself was something of a wonder. As it turned out, Dennis lived about five houses down the road from me, at the bottom of a steep incline perhaps three hundred yards away. Had we not been in Scouts, we might not ever have met—the lots are long and wooded, and the only people who really get out are the few, like me, who walk their dogs rather than let them roam around and bark neurotically behind their electric Invisible Fences. Plus his son, the famous Eric, and mine were different enough that they were not likely to have become great pals even if they rode the same school bus every day. To the rest of the world, Eric was one of the swaggering *Über*-sized *Über*-Dogs of the troop. But in his dad's forgiving eyes, pretty much like the ones with which I viewed my son, he was a gentle soul who could be a minister, a teacher, a therapist, or certainly an actor if he wanted to go that route. Dennis went on for a while and then segued to a reminiscence of growing up in Mississippi.

"Our big thing when we were kids was swinging from the hickory trees," he said. "That was the Six Flags Over Georgia of its day. It had to be hickory, they're the most flexible; otherwise the branch might break. So what I did in my backyard was we had a whole stand of hickory trees out back in the woods. You would climb about ten to twelve feet up and grab a branch. Then you'd swing back and forth and reach for the next one and do like a Tarzan thing, swinging from hickory tree to hickory tree. It got so I could go through five trees. That was magic. Now it's a lawsuit. The other thing I'd do is I had all these Japanese and Axis toy soldiers, and I'd get out my BB gun and kill them all. Plus I had my individual lady-finger firecrackers. I'd put some of them out there and blow up some of the enemy. I describe this to Eric and he says, 'Dad, you had such a great childhood.' I say, 'Well, my dad beat me with a belt when I disobeyed. I had to take out the garbage, and I didn't get paid anything for it. There were no video games and no computers.' But he still thinks I had a better childhood. I had more freedom. I could go out and risk killing myself without my mom even worrying about it. So he thinks that would be the coolest thing. To be free, which is the way he describes it. To do what you want."

We refilled our containers and headed back down, light-headed from the exercise and the utter remove from life as we usually knew it. Back when I had time to read books, I was a huge fan of Thomas Pynchon, particularly *Gravity's Rainbow,* his long, twisted masterwork about rocket science, anomie, and World War II. Near its end, Pynchon's schlemiel/hero Tyrone Slothrop, exhausted from his role at the intersection of history, weaponry, and his own libido, finally finds himself peacefully mindless and blissed out, his normal sense of consciousness so overloaded it has shorted out as he watches a thick rainbow after a heavy rain he doesn't even recall: "His chest fills and he stands crying, not a thing in his head, just feeling natural." I hadn't reached quite that point, but I knew what he had in mind.

But it wasn't just Dennis and me. Maybe there was something in the air, maybe all the stars of Waubeeka were somehow aligned for a day with B-P. Not B-P "the Hero of Mafeking," but B-P "the inspired mystic of Scouting." Because the campfire that night seemed to pick up where we had left off on our hike. First Tom Logan got up and asked us to let our eyes sweep over the slumbering lake, black under the gaggle of stars, and the curtain of trees encircling it.

"I remember the first time I ever came to this camp," he said. "It changed my life forever. The appreciation it gave me for nature. The people I've met. I had some of the best times I've ever had in this camp. Can anyone tell me what the outdoors code means to them? Anybody?"

One little kid—he looked about ten or eleven—got up and said, "Nature's given us so much, and what you really need to do is, you need to be aware you just can't take things from the environment. You can't chop down a bunch of trees for no reason or capture animals for no reason. You have to protect nature or one day it will all be gone."

Tom looked beyond pleased.

"'We have to take care of nature or one day it will all be gone.' That was very nice. Thank you. Now all of us are sitting here and we're staring at something which can be amazing. This fire right here. All of this fire is energy. And that's something we need to be very safe with. But tonight I want to draw from that energy. So everyone sitting here tonight is going to go down in Waubeeka history. And the story is going to be passed down to everyone who comes after us. I want us all to put our heads together and create a Camp Waubeeka Outdoor Code. I want us to come up with a sentence, a couple of words, a phrase that will be the outdoor code only for Waubeeka. Who has an idea? Anyone?"

Silence. Then another boy stood up. He was, of course, from Lester's troop. He paused, and then in a surprisingly firm voice for a small kid, announced: "I will do my best to be a guardian of the beauty of Camp Waubeeka."

"Perfect," said Tom. "Perfect. From now on that will be the Outdoor Code for Camp Waubeeka."

We didn't know quite what that entailed, but we were all suitably impressed by the gravity of what we'd just witnessed.

No doubt inspired by the sense of history in the making, the camp commissioner, Lenny Harris, got up next. He was a thin Floridian in his early twenties who wore his blond hair long, in a ponytail. His job was to care for the physical plant at Waubeeka while Tom took charge of the programs. If Tom seemed inspired, Lenny seemed in the throes of mystical revelation. He talked about spending much of the day in the caves, just thinking of Waubeeka and Scouting and what he wanted to say at the night's campfire. Then he started talking about the ideals of Scouting.

"When I was in the caves, I tried to visualize a perfect person," he said. "We all know no one's perfect. But I dreamed of a man who was clean, manly, strong, fearless and kind, gentle with his strength, dignified, silent, and friendly. He was equipped for emergencies and filled with religion that was not only built from creeds or occasional observances but a desire to help those who needed help. This perfect man was athletic, fearless, kind, picturesque, wise in the ways of the woods and without any regret for the way he lived his life. And with this vision, I was led as many before me to choose the life of a Scout. Scouting is my travel guide on the path to being a perfect man. I may never reach being perfect. But I will live my life knowing I'm always striving for the one single goal, to be the best man I can be. And I want all of you to leave here with a vision of how you can be the best you can be. And I know you will never forget what went on here. Thanks for being here with me."

He sat down, and then we all sat in silence for what seemed like an eternity, the fire crackling and snapping in the darkness, the stars dazzling overhead. Who knows what the kids made of it. But I was transfixed by Lenny's intensity and the simple, direct way he had tried to do what most of us, man or boy, almost never do—come to terms with male identity. It was like picking up an "Archie" comic book and getting *War and Peace* instead. After a while, we repeated the new outdoor code and sang "Taps" and filed out, much more quietly than we ever had before.

No one said much about Lenny's oration. Chances are it registered more with the dads than the kids. But when we got back to Wolfjaw, the kids did seem quieter than usual, as if the lofty thoughts of the campfire had stuck with them. They ended up going to bed, for a change, not long after ten. Then Harry and Dennis and I met at the lean-to for our own private observance. In the afternoon, I had gone into town and bought us a bottle of tequila and some margarita mix at the one liquor store in Brant Lake. I barely drink, and didn't have any great need for a beverage more serious than our usual bug juice or Cokes. But we figured we deserved our own little senior management retreat, and this seemed the way to do it. Alcohol is forbidden at Scout camps or activities, but, truth to tell, we weren't exactly the first dads in history to bring a bottle of one kind or another to camp or a camp-out. So we fired up the two Coleman lamps, filled our plastic cups, broke out some peanuts and chips, and sat around talking about the week, about whether Bernie had perhaps learned to curb his instincts to function as class clown as the week went by, about how Louis and Jimmy had struggled as Patrol Leaders but perhaps had learned a bit, about Harry's abilities as a hiker and mine as a swimmer. We didn't talk much about the campfire, but we didn't have to. It was just part of the air that night.

We spent the last day cleaning up the site and turning in our gear. There was a staff barbecue, so the kids didn't have to cook, and then another camp-wide campfire, where, to no one's amazement, Bronxville 4 was declared winner of the Waubeeka Award. During the afternoon, Harry had driven into town and come back with Cokes and Sprites and marshmallows, graham crackers and Hershey's chocolate for s'mores, and various chips and nuts. We piled them on the picnic table at the upper site, and lit the fire.

Harry had come up with his own informal awards for the kids. The meeting that preempted the Staff Hunt had long since been forgotten, and I admired Harry's skill in presiding over the gathering. His awards were the main event, but when we all hung around the campfire afterward telling stories and jokes, my jokes during the open-mike campfire that followed probably came in second. It shouldn't have mattered whether I could entertain a bunch of twelve-year-olds. But just as I admired Harry's skill, I felt some little sliver of pleasure at playing my part too, as if this were my advancement activity for the week. The kids gorged on junk and then straggled back to their tents. By 11:30 all you could hear was a thunderous chorus of snores over the nattering of the crickets and cicadas.

The next morning, we finished our packing. I made a point of paying homage to Lester and saying good-bye to our long-suffering neighbors from Greenwich. Mark and Jonah were coming home with Ben and me, which made our trip back feel like a nice fade-out. We loaded up our gear in my dusty station wagon and headed out. Within thirty minutes, all three boys were sound asleep.

One of Norman Rockwell's most famous works is his 1956 painting *The Scoutmaster*. In the foreground is a Scoutmaster looking like a young John Wayne with his full uniform and yellow neckerchief, tending a campfire under a starry sky as four young Scouts slumber away, their heads poking out of their old-fashioned military surplus tents. I didn't flatter myself by seeing myself quite in that light, but I thought of that painting as I drove along and of how amazingly peaceful and rewarding the whole week had been. I was sorry it had to end.

Year II

11: Peaks and Valleys

Our second year of Scouting began the way the first had, with Dr. Flank's annual exercise in schedule reconciliation where we made up the calendar for the year. The difference, of course, was that rather than something odd and foreign, the troop and its rituals now felt like a central part of our life. So when we loaded up the cars and vans two Saturdays later for the canoe outing, it felt like a welcome return to a thoroughly familiar place. We got a pleasing jolt of déjà vu from the most scenic part of the drive, a serpentine stretch of road winding above the Delaware, and from the lecture on the J stroke and the risks of hypothermia and following the black snake. Then Ben and I shoved off confidently into the water like two of Seton's Indians on our way down the Delaware.

A month or so later we had a new outing scheduled, a hiking trip up Hunter Mountain, about two hours away. We drove up with Fly Guy and got his personal fishing travelogue of upstate New York. He pointed out places like the fishing cemetery, where you park at the end of a roadside graveyard so full of wild oregano that the scent overwhelms you as soon as you open the car doors. When we arrived at Hunter about 10:30 in the morning, there was still a serious chill in the air. It was early October. The week before had felt like Indian summer, but now I felt the first unwelcome tendrils of winter. There was a forecast of a freeze for the night, and we all had been advised to pack for cold weather. We lugged our gear to the campsite and set up our tent. The kids were dispatched to gather firewood, and once that was done, we trekked across a broad trail to the base of a narrower trail heading up a steep slope.

"Gentlemen," began Mr. Johnson. "Well, gentlemen is really exaggerating a tad. Some of you have contour maps. The ones who don't should look at the maps with the ones who do. Where the lines get close together is what? The steepest part of the hike. Basically we're going to follow this up past where it's marked *L* for the lean-to, to the top where there's a state fire tower. That's up to about 4,040 feet. Down here where we are, it's a little over 2,500 feet. So you can see we've got a pretty good stretch to climb."

And with that we started off. The temperature on the thermometer on Mr. Toonkel's backpack read 48 degrees. I walked along in the middle of the pack with Fly Guy. Behind us, I could hear Ben and Mark. "What do you do," Mark asked in his usual deadpan, "if you see an endangered animal eating an endangered plant?" The trail got very wet and sloppy. Before long we saw little patches of snow like a thin glaze over the landscape. It was a bit of a shock. A few days before it had been in the 60s back home, and now we'd suddenly journeyed from one season to another. We passed the lean-to on the contour map and kept going up. The heavier kids, as usual, were groaning and complaining of incipient collapse, dehydration, heart attack, and various forms of ankle, knee, or hip distress. Somehow, they heroically kept going. The snow on the ground became more than a dusting. It was wet and clearly suitable for packing and there was enough to make snowballs—a matter of almost unbearable temptation for the kids. We continued on with a growing sense of excitement. There's always something magical about the first snowfall of the year—especially if you're a kid and you don't have to shovel or drive in it. But this was more than that. Instead of the first snow finding us, we were finding *it*, climbing ever farther into an ever snowier realm, with pristine coatings on limbs and branches and a few inches on the ground.

Finally, the trail widened, and we found ourselves in an open expanse of snow glistening under the mottled blue sky. We had made it to the top. But there was an additional reward in store. Brooding over it, in the most unlikely fashion, was a giant tower—the fire tower Mr. Johnson had mentioned at the beginning. Not only had we reached this startling expanse of untouched snow maybe three or four inches deep, but we had the opportunity to view it from the vantage point of a seventy-foot tower. "Thees ees the promised land," proclaimed Louis in a cartoonish Latin accent that made him sound like a crazed bit player in *The Treasure of the Sierra Madre*.

By this point, Mr. Toonkel's thermometer read 28, and it felt much colder. Some of the dads were perfectly happy to huddle under the eaves of a little ranger station that was the only other structure at the summit and forgo the final trek to the top of the tower. But the rest of us clambered upward, the metal steps slippery with ice and noisy under our clomping boots, the winds snapping like mad the higher we went. The wind was enough to intimidate some of the smaller kids—who seemed in danger of blowing away—into turning back. But most of us kept going, finally bunching up near the top as we waited our turn to linger at the upper level with its spectacular view of the hills and valleys below. Some of the kids scooped the wet snow off the railings as they ascended and had a pretty substantial snowball to hurl down at the ground below. It landed with a triumphant splat. It was not hard to figure out what was coming next. It began with a random snowball Bernie tossed at Allen. Before long snowballs were flying left and right, kids were trying to dump wet piles of snow down one another's backs, and all of them were enjoying the freedom of being rowdy in a mom-free zone. Ben didn't have gloves, a disincentive to snowball-making, so he and I for a while watched at the periphery of the action. But bit by bit almost all the onlookers got sucked in, and before long he was getting his licks in too. After a while, the snowball fights played out. Instead, kids made snow angels, sucked on snow, threw snowballs at trees, and just wandered around, appreciating the unexpected scene. If a huge part of parenthood is vicarious pleasure, being happy because your kid is, this was one of the days you figured to remember for a long time. It just felt magical up there.

We lingered for perhaps a half hour before Mr. Johnson yelled, "Let's go saddle up." In a few minutes we were headed back down, treading slowly and gingerly on the wet trail to avoid slipping. I walked much of the way with Bernie, who drove some of the other dads crazy but struck me as rather endearing. He talked about his Web site, what he programmed onto his Palm Pilot, and his skills with PowerPoint presentations.

By the time we got back, the sky had turned overcast and temperatures were beginning to fall again. Fly Guy boiled some coffee, and the huddled dads broke out some snacks. "Ahhh," said Fly Guy happily. "Donuts, chocolate chip cookies, and Starbucks. The building blocks of life." It was getting cold as hell. I put on an extra fleece for warmth and wandered off to get some more wood for exercise. Suddenly, our epiphany at the top of the mountain seemed a long time ago.

We did our cooking and cleaning and listened to the campfire stories. Dr. Flank had passed on the hike, but he returned for the campfire and a brief benediction. "Troop 1," he said, "has been coming to this place for many years. But this group and this day will come just once. I hope you remember this day for many years and the good friends you shared it with. May the Great Master of all Scouts be with us until we meet again."

When we finally made it back to the tent, Ben was complaining of stomach pains. He attributed this to the chili we had had for dinner and the fact that he had brought only one Sprite for lunch, leaving none as a dinnertime digestive aid. Whatever the cause was, he continued to experience a measure of intestinal distress as he lay reading by flashlight. Chances are it was nothing much. But more dire scenarios also flitted across my brain, like the possibility of a bout of appendicitis here in these too-cold woods, which felt like they were a thousand miles from nowhere. I stayed up half the night listening to him toss and turn and trying to figure out what I'd tell my wife if some major medical emergency was transpiring.

"How was the hike?"

"Well, good and bad."

"How so?"

"Well, we had a wonderful hike to the top of the mountain and experienced an epiphanic bonding moment at the top of a snow-covered peak."

"And what was the bad part?"

"Uh, Ben's appendix burst, and he's at some semipro hospital in Phoenicia being attended by a half-awake guy wearing a baseball cap backward and regularly consulting a medical textbook."

When we woke up the next morning, I was pleased to find that Ben was still alive and apparently recovered. "New rule for hikes," he said. "Two Sprites or we be sure to bring Pepto-Bismol." A thin dusting of snow had fallen overnight on the tents, like the meteorological analogue of a musical theme repeated softly at the end of a symphony.

As soon as breakfast was over we cleaned up, took down our tents, packed up, and headed home. Fly Guy found a '60s rock oldies station that played Fleetwood Mac, the Temptations, Credence Clearwater Revival, Jackson Browne, and the Stones. Fly Guy was in an expansive mood, remembering how he first danced with his wife to "Stairway to Heaven," his experiences with Texas barbecue, his plans to eventually quit the New York rat race of his job as a lawyer for a major financial company and do something like open an outdoors shop. "The End" by the Doors came on.

"This is the Doors, George," he called out to his son in the backseat.

"Sounds like good music," his son replied in an agreeable show of multigenerational musical consensus never heard in my house. From our paternal perch in the front seats, the song's Oedipal Sturm und Drang ("Father," "Yes, son." "I want to kill you. Mother, I want to...") seemed, for some obscure reason, darker and less wonderfully anarchic than it had when I was on the other side of the Oedipal equation as a teenager. But we listened like nostalgic geezer dads while the kids, barely tuned in, remained oblivious to any grand meaning at work. It seemed like a nice way to end the trip, not the transcendent high of the climb, not the chilly hangover of the camp-out, but a comfortable balance point in between.

Whether it was in spite of our epiphany on the mountain or because nothing could come close to it, my enthusiasm for troop life began to wane over the next few months. We did the tree sale, but Ben seemed less thrilled to have his dad around and the seasonal cheer didn't quite get to me. Our second version of the Klondike Derby actually had snow, which was a distinct improvement over the first. But once had been plenty for me, and the highlight was getting our donuts and going home.

We had one event over the winter, a five-mile hike to the cabin at Camp Siwanoy. The Siwanoy trip posed a particularly knotty dilemma. Concomitant with the hike was a critically important event back in Couch-Potatoland, the Duke–Carolina season-ending basketball game, an event that looms on my calendar with the urgency that Christmas mass does for a devout Catholic. I am perfectly aware that there's no rational defense for some middle-aged man planning his schedule around the exploits of a bunch of ectomorphic kids who weren't even born back when he attended the university they were attending now. And this wasn't, say, Duke playing for the NCAA Championship, an event I sure as hell wasn't going to miss for a Scout hike. Still, we all have to have some indulgences, and if this was mine, so be it. I had been perfectly willing to pass up that poetry reading at the White House to make it to Ben's Little League game a few years past, but, the Duke–Carolina game loomed larger than the poetry at the White House. I had said I would go, a promise I planned to honor. But I had not said I planned to stay.

We set off on a gray, windy early-March morning. It felt much more like winter lingering than spring making an appearance. Ben and I drove to Siwanoy with Jeffrey, one of the older kids, a garrulous high school senior who hoped to attend the Air Force Academy and become an astronaut. This was the camp's last year in operation before it was sold, and when we got to Siwanoy it looked even bleaker than I had remembered. We carried our gear to our cabin, a mud-brown building with green trim and a yellow Smoky the Bear fire-prevention sticker outside. All the cabins were named after towns in Westchester County—Pelham, New Rochelle, Port Chester, Larchmont. This one bore a plaque reading "This cabin donated to the Boy Scouts of Harrison by the Lions Club of Harrison. 1981." It looked a heck of a lot older than that. We claimed our bunks, not that there was anything much to choose among, then headed to the Appalachian Trail to begin the hike.

The previous year we had begun at the scenic waterfall in Connecticut. This time we just began by trekking across an open field. There were no surprises as dramatic as the Hunter Mountain snowfall, but the trail twisted agreeably through fields, groves, and swamps. About midway through we came upon headstones from what looked like an old family graveyard. "Dear Brother Max Shenkman," read one, its Hebrew lettering incongruous in the lonely field. "Died Aug. 6, 1946. Age 60 years." Another had a menorah and the words "Sarah Brokaw. Beloved Mother. Died Jan. 18, 1937. Age 48 years. Forever in our hearts."

As the hike went on I found myself increasingly checking my watch, calculating what time we might be back and whether that would be early enough the catch the game, which began at 3:00 P.M. We made it back to the cabin around 2:30. I conferred with Ben, who looked at me indulgently as if counseling someone with an untreated mental disorder. "Why don't you just go watch the game and then come back," he said. This was pretty much what I had in mind. I had mentioned my spiritual crisis to Dr. Flank earlier in the day, as if confessing some dark sin to my parish priest. I assumed that leaving a Scout camp-out to run off to some dark bar to watch a meaningless basketball game must have violated any number of codicils and subclauses of the Scout Oath or Law, but Dr. Flank seemed willing to absolve my sins. "We'll be here when you get back," he said indulgently. "Don't worry about it."

With both Ben's and Dr. Flank's blessings I figured I was OK, so I ran to my car, raced back toward Pawling, the last town we had passed on the way up, and drove frantically around its tiny downtown looking for an appropriate place. Finally, I spotted something called the Pawling Tavern and walked in. There was a television showing not Duke, but some Big Ten game no one seemed to be watching. I sat down, ordered a Bud, and trying to sound as casual as possible, asked the bartender if he minded switching to the Duke game. A refusal would have blown up my whole nutty escapade. But he was happy to change the channel, and voilà! there was the game with Duke up by nine points late in the first half. The tavern, which had a pressed tin ceiling and a regal cavalcade of sports trophies behind the bar, suddenly seemed an amazingly agreeable and comfortable place—much more my world than the drafty cabin and manly cookcraft of Siwanoy. A woman planning to get married was discussing her plans with a guy who had just gotten divorced. Some local firemen had just gotten off from work. I sat alone, watching the game in complete and utter bliss. Duke was in the middle of a 21–8 run, aided by the fact that Carolina's point guard, who apparently needed work on his orienteering merit badge, had run into a teammate and had to leave the game to get five stitches.

I noticed a guy a few stools down who seemed to be following the game too, and out of the blue he looked over at me, as if realizing we were on the same wavelength.

"You really feel good for Carrawell," he said.

Talk about getting it right! Carrawell was Chris Carrawell, who had overcome various injuries to build himself into one of the really reliable Duke players of his era, not the biggest star but a spirited, resilient, likable kid. He was playing his last home game, and had been honored at Duke's version of a Court of Honor before the game. I found myself thinking that, for all its mindless frivolity, sports—my world—at its best could teach values to twenty-first-century kids the way Scouting once did.

"Nice to see him go out on such a good note," I said.

We watched the rest of the game not saying a lot, but musing on Duke's chances in the NCAA tournament. In the interest of not seeming like too much of a freeloader, I ordered another beer and then a bowl of homemade onion soup. We happily watched the game end with Duke winning 90–76.

When it was over I lingered for a while, nursing my onion soup more than my Bud, half watching the next game that came on, perfectly happy to be alone and anonymous in this dark little cocoon. Staying there seemed a heck of a lot more appealing than trekking out into the cold to return to a dank cabin full of flatulent twelve-year-olds. But duty called. So I left a few bucks on the bar, said good-bye to my one fellow fan, and walked outside. It was freezing. My car took a while to heat back up, I drove in discomfort, and I almost missed the turnoff to the camp.

Half the kids didn't know I had been away, and the other half didn't much care. I told the few who were curious—Ben, Dr. Flank, Mr. Toonkel—that the right team had won. It was just about time for dinner. Not that I needed any after my onion soup, but what the heck, there wasn't much to do other than eat. So I had my share of salad, onion bread, and spaghetti with meat sauce. We were all cleaning up when we heard a thunderous knock on the door. It was then flung open to reveal . . . Todd Davis. He had had a swimming meet or choral concert or one of his eight thousand activities in the afternoon but had decided to drive up anyway. It felt like some grand celebrity had appeared.

After dinner Mr. Toonkel broke out some ancient board games, and we played those, played cards, told stories, and told jokes until bedtime. When I crawled into my sleeping bag, which was laid out across one of the hard wooden bunks, it felt like sleeping on cement. Even with the foam mattress underneath, I woke up the next morning—if I ever really went to sleep—cold, sore, and exhausted. Breakfast was pancakes, unless you were Todd. Using his Leatherman tool, he cut up a big hunk of sausage into thin slices and cooked them in a skillet, then added some packaged potatoes and cooked them up too. He had even brought his own kind of hot chocolate. The kids crowded around his sausage like hungry hounds waiting to get a small piece, which he dispensed with his usual magnanimity.

After we cleaned up, I took off by myself for a walk. Siwanoy was even drearier in the early-morning chill. Every building needed repainting. Almost nothing seemed to work. By the camp's lake was an old pavilion—the building had burned, and what was left seemed like it could have been an open-air dance floor in *The Great Gatsby* that had also gone to seed. Around it were old supplies, piles of lumber, old tables, roofing, and shingles, as if someone had wanted to rebuild whatever was there but never got around to it. I circled down toward the water and came to a spillway, where a small calf, much smaller than a Shetland pony, lay entombed in the frigid water, caught in a pile of limbs and brush. One of its hind legs was crossed over the other like a girl primly positioned in the first row of a classroom. Its inky wet skin, glass-eyed stare, and frozen repose gave it an otherworldly appearance, like something out of one of Mr. Toonkel's ghost stories.

I was about ready to get out of there. It was freezing; there was work to be done at home, I wanted to take a shower and change my clothes. We had hiked our hike. Duke had clobbered Carolina. Todd Davis had made sausage. The dead calf was still dead. We had done whatever this trip had called for. It was time to get out of Dodge.

Unfortunately, I saw no sign this was about to transpire any-time soon. To the contrary, Mr. Toonkel was outside, striding across the field with great vigor, stopping purposefully to write something down on a pad. My heart sank. Mr. Toonkel was ob-viously walking off a compass course, which meant, one as-sumed, that kids would then be expected to show they could navigate it. I didn't even want to think how long that would take. Sure enough, a few minutes later, I heard Mr. Toonkel's voice: "I want you to get your compasses and line up." For the first time in my brief Scouting career I felt totally alienated from the whole damn thing. I'd gone through life perfectly well without using a compass, and though I could improve on myriad things, I could think of none that would be aided in any way by the knowledge of how to use a compass. It was cold in the stupid cabin and colder in the stupid outdoors. Mr. Toonkel's zeal was, I knew, admirable, but at this moment it struck me as borderline fanatical, like Alec Guiness in *Bridge Over the River Kwai*.

"Who can tell me how a compass works," he barked. "And not you, Todd," he added. We were going to have not just the hands-on course, but the oral exam as well.

"Magnetism," said Louis. "The earth has a magnetic pull that makes one end of the compass point toward the magnetic north."

"Tell me about declination," Mr. Toonkel said.

"Compasses don't point to true north, the North Pole, they point to magnetic north, which is part of Canada one thousand miles away. The angle between them is called declination, and you have to adjust your compass for true north rather than magnetic north."

"OK, we've done this before," Mr. Toonkel barked. "I've mapped out a course. I'm giving you each a sheet with compass directions. Hold the compass in your hand in front of you about waist high and follow the directions, and you should all end up in the same spot."

One by one the kids started off, with Mr. Toonkel checking on their progress and Mr. Johnson hovering around to help. Kids paced off their course, and the ones who got it wrong got to try again. Finally, about 10:30, they all finished up. But we still had plenty to do. All the kids had to pack their bags or backpacks and line them up neatly with the others outside. Then we had to clean the cabin and grounds, sweeping out all the rooms of the cabin, replacing all our wood, cleaning out the fireplace, and scrubbing the kitchen. By the time we were through, you could have performed brain surgery there. Then we had our final lineup, Mr. Johnson told the kids what a swell job they had done, and we were free.

I didn't even think of trying to get to the next camp-out a month later. But I figured I should make a showing at the final event of the year, the overnight canoe trip down the Delaware. This was a big event, a camp-out that often served as a reunion with troop graduates who were off in college. Often it was a two-night camp-out, but this year we were doing just one night. It was probably a good thing. The weather report called for intermittent showers, and if we were going to get a little damp, why not keep it to a minimum? The main group, most of the kids, Dr. Flank and Mr. Johnson, Fly Guy, and two more dads with inexplicably flexible schedules left at 5:00 P.M. I got a ride with Mr. Toonkel and his son Jon, an Eagle who was now in college. There were two kayaks lashed to the top of Mr. Toonkel's van, whose interior bore a little plaque reading "Custom Designed. Marc Toonkel." We drove up listening to a wonderful tribute to Stephen Sondheim, full of snatches of music from *Sweeney Todd,* on NPR, stopped for dinner at a McDonald's, and arrived at the campground at about eleven.

Kids and dads were milling around a picnic table that was shrouded in a soupy fog so thick you could almost see the droplets of water hovering above the Coleman lamps. Still, it wasn't raining, which seemed a good omen. Ben was in the group at the table, and he escorted me to the tent, which was wet on the outside but warm and snug inside. "You think it's gonna rain tomorrow?" he asked. "Nahhh," I said, figuring a show of can-do optimism was part of my dadly duties. "I predict we dodge a bullet, and it's gray but dry while we're on the water and rains all the way home."

We awoke around 7:30 the next morning. I did not hear the sound of raindrops falling. That was good. It was still dry inside the tent. That was good. I looked outside and did not see any evidence of precipitation. That was good too. But the air was still wet and clammy, like a giant sponge. That was not so good. Mr.

Toonkel went down to the water and stuck in a thermometer. The water temperature was 50 degrees. The air temperature must have been about the same or a little cooler, and the sky was a solid wall of misty gray.

"What do you think, professor?" Mr. Johnson asked Dr. Flank.

"Not exactly a perfect day," Dr. Flank replied. "What do you think? Do we take the canoes or do we play it safe and go for the rafts?"

"I can't see how we have much choice," Mr. Toonkel said. "If we're caught in a real downpour, which we probably will be, do we want the kids in the canoes or in the rafts?"

"I'll tell Jerry we want the rafts," Dr. Flank said. "He probably wouldn't let us go out in anything else anyway."

Dr. Flank went from tent to tent, like a captain preparing his regiment for battle, telling everyone to bring their best raingear. Then we proceeded to Jerry's parking lot, where his minions hoisted great, big rubber rafts on top of the battered old buses and tied them on. Unlike the canoes, the rafts, which sat three or four as opposed to the two in a canoe, were almost impossible to sink. They were also fat, slow, bulky things, so you were guaranteed a longer, slower trip, and you had to paddle like a madman to get up any speed at all. We all jumped in Jerry's old vans and buses for the fifteen-minute drive to the place where we would shove off. The drizzle began as we were waiting in the parking lot, ready to leave. It picked up substantially during the ride.

"I feel like we're riding to the top of a roller coaster, and I hate roller coasters," said Doug.

"Nice weather for ducks," said Jonah.

"Or schmucks," said Mark.

By the time we got out, it was pouring. Not raining. Pouring. Pouring like get out the umbrellas or get inside. Pouring like alert the ground crew to roll out the tarpaulin; we're not playing in this. Pouring like no one sane would choose to travel down a river, whether in rafts, canoes, or ocean liners, in this. We stood miserably in a soggy field as Dr. Flank ran through a truncated version of the normal spiel—no worries about downstream gunwales and following the black snake in our bulky, unsinkable rafts. Mr. Toonkel, his respectable belly giving his wet suit something less than a perfect aerodynamic contour, had brought the kayak and seemed, as usual, unfazed by minor issues like being caught in a monsoon. The rest of us felt like laboratory rats being prepared to test the absorption capabilities of our fur. We divided up into groups of three or four for the trip. I was with Rich, an Eagle and a sophomore at Johns Hopkins who had graduated from high school two years ago, and two new kids, Dave and Marty, fifth graders who had just graduated from Webelos and were taking their first trip with the troop. Some introduction.

As usual, I was less than fully prepared. I had on my blue jeans, wool socks, sneakers, teal Charleston River Dogs baseball cap, and a gray Patagonia windbreaker that looked vaguely waterproof. The cap had been soaked with cold rain that spilled down onto my sparsely populated scalp before Dr. Flank was finished with his instructions. My feet got wet shoving off into the water. Within two or three minutes, my jeans were soaked completely through. The jacket turned out not to be even vaguely waterproof. About five minutes into what was supposed to be an all-day canoe trip, I was soaked from head to toe.

Now, it is true, we were not the most afflicted creatures ever to set out on the Delaware or its environs. When George Washington crossed the Delaware near Trenton, New Jersey, on Christmas Eve 1776 with his exhausted, freezing, and ill-equipped men, it was snowing and sleeting like mad and the river was a gauntlet of ice floes. And no one had even invented Gore-Tex. Historical markers nearby commemorated the bloody battle of Minisink between colonial militia and Mohawk Indians and their Tory allies in July 1779. It left a colonial colonel haunted by "the cruel Yellings of these bloody monsters," a sound so awful that "all the fiends in the Confines of the Infernal Regions with one United Cry could not Exceed it."

So, it could have been worse. But that was cold comfort as we began paddling downstream at an excruciatingly turtlelike pace. Dave and Marty looked shell-shocked. Rich, on the other hand, was maddeningly chipper. "I've been in a lot worse," he said. "It's good training. People may talk about the Boy Scouts being in decline, but it's not going to happen. Scouting will be stronger in thirty years than it is now. It's part of Americana. And being an Eagle looks good on your college application." Then he went on at length about how much he loved the *National Review* Web site and William F. Buckley's word of the day, the most recent being *badinage.*

Maybe an Eagle could keep up cheery badinage floating down the Delaware in a chilly gray soup, but not many others could. Instead of the usual intraflotilla horseplay and splashing, there was just the long, slow process of paddling down the river, like slogging through chilled molasses. The rain had slowed to a steady drizzle instead of a downpour, but the temperatures remained in the high 40s. The little kids paddled listlessly. Rich chattered happily. I found myself, for some reason, harkening back to the Sondheim show on NPR and humming "Pretty Women," from *Sweeney Todd,* the duet sung by the demon barber Todd and his prey in his barber's chair whose throat Todd is about to slit. It didn't really take my mind off this soggy debacle, but it helped a little. I don't know how long this went on. Like prisoners of war or victims of dementia, we began to feel like time was a meaningless concept. Finally, the rain stopped, though we were too waterlogged for it to make much of a difference. And soon after that, like sailors spotting land after a transatlantic crossing, we caught a glimpse of a familiar spot on the riverbank. It was a sturdy-looking, two-story frame house with a wide front porch painted white and a sign out front reading ZANE GREY MUSEUM. Zane Grey, famous for his novels of the American West, fishing and baseball, quit his dental practice in New York and moved to Lackawaxen, Pennsylvania, on the Delaware in 1905, where in 1912 he wrote his most famous novel, *Riders of the Purple Sage.* In this watery hell, the notion of a desert landscape of purple sage seemed as foreign as Byzantium, but his home from 1914 to 1918, preserved by the National Park Service, was our midway point. We paddled over to the landing in front of it and clambered out of our rafts.

I was so cold my legs didn't seem to want to bend at the knee, so I hopped straight-legged up toward the front porch. The little kids were huddled together, their teeth chattering, looking vaguely blue. The museum was closed up, and it wasn't any warmer on the porch, but just being out of the raft and off the river seemed a small blessing. Mr. Johnson had a red ice chest full of bologna, turkey, and salami sandwiches. There was Kool-Aid, not precisely what we needed, to drink, and cookies.

I'm not sure why I saw the need to augment all that, but I hobbled off to the Hawk's Nest Café and general store about three hundred yards down the road to get Ben and me Snickers bars and sticks of beef jerky. I lurched in the door shivering and dripping in my wet hat, wet windbreaker, wet jeans, wet wool socks, and wet sneakers. Everyone in the place turned and stared. On the radio, Elvis was singing, "Are You Lonely Tonight?" There were arcane fishing accessories all over the place. It occurred to me that all we lacked was a bunch of nubile coeds in tank tops on their way to a deserted cabin in the woods for me to look like the deranged killer in a slasher movie. I picked up two Snickers bars and two sticks of teriyaki beef jerky—probably what your average slasher dines on—and brought them to the register. "Boy Scout camp-out," I stammered. "Bad day for a canoe trip." It probably sounded more like a threat than a neutral bit of reportage. Good thing I wasn't humming anything from *Sweeney Todd*. I gave the guy a waterlogged $5 bill and waited for my change. "I'm *with* the Boy Scouts," I added. "One of the leaders. Have a nice day." He seemed glad when I left without harming anyone.

I hobbled back to the Zane Grey Museum, gave Ben his Snickers and jerky, and shared some with his friends. By this point Dr. Flank, Mr. Johnson, and Mr. Toonkel were deep in conversation. The question was whether we should abort the mission halfway through and head for home. Finally, Dr. Flank went to the phone, made a call, and came back. "I called Jerry's," he said. "They're coming to get us."

I'm not big on gender absolutism, but those who think that men are inherently irrational could take comfort in my reaction. Because when I heard the words, my first reaction was not relief or elation. Instead, my heart momentarily sank. It had stopped raining, after all. We were all a bit fortified by our sandwiches and snacks. I was beginning to get some feeling back in my lower extremities. Maybe we should have pushed on. This, of course, was pure idiocy. The kids, particularly the little ones, were too cold to keep going. By the time we finished, who knew how cold and nasty it might be? After all that talk about hypothermia, this was the first time it was a potential issue. Even gung-ho types like Fly Guy were ready to pack it in. Still, it left me with the feeling that we'd managed to achieve the worst of all possible outcomes—we were utterly miserable, and we hadn't even managed to complete the trip. We drove back to the parking lot in Jerry's ancient buses and vans, then Ben and I piled into Mr. Toonkel's van. We stopped at a Quik Stop, where I got some French vanilla cappuccino and Ben got some hot chocolate. It helped a little, but our clothes were still soaked, and we were too uncomfortable to fall asleep during the ride home.

"It was an experience," Mr. Toonkel said. "That's what we go for, the experience. Sometimes it's the things that don't turn out so well, that you learn the most from."

Well, that was one way to look at it. I just sat there thinking that it could not get any worse than this.

12: *Boy Scouts of America v. James Dale*

But it did.

On June 28, 2000, a month or so after our disastrous rafting expedition, the U.S. Supreme Court, in the case of *The Boy Scouts of America v. James Dale,* ruled by a 5–4 margin that the Boy Scouts have the constitutional right to exclude gays from Scouting. It was a decisive legal victory for the Scouts that culminated two decades of litigation over whether they could exclude homosexuals. But as public relations, it was madness. It pleased some, enraged others, and put Scouting in the middle of a bitter national debate certain to do it more harm than good. Many people inside and outside Scouting agreed with the decision and applauded the organization for taking the stand it did. Many did not. And for those of us who felt that the B.S.A.'s stance was a betrayal, not a defense, of Scouting's core values, it raised an inescapable question—was this an organization we wanted to keep supporting?

After the past few months of Scout activities, there was some obvious appeal to an excuse—any excuse—to put Scouting behind me. If it involved declaring the moral high ground, so much the better. But, of course, jettisoning Scouting wasn't so easy. By this point Scouting was a huge part of my son's life, and the past few months notwithstanding, an interesting adjunct to mine. That said, how much were we willing to excuse to remain part of it? If Scouting decided to exclude blacks or Hispanics and that was upheld by the Supreme Court, would I stay a part of the organization? The easy answer there was, of course not. So why should it be any different in the case of gays? Could you separate out the values of the troop from the values of the B.S.A.? Could you decide to agree with this part of what Scouting professes but not that part, as if picking and choosing from an ethical smorgasbord? Whatever the case, it soon became clear this was not an issue that would surface and quickly disappear. Instead, the Supreme Court ruling, rather than settling the issue, just magnified it.

James Dale, who had mercifully changed his name from James Dick, was a walking advertisement for Scouting. The son of a lieutenant colonel in the U.S. Army, he joined Cub Scout pack 142 in Middletown, New Jersey, at the age of eight and became a model Scout, earning more than twenty-five merit badges, his Eagle, and membership in the Scouting honorary society, the Order of the Arrow. He was chosen by his council to speak to civic groups about Scouting, recruiting members and seeking donations. When he turned eighteen and had to leave Scouting, he continued on as an assistant Scoutmaster at Troop 73 in Matawan, New Jersey. In July 1990 all that changed. At Rutgers University, Dale, who had attended a military high school and voted for George Bush three months after he turned eighteen, came to accept something else about himself—that he was gay. He came out of the closet as a homosexual in his sophomore year and became active in the Lesbian/ Gay Alliance. He kept that world separate from Scouting until July 1990, when his photograph appeared in the *Newark Star-Ledger,* identifying him as copresident of the alliance. Soon afterward, he received letters from the Monmouth Council of the Boy Scouts and from the district council. They said that "avowed homosexuals" are not permitted in Scouting, and he was being expelled. Eagle or not, as far as the B.S.A. was concerned, he was history.

That began a long legal odyssey. Dale filed suit in Monmouth County seeking reinstatement and lost at the trial level in 1995, where the judge's ruling was an antigay screed. "Men who do those criminal and immoral acts," sputtered Judge Patrick J. McGann, "cannot be held out as role models. B.S.A. knows that." In 1998 an appeals court overturned the ruling, saying that the Scouts "are essentially a public accommodation like a hotel or restaurant" and bound by state discrimination laws. And on August 4, 1999, the New Jersey Supreme Court, in a unanimous 7–0 ruling, said Dale's ouster violated the state's antidiscrimination law, and the B.S.A. could not ban gays any more than it could ban blacks, Jews, or Hispanics. His dismissal, Chief Justice Deborah T. Poritz wrote, "was based on little more than prejudice. The sad truth is that excluded groups and individuals have been prevented from full participation in the social, economic and political life of our country. The human price of this bigotry has been enormous."

Similar cases were percolating around the country, with the most closely watched playing out in California, where a gay Eagle Scout named Timothy Curran filed suit in 1981 after being banished from Scouting. It took seventeen years for the California Supreme Court to hear the case and then come to the opposite conclusion that the Supreme Court in New Jersey did: Scouting is a private-member group, not a public accommodation, and thus can bar gays, atheists, agnostics, and others who it feels do not share—or whose conduct goes contrary to—its core values.

The California case did not make it to the U.S. Supreme Court, but the New Jersey one did. In oral arguments in April 2000, the justices focused not on the Boy Scouts or the future of gay rights but on the legal implications of the case. If the Boy Scouts cannot exclude gays, are they allowed to exclude girls? Is a Jewish group obliged to accept non-Jews? If a group says a particular kind of exclusivity is central to its mission, are the courts required to accept that, or can they interpret for themselves the essentials of the group's identity? And if the Scouts can discriminate on the basis of their own sense of their identity, how many other groups could claim the same right? Most observers who heard the questioning felt the justices were more receptive to the B.S.A.'s case than to Dale's. They were right. Two months later, the judges found for the B.S.A., saying the First Amendment's protection for freedom of association meant the Scouts were entitled to set membership standards in accordance with the organization's expressed values. Writing for the majority, Chief Justice William H. Rehnquist argued that the forced inclusion of an unwanted person in a group infringes on the group's freedom of "expressive association" if that person undermines the group's ability to convey a message. "Dale's presence in the Boy Scouts," he wrote, "would, at the very least, force the organization to send a message, both to the youth members and the world, that the Boy Scouts accepts homosexual conduct as a legitimate form of behavior."

In the end, the case centered on two questions. Are the Boy Scouts a public accommodation, or a private group? And is the exclusion of homosexuals central to its "expressive message"? The New Jersey court found that the Scouts, who after all were chartered by Congress, receive money from the United Way, and regularly use public facilities like school buildings, are indeed a public accommodation. And it found that there is virtually nothing in Scout literature that in any way calls for the exclusion of gays. One Justice said he had pored over the group's literature and Web site without finding anything at all that advocated an antigay policy. The four dissenters on the U.S. Supreme Court found the same thing, scoffing at the idea that the phrases "morally straight" and "clean" in the Scout Oath have any bearing on the issue. "It is plain as the light of day that neither one of these principles 'morally straight' and 'clean' says the slightest thing about homosexuality," wrote Justice John Paul Stevens in his dissent. ". . . B.S.A.'s mission statement and federal charter say nothing on the matter; its official membership policy is silent; its scout oath and law and accompanying definitions are devoid of any view on the topic; its guidance for scouts and scoutmasters on sexuality declare that such matters are not construed to be scouting's proper area, but are the province of a scout's parents and pastor."

The one-vote U.S. Supreme Court majority, looking at the same facts, said the Boy Scouts was not a public accommodation—it was not a restaurant or hotel where anyone had the right to expect service, but a group espousing certain values that admits only those who share those values. And it ruled that if the purpose of the Scouts was to instill values, it had the right to define those values as it saw fit. "Who is better qualified to determine the expressive purpose of the Boy Scouts," Justice Anthony M. Kennedy had asked an attorney for Dale during oral arguments, "the Boy Scouts or the New Jersey courts?" And its ruling was consistent with an earlier unanimous decision in a Massachusetts case that Boston's privately sponsored St. Patrick's Day Parade could exclude gay marchers.

I'm no lawyer, and probably would have voted with the dissenters, but this is one case where a good lawyer could argue it round or argue it flat. Even some generally liberal civil libertarians, like the writer Nat Hentoff, argued forcibly that the right of free association needs to be protected whether the views expressed are popular or not. The Ku Klux Klan should not be forced to accept blacks. The Catholic Church should not be required to accept Jewish priests. If the B.S.A. exists to teach its values to boys, and one of those values is that morally straight means, among other things, heterosexual, it should not be forced to include gays as leaders. On that issue, more than any other, the court based its ruling.

But just because five members of the U.S. Supreme Court found the Scouts' policy legal didn't mean it was admirable or wise or consistent with Scouting's oaths and laws. There is virtually nothing in the Handbook or other Scouting literature specifically about homosexuality, but the handbooks are full of advice about being tolerant and respectful of differences. "Your conscience speaks to you about your relationship to other people," reads the 1959 Handbook, "respecting their rights, treating them justly, giving them a fair chance." The phrase "morally straight," used well before "straight" and "gay" were colloquially used as opposites, is usually invoked in a religious and moral sense—living a moral life that's reverent toward God and respectful and considerate of the rights of others. And Scouting from its start had tried to steer clear of divisive controversies. It embraced such disparate figures as Seton and Beard largely as a way to make it clear that this was a big, rugged tent, open to Indians and to cowboys and to other seemingly opposite constituencies as well.

But that was then. Now, with wearying frequency, Scouting has found itself in the middle of legal scuffles over what it has come to see as the three Gs—God, Girls, and Gays. It has fought to oust and exclude those who don't claim a belief in God, most recently in November 2002, when the Scouts expelled Darrell Lambert, an Eagle Scout from Port Orchard, Washington, because he said he did not believe in God. Lambert, a college freshman, had planned to volunteer as an assistant Scoutmaster. He was told that unless he professed a belief in God he was not welcome. He refused to comply and was told his participation in Scouting was no longer needed. It has gone to court to fight against suits seeking to include girls in Boy Scout activities. And, as we've seen, it has been fighting to keep gays out since 1980. We'll skip over the girls part. Baden-Powell, Seton, Beard, and West would, for once, have been united in their utter bafflement at the notion of girls as Boy Scouts. There does seem to be an awfully high definitional hurdle to the argument that the Boy Scouts have to include girl scouts. And over time, more out of practicality than conversion, Scouting has begun to accept women as troop leaders.

The Gays and God issues were harder to resolve. But they were enormously illuminating about how Scouting has evolved and who controls it today. And those issues reveal two things about Scouting. The first is the way Scouting's identity was forged in the 1950s in an image that's still with us today. The second is that it has come to be dominated by religious groups and the conservative voices of the nation's culture wars. Once the Scouts sat square in the middle of a relatively homogeneous civic culture. Now, if there is a middle, the Scouts don't seem to know how to find it.

We think of Scouting as a consistent, immutable entity, and many of its values are consistent—think of those in the Scout Oath and Scout Law. But on religion, Scouting has veered back and forth between the church of the wilderness—essentially the vision of Baden-Powell, Seton, and Beard—and more conventional expressions of reverence and faith. The early editions of the Handbook have relatively muted references to religion. But as Jay Mechling pointed out in *On My Honor: Boy Scouts and the Making of American Youth,* in the 1950s, both the references to religion and the linkage between religious faith and patriotism became much more explicit. Scouts read about Washington kneeling in the snow to pray at Valley Forge, and Lincoln and Eisenhower praying before making momentous decisions. It was the era when the government added the words "In God We Trust" to coins and paper money and "under God" was added to the Pledge of Allegiance. The sixth edition of the Handbook, published in 1959, reflected the same spirit: "Take a Lincoln penny out of your pocket and look at it. What do you see on it? Just above Lincoln's head are the words 'In God We Trust.' Twelve little letters on our humblest coin. Not only as individuals, but as a nation too, we are committed to live and work in harmony with God and his plan."

It was the same time that Norman Rockwell was giving us the powerful, iconic images of Scouting that still define it in our minds. Even now, Rockwell's reverent, patriotic images still shape our views of Scouting. But what we see is the world Rockwell saw—not that of Baden-Powell or Seton or Beard, but that of America in the 1950s. Of course, the reality of the 1950s was more complicated than the myth. (You can start with Rockwell. He was married three times, was a liberal Democrat, and was an early believer in the civil rights movement and a driven workaholic who worked seven days a week, including holidays.) But in a period of relative political and social consensus, Scouting became a symbol of the nation's shared values and virtues. When the consensus frayed in the 1960s and '70s, Scouting's role became more complicated as well.

And the issue of gays in the organization seemed almost destined to emerge as a flash point for Scouting. As an all-male culture, Scouting has always struggled with the issues of intimacy, homosexuality, and abuse that in recent years have exploded into the devastating scandals that have rocked the Catholic Church. One need only think of Baden-Powell, savoring his pictures of naked boys and swooning over "the Boy," to realize how close sexual issues can cut to the core of Scouting. Baden-Powell often wrote of the male form in a gushing voice ("I see in my mind's eye my friend Jack, a great strapping lumberman...I could watch him by the hour"). He took particular pleasure in watching boys swimming and sunbathing nude at the Scouts' campground at Gilwell Park. He was adamant about rooting out pederasty in Scouting and once said he would have approved of flogging (make of that what you will) as a punishment had the law allowed it. But, as Jeal notes, though many of his early associates saw homosexuality as a huge potential problem for Scouting, Baden-Powell showed very little interest in either discussing or addressing it.

Homosexuality has ebbed and flowed as a concern ever since, but mostly it plays out as a recurring theme for adolescent verbal abuse. Go to almost any troop meeting—or any gathering of adolescent boys, for that matter—and it is soon obvious that few insults are as common as taunts of "queer" or "faggot." Little would be less acceptable, even in a troop in a generally liberal area like ours, than for a kid to be openly gay. It has nothing to do with any policy and everything to do with the insecurities of boys trying to find their way through the adolescent minefield beginning to open up in front of them.

But, if the reflexive name-calling reflects one sort of unease, worries about men preying on boys reflect a far more serious and substantive fear. And Scouting officials have long been aware of pederasty as a concern. In *Scout's Honor: Sexual Abuse in America's Most Trusted Institution,* Patrick Boyle cataloged the long, ugly history of sexual abuse in Scouting, finding that during the 1970s and '80s, more than half of the four thousand people banished by the B.S.A. were accused of sexual abuse. The most sensational case played out in New Orleans, where a group of men had started Scout Troop 137 in a low-income neighborhood. In

August 1976 one of the assistant Scoutmasters took a roll of film to be developed that contained pictures of men having sex with boys. Employees at the store where the film was developed alerted police, who raided the homes of the troop leaders and found caches of pornographic magazines, pictures of men having sex with boys, and evidence of a nationwide network of pedophiles. The Scoutmaster and his two assistant Scoutmasters, it turned out, were regularly having sex with four Scouts as young as nine years old. The New Orleans case gained national attention, but most cases never made the papers, and the Scouts, like the Catholic Church, preferred to handle them quietly, sometimes allowing abusers to go from one troop to another.

Michael Rothschild, an attorney from Sacramento who represented a youth claiming abuse, obtained documents from the B.S.A. in 1992 showing that more than 1,800 Scoutmasters suspected of molesting boys were removed by the B.S.A. between 1971 and 1991.

All in all, the Scouts were forced to hand over 4,000 pages of documents, kept in shocking pink files that around headquarter were known as the "pervert files," on case after case of troop leaders, many of them respected community leaders, suspected of abusing the children in their troops. At least 2,071 Scouts reported being abused by their leaders during that period, though the number is almost certainly several times that. For all the cheap jokes about the dubious motives of Scoutmasters, the truth is the Boy Scouts are very lucky that there wasn't broader news coverage and general awareness of the extent of the abuse within troops.

As litigation became more a part of American life, molestation increasingly became a public issue, and an enormously expensive one for the Scouts. Between 1987 and 1991 alone, the Scouts were ordered to pay at least $15 million in damages in dozens of cases. Throw in the costs of legal fees and increased insurance premiums—not to mention the potential for disastrous public relations for the B.S.A—and it was clear molestation had the ability to do irreparable harm not just to kids who were victimized, but to Scouting itself. What to do about it?

One thing Scouting did, less than a year after the New Orleans verdict was put in writing for the first time a policy that said anyone who declares himself to be a homosexual could not participate in Scouting as a Scout, a volunteer leader, or an employee of the B.S.A. In a March 1978 memo to executive committee members, the President of the Boy Scouts, Downing R. Jenks, and the Chief Scout Executive, Harvey Price, said the policy was aimed at sexual preference, not misconduct, and that the organization knew of no laws that prohibited it.

It was probably a popular and noncontroversial pronouncement within Scouting, and codified the existing practice in which troops routinely kicked out men who were openly or transparently homosexual. But it did very little to deal with pederasts preying on boys. Study after study has shown that pederasty is a twisted sexual preference of its own, engaged in more often by men with female partners than men who are overtly homosexual. More often than not, the abuser is someone who shows no signs of aberrant behavior and gains the trust of a boy, then betrays it. On a practical level, a Scoutmaster who is openly gay and identified as such by other leaders, children, and parents, would probably be far less likely to be able to operate in perverse anonymity and abuse a child without anyone paying attention. And, to its credit, Scouting has since acknowledged that eliminating homosexuals in Scouting and rooting out pederasts are two entirely different things. In 1986 Scouting took a far more effective step, beginning a child abuse prevention program that has since been expanded and given extraordinary visibility within Scouting. Adult leaders are not allowed to sleep in tents with Scouts other than their own sons. They are not allowed to have Scouts over to their own homes. At Waubeeka and other Scout camps there are rigid schedules for use of the showers, mandating that Scouts and adults shower at separate times. The Handbooks now offer extensive information on spotting and reporting abuse, and they quite explicitly say homosexuals are no more likely than heterosexuals to abuse boys. And in late 2002, the Scouts for the first time authorized criminal background checks for all new volunteers applying for leadership positions in Scouting. Whether to protect its Scouts or to protect itself, the B.S.A. has taken enormous strides toward rooting out sexual abuse since the period reflected in the shocking pink files.

But a more realistic approach to the issue of sexual abuse did not resolve the issue of gays. Instead, in the face of lawsuits and public scrutiny, the B.S.A. increasingly took a hard line based on the relatively new argument that the Scout Oath's requirement that boys be morally straight and the Scout Law's demand that they be "clean" necessitated that gays be barred from participation.

To many in Scouting, this was just common sense. It's often argued that just as an adult male would not be an appropriate guide for a Girl Scout camp-out, a gay man would be problematic at a Boy Scout one. When I discussed the issue with Dennis, my berry-picking pal from summer camp, he was stunned that I might think otherwise. "It all goes back to what I believe is the standard—and I know not everyone does—which is the Bible," he said. He had that wide-eyed, open-faced look he has when saying something that to him seems as obvious as a sunrise. "When the Bible says that homosexual love is considered an abomination, I don't see too much wiggle room there. It doesn't mean I hate gays. One of my best friends turned out to be gay. Fine, but I don't want him to be a Scoutmaster. I think if I was an Eagle Scout and I was gay, I'd be majorly ticked off if someone told me to leave Scouting. It must be awful. But I also don't think we should say that what this guy is doing is exemplary behavior, which is what Eagle is. The idea that homosexuality is just fine is just not part of the aspirational message of Scouting."

We don't have too many Southern Baptists in Troop 1, but there are plenty of religious conservatives around the county who feel the same way. Most national polls show a majority of people disapprove of homosexual behavior. In a popular election between the Boy Scouts and, let's say, Queer Nation, it's not hard to deduce who would win. And in the culturally divided nation we've become, the gay issue was a particularly charged marker of which side Scouting was on. Scouting had made a big philosophical statement in 1979 when it moved its national headquarters from New Brunswick, New Jersey, to Irving, Texas, just down the road from Texas Stadium. It was more than just a real-estate transaction. At a time when the culture war was becoming an inescapable part of American life, the Scouts were voting with their feet, moving south and west, reflecting both the nation's demographic movement and the increasing influence of Sunbelt cultural conservatives. The increasing ties to conservative culture made sense in other ways as well. Individual troops are chartered by service clubs, or schools, or churches. But service clubs like VFW posts or Kiwanis Clubs are disappearing from American life, so increasingly sponsoring organizations are churches. Methodists, Mormons, and Catholics charter troops that enroll more than 1.2 million Scouts, or about a third of all Scouts. The Mormons in particular are an enormous source of manpower, Scouts, and financial support, chartering 33,272 troops, far more than any other group. The 12,102 troops chartered by Methodist churches enroll slightly more Scouts: 412,864 to 410,805 for the Mormons. But the Mormons almost certainly will take the lead in total Scouts enrolled in a year or two, and it's clear they play a role in the Boy Scouts that is wildly disproportionate to their numbers in the overall population. Scouting is not just something that appeals to many Mormon families; it is the official youth activity of the Mormon church, meaning virtually all Mormon boys are Boy Scouts. And the Mormons have made explicit threats to leave Scouting altogether if gays are admitted. The position of the Catholics is clear as well. Reversing the ban on gays could immediately cost the Scouts almost a quarter of its members.

There's also a financial consideration at stake. In 1993 Jere Ratcliffe, then beginning his tenure as Chief Scout Executive, made a speech to Scout executives around the country. He said that between then and 2006, $6.8 trillion would pass from one generation to the next—"the largest transfer of wealth in the history of our nation." He went on: "The individuals holding this wealth agree with our values and will be passing it to a generation that has demonstrated a lesser charitable attitude." In other words, if Scouting wanted to get its share of the pile of money about to be disbursed, it needed to make clear that its values were those of a generation getting ready to die off. And when he listed some values of particular importance to older Americans, a commitment to keeping homosexuals out of Scouting was a central part of the agenda. In short, Scouting had economic as well as philosophical reasons to stand firm against gay participation.

But if you don't see homosexuality as a sin, you know it's not a predictor of pederasty, and you have gay friends who are pretty much as virtuous and as sinful as you are, it's hard to see the policy as anything other than discrimination. To be honest, gay rights is not a huge part of my political agenda. But just as Harry or Dennis's sex life is none of my business, neither is James Dale's. If he was a model Eagle Scout and an esteemed assistant Scoutmaster before anyone knew he was gay, why should he suddenly be deemed a pariah afterward? If Todd Davis turned up in his college's gay student association, should we ban him from being part of Troop 1? And Scouting's formulation of don't ask, don't tell—the B.S.A. said it had no interest in ferreting out homosexuals, but was only barring out-of-the-closet ones— seems only to compound the moral mess. Being an "avowed" homosexual was a crime punishable by expulsion, but if you kept it secret that was OK? What kind of a lesson for Scouts was that? The deeper you went, the less sense it made.

The Supreme Court ruling came after we were all but done with the yearly Scout calendar, so the troop did not have to address it in any way. But it was still impossible to ignore. The weekend after the ruling, for example, there was the phone call from a friend who is a lawyer in a nearby town and the father of three boys.

"Your son is in Scouting, isn't he?" he asked.

I said he was.

"Are you planning to drop out or stay a part of it?" he asked. It was obvious what the right answer was.

I was taken aback a little by his directness, but said we planned to stay and that I didn't think one position I don't agree with should obliterate all that I did.

"I'm planning to pull my son out," he said. "We've talked about it, and we both agree it's not something we feel comfortable with. You can't teach a kid that discrimination is wrong and remain a member of a discriminatory organization. If this were 1966 and you were part of an organization that kept out blacks, would you stay part of it? By remaining a member aren't you condoning the policy?"

We must have talked for an hour. I said that in the real world, the policy was more symbolic than functional and that in the vast, vast majority of troops, no one, leader or Scout, was going to be openly gay, ruling or no ruling. In the others, in big cities and on the coasts, if someone would have been accepted before,

248

he would probably be accepted now, even if it meant ignoring the policy. To compare the Scouts' policy on gays—a policy I disagreed with, but one with minimal real-world implications—with the legalized apartheid of the segregated South that relegated blacks to separate and unequal versions of everything society had to offer was to engage in the kind of overblown moralizing that gives liberals a bad name. I said the only real way to change the policy was from within, not from the outside. And I thought, but didn't say, that Scouting provided one of the only forms of affordable outdoor recreation that's available for middle- and working-class families who can't afford the $5,000 summer camps and exorbitant wilderness outings that well-to-do families in Westchester County send their privileged little princes and princesses off to. Easy for the privileged classes, who seemed to be the most aggrieved, to write off Scouting.

Still, I couldn't dismiss my friend's misgivings, because I shared them. If my son was just starting out in Scouting, as my friend's son was, it might have been a reason not to join or to drop out. But, in the way that the messiness of real life often obliterates abstract judgments, I could not see punishing Ben and Troop 1, which doesn't discriminate against anyone, by pulling out. And I wondered just how much damage should be inflicted on Scouting because of this one policy.

Others I knew were similarly torn. One woman I know called up in distress to try to figure out what to do and then ended up writing about her dilemma in the online magazine *Salon.* She wrote about the Webelos handbook her son was getting as a prized present on his ninth birthday and concluded:

> In commenting on the court's ruling, defenders of the Boy Scouts pointed to an ongoing increase in enrollment as proof that American parents support the organization's condemnation of homosexuals. I thought I heard a dare in

those words: If you want to be around gays, start your own club. So if I allow Jonathan to stay with his pack now, I'm allowing the current Boy Scouts leadership to continue to misrepresent our family as antigay. The alternative is to quit in protest. And break the birthday boy's heart.

(Since enrollment has been dropping in recent years, it's not clear what growth the B.S.A. was talking about. And, on the other hand, when the gaping discrepancy between real enrollment numbers and the officially reported ones first surfaced in the 2000 investigation in Dallas, officials first attributed some of the gap to attrition because of Scouts quitting in response to the gay policy ruling. As a friend in Texas noted, maybe the Scouts need to add a new merit badge for spin.)

Less conflicted was the *New York Times*'s "Ethicist," a column in the Sunday magazine that often captures the finger-wagging voice of New York liberalism at its most politically correct:

My son had been a Cub Scout for three years, and I've been a den leader for one, a wonderful experience for us both. But I was appalled by the Supreme Court's decision upholding the Scouts' right to exclude gay people. I cannot feel proud to see my son wearing a uniform that represents bigotry, and we are withdrawing from Scouting. Many of my friends also oppose this discrimination but plan to continue in Scouting anyway. Aren't they wrong to do so?

Resigning as you did is the ethical thing to do. Just as one is honor bound to quit an organization that excludes African Americans, so you should withdraw from Scouting as long as it rejects homosexuals. That Scouting has a legal right of free association does not clear you of this obligation. The right to shun Jews is no less anti-Semitic for all its legality.

Did the Scout uniform now really "represent bigotry"? Ninety years of mostly good works and the uniform was akin to a Klan robe? Maybe I had too much invested in the wrong side, but, though I felt offended by the Neanderthal tendencies of the B.S.A. officials, I also found myself offended by the glib moral hauteur of the antigay side. I know we've got a culture war to fight, but don't the kids fit in here somewhere? Still, these were just the first of the rumblings around the country as people lined up to agree or disagree with the court, to voice their moral outrage against Scouting or their moral outrage against those who would voice moral outrage against Scouting.

Dozens of corporations, local governments, school districts, and United Way chapters withdrew funds or the free use of school facilities for meetings. More than one hundred Eagle Scouts handed in their badges in protest. (To which the B.S.A., always prepared with its numbers, proclaimed in March of 2001 that 47,582 Scouts had made Eagle in 1999 and there were more than a million Eagles overall, so a measly one hundred badges didn't amount to squat.) Steven Spielberg, an Eagle Scout who has been the Scouts' one prominent culturally plugged-in ally, quit his post on Scouting's advisory board, saying, "The last few years in scouting have deeply saddened me to see the Boy Scouts of America actively and publicly participating in discrimination. It's a real shame." The presidents of urban Scout Councils in Chicago, Los Angeles, New York, Philadelphia, Boston, Minneapolis, San Francisco, and Orange County, California, called for the national organization to change its policy. One leader in New York called the Scouts' national board "a bunch of rednecks from Texas." On the other side, the U.S. Senate, by a 51–49 margin, passed a measure proposed by Jesse Helms that would block federal funds for school districts that restrict access to Boy Scouts troops. The American Legion passed a resolution supporting the Scouts' policy. In Cleveland, a ninety-year-old troop lost its sponsoring church because the church had a nondiscrimination policy, and the troop failed to put in writing a pledge not to follow the B.S.A.'s policy on gays.

Sometimes, it just became absurd. In Berkeley, California, a gay member of the city council got the city to cancel a reception for Japanese Girl and Boy Scouts on a goodwill mission to the city, saying it would be an endorsement of the B.S.A.'s discriminatory policies, even though the Japanese Boy Scouts have no such policy, nor do Girl Scouts here or in Japan. But if the most agitated outrage occurred in the usual places (Bay Area gay groups protested an Oakland Raiders charity golf tournament that raised funds for Scouting), the issue cropped up everywhere—in Fort Lauderdale and Boston, Denver and Columbus, Hartford and Kansas City, Sacramento, Raleigh, and Des Moines. Among the United Ways withdrawing support from Scouting was our own, the United Way of Westchester and Putnam, which cost the Westchester–Putnam Boy Scout Council $150,000, or 7 percent of its budget. "There is a recognition that the Boy Scouts have provided a lot of good programs," the local United Way president said. "On the other hand, our organization has always stood for inclusion, and it was extremely important to us to be able to say that all our donor dollars go to programs that are consistent with inclusiveness."

The more the debate raged, the more alienated I felt from both the moral superiority of the Scouting-averse constituency on the left and the moral superiority of the antigay minions on the right. We weren't going to pull out of Troop 1. So the real question wasn't whether I would quit Scouting. It was whether I'd ever be able to reconnect to the whole archaic and now embattled enterprise.

13: Summer Camp 2: Baden-Powell Meets Bob Dylan

I didn't have much time for abstract reflection on our future in Scouting, because two weeks after the ruling I was headed back to Camp Waubeeka. Whether because of my fond memories of last year, my desire to accumulate Good Dad points, or a taste for masochism (probably a bit of all three), I had volunteered months earlier for a second summer at camp. Even if I had decided that Scouting was America's answer to the Hitler Youth, I was obligated to show up or we wouldn't have enough dads for the second week of camp.

Not surprisingly, given the events of the prior few months, Year Two began with a wary, conflicted sense of duty rather than the last year's buzz of anticipation. And there were other changes right from the start. Unlike that year, there was no dads' caravan. Harry was not coming. His three kids, with the usual perverse logic of adolescence, had declared that they had either no interest in or active contempt for Scouting and had already dropped out. That left Harry, reluctantly, once again out of Scouting. Dennis, thank goodness, was coming, but had gone up a day early, so I headed out on my own, the day a mix of clouds and drizzle.

Under the gray sky, Waubeeka looked somehow smaller than I remembered. But, to my relief, it felt kind of nice to be there, and I found myself remembering the good feelings I had taken from the last year more than the not-so-good ones I was bringing with me this year. The first familiar faces I saw were Fly Guy and Dr. Flank, carrying their fishing poles, returning from the Waubeeka lake where they hoped for bass and were lucky to get perch. A moment later Ben and Mark came up the path, and I was thrilled to see that Ben's face this time bore no swollen purple splotches or other signs of blunt-force trauma. Ben and Mark helped me carry my gear—overnight bag, pillow, sleeping bag—down to Wolfjaw. I stowed my stuff in Ben's tent and surveyed the site.

Ben gave me a quick rundown of the group dynamic so far. Most of the kids from the last year, except for Bernie, were back this time. The only newcomers were Dave and Marty, the little kids who had barely survived our soggy canoe trip. There were, Ben said, three main campsite factions, though factions sounded a bit more nefarious than was appropriate. They were more like the three rings of a circus. There was Sam 'n Eric Enterprises, Inc., in which our two heroes and their cronies huddled in The Underworld, dissing the adult leaders; discoursing on their three favorite topics—music, girls, and dropping a deuce; and resuming their performances of "Scout Socks." There was the Magic Card crowd, led by Doug and Elliot, in which the hard-core computer kids spent hours playing a fantasy card game with wizards and elves and other evil or virtuous creatures who can cast spells or kill off their enemies in a pallid but acceptable real-world substitute for Starcraft, Counterstrike, or their other preferred computer games. This group tended to gather at the cooksite and picnic table I thought of as Middle Earth. And then there were the pyros, mostly younger kids, whose idea of a good time was finding an excuse, any excuse, to make a fire—for cooking, warmth, a troop campfire, or for recreational purposes. Failing in that, they preferred to sit around lighting matches. The groups were not exclusive, and kids went from one to another as they saw fit. And there were some kids, like Ben, Mark, Jonah, Louis, and others, who were more likely to sit around reading or playing cards than joining any of the three factions.

It rained on and off all the next day. The evening was supposed to be the first-night-of-camp barbecue at the handicrafts shed, where the staff prepared hot dogs and hamburgers. The idea was to have a serving line outside, with some troops eating inside the shed and others at picnic tables outside. But by the time the barbecue began, it was pouring in sheets. So everyone was crammed inside the shed, there was not enough room to sit, and the lines of Scouts and Scouters waiting to fill their paper plates moved at a crawl. When I finally got my hamburger, I took one bite and almost coughed it up. It was half cooked, and like everything else it felt cold and soggy. I threw it away and didn't eat anything else until the watermelon for dessert.

After dinner was merit badge sign-up, which also played out amid the chaos of the overcrowded shed. The campfire was canceled by the camp director this year, a dark-haired, loose-limbed, athletic-looking Dartmouth student named Nick Reynolds. He didn't try to recreate all the campfire activities inside, but he did want to put together an appropriate opening-night convocation. So after the merit badge sign-up ended, he climbed onto a bench and hollered for everyone's attention. The room instantly went silent. Nick had short black hair and was wearing green Scout shorts, hiking boots, a T-shirt, and a long red stocking cap with a puff ball on the end that flopped halfway down his back.

He began with the Scout camp call and response:

"Hi, Guys!"

"Hi, Nick!"

When he did the obligatory "I can't hear you," he lifted one leg, put it down like a sumo wrestler preparing to face off, went into an exaggerated crouch, and put his cupped hand over his ear in an artful pantomime, like someone who was either a natural ham or a trained actor.

He then introduced each of the staff members with exaggerated World Wrestling Federation–style bombast, and they improvised various skits with hyperactive bursts of Y-chromosome energy. With the rain pouring down and the kids crammed in, it should have felt miserable in there, but Nick somehow had them mesmerized. I was sorry when the program ended.

By this time we were almost used to the rain. Allen, our ace chef and walking jukebox, broke into a spirited rendition of "Singing in the Rain," and kept singing most of the way down to Wolfjaw. But that was it for the evening's merriment. The muddy, waterlogged camp and everything in it felt like a giant saturated sponge. Ben seemed reasonably content, reading his Tom Clancy novel by flashlight in our tent. But my sleeping bag felt clammy, and the rain pounding on the tent, which was probably Korean War surplus, gave me the sense of being at sea in a leaky dinghy. Worse, there was a puddle on the wooden pallet supporting the tent, and you could hear the dripping water plopping onto the puddle on the floor. I burrowed as deep as I could into my clammy sleeping bag, but the rain outside and the various drips and drabs and puddles and leaks inside were like a noisy, waterlogged Rube Goldberg machine. Our Canoe Trip From Hell, as awful as it was, at least had seemed finite—it had to end that day. But as I lay in bed unable to fall asleep I found myself thinking in horror: What if it rains for days, for the rest of the week even? I'd never make it.

"Hey, Ben," I called.

No answer. At least one of us had fallen asleep.

So I lay alone in the damp darkness, not sure whether to feel depressed or just amused by the masochistic purity of it all. How perfect to be stuck at Waubeeka for a week in the rain, not just suffering, but suffering for an organization now reviled—*its uniform representing bigotry!*—by all right-thinking members of my social class.

This should have felt like the last circle in my Scouting death spiral. But I realized that, rather than scraping bottom, I was feeling a not entirely unpleasant jumble of disparate emotions. Yes, it was uncomfortable as hell, but even in the rain, there was a powerful, primordial appeal to being in this ancient, stupid, leaking tent with my son. I was intrigued by Nick and wanted to know more about him. I had seen Lester and Igor at the festivities earlier in the evening and was eager to catch up on what was new with Bronxville 4 and get their take on the Scouting news of the past year. As the rain continued to pound on the tent, I found myself more discomfited than unhappy or alienated. And after a while I began to feel utterly unhitched from the usual mad rush of daily life with no distractions and no static, nowhere to go, nothing to do. Time seemed to stop. I had those moments all the time as a kid, lying alone in bed thinking about how you crossed the line from consciousness to sleep, too intrigued by stray thoughts to nod off. This didn't have that kind of restless excitement. But the moment did have a solitary, peaceful sort of gravity, disconnected from daily life but reconnected to myself in a way I seldom experienced anymore. If we had background music, it would have been the langorous reverie of "Rainy Night in Georgia." More specifically, it would have been the breathtaking duet Sam Moore, of the soul duo Sam and Dave, and the late country singer Conway Twitty did on a 1994 album of duets between soul and country singers called *Rhythm Country and Blues.* "Lord," sighed Twitty, who died just a few months later, "I believe it's raining all over the world." We weren't in Georgia, but, Lord, it felt to me like it was raining all over the world. I found myself flashing back to a long-forgotten spring afternoon in college. Some friends and I, caught in a powerful soaking downpour, just decided to go, as it were, with the flow. We threw down our umbrellas and shed our rain gear and started doing handstands and somersaults and rolling around on the ground in giddy youthful abandon, cavorting like waterlogged loons on an isolated corner of the campus. I remembered the old folks at a group home across the street watching us all but expressionless as they sat on their front porch, the smell of magnolia and pine, and how conscious I was of being one of the lucky young fools cavorting in the rain and not the tired old folks watching from their rockers and straight-backed chairs from the porch. It seemed a long time ago. It *was* a long time ago. But after a while the memory of that magical rainstorm merged with the reality of this more prosaic one, and without knowing it, I fell into a deep, peaceful sleep, like a pebble dropping into a lake.

I awoke the next morning and poked my head out from the tent. It was gray and foggy, but the rain had stopped. Ben was still dozing, but I pulled on my sneakers and a warm fleece and wandered outside. The familiar ritual of Waubeeka breakfast was getting underway. Kids trekked into camp with those plastic garbage cans strapped to their back. Dr. Flank, who had stayed over for the beginning of Week 2, was preparing coffee for himself and Dennis. The kids were doing their best to get a fire started with the wet wood but had the cereal stacked up just in case.

Before long the sun began to peek out. The kids managed to get a fire started and made some slippery globs of scrambled eggs and mounds of toast slathered with butter. And there I was back with Ben and Mark, Jonah and Doug, Hal and Herb and whoever else came and went, glancing at our copy of the "Waubeeka World News," wondering which of the staff from last year would be back and what Sam 'n Eric had up their sleeves. We finished our breakfast, the kids cleaned up, then they all decamped for their various activities and the adults were left alone.

Dr. Flank, Dennis, and I gathered at the picnic table at the upper cooking site to plot strategy. The last year Harry was the clear heir apparent as soon as Dr. Flank left. Dennis and I, despite our baptism at Waubeeka, still felt clueless. Dr. Flank didn't seem worried—he'd seen dads even less prepared than we were figure out how to get through the week. But we went down the list of kids, determining which ones were homesick, which ones were handfuls, which ones you had to watch, and which ones you could pretty much leave alone. Dr. Flank figured to leave later in the day. But in the meantime he had more important things to do, namely fishing. He headed for the lake with Dennis and his tackle box and fishing poles, while I headed for the camp office to see who was around. Sitting on one of the benches playing his harmonica was Igor, Lester's loyal aide-de-camp. Igor was short and squat to Lester's tall and solid, but like Lester he had an opinion on everything, from the literary quality of Martin Luther King's "I have a dream" speech to Scout camp aquatic training now as opposed to ten years ago. Indeed, often he had so many opinions on the same issue you weren't necessarily sure what his true opinion was. So we chatted idly for a few minutes, and then I asked him about the gay issue. He didn't hesitate.

"The problem is not homosexuals, it is people who are pederasts," he said. "Everyone gets behind an easy victory, and they avoid the hard problems. Really dealing with sexual abuse? That's hard. This is something they could win. They won the Bible Belt. Is it worth it? They think it is. They'll take an easy victory anytime."

I figured this meant he was going to condemn the Scouts' policy. But then as he went on, I wasn't so sure.

"But here's the problem. No one wants to hear about someone's sex life. Don't ask, don't tell. That's fine. The trouble is when someone comes out of the closet. Should a heterosexual swinger be a Scoutmaster? It's the same issue. It's promiscuous sex we're against, and it's a promiscuous lifestyle. Even Allen Ginsberg and Peter Orlovsky, the longest-running gay marriage I know of, broke up a number of years ago and even during their long marriage they had affairs."

This was a reference to the beat poet Allen Ginsberg and his longtime partner, who were immortalized in a nude Richard Avedon portrait, which helped galvanize the gay pride movement back in the 1960s. It wasn't a standard Scout camp reference, but you never know what to expect these days.

"A young man joins the Scouts to learn how to become an adult male. One doesn't push one's own biases; one wants them to discover who they want to be. You want to be—what is the expression? Transparent. Your job is to help them with their problems and keep your own lifestyle out of sight. My father died last Friday. I mourned and buried him and came here Tuesday and did my job. The kids don't know my father died. They're having summer fun. They're only young once. It's not our job to create an unofficial barrier that shouldn't be there. In this case, it was Dale who made it the issue."

The logic was a little threadbare—a gay man is not transparent when he comes out of the closet, but a married man with two kids and a wife who brings three-bean salad to the Court of Honor is? Still, just when I thought that meant he supported the ruling, Igor turned around again. Sort of.

"I know people who after twenty years of marriage, women go off to marry women, men decide they're gay, men become women, women become men. Who can understand it? It's really no one's business what a private life is. It's never been an issue, and we're crazy to make it one. That's why the Scouts can't win in this. Or they win in court but end up with a public relations disaster. Scouts are like Shakers after the Civil War. We're dying off."

By this time, Lester had ambled over. Lester had me pegged as a hopeless liberal and liked starting arguments over almost anything—Vietnam, the war on drugs, school desegregation, the *Times*'s coverage of presidential politics. I figured he'd come out guns blazing on this one, but like Igor, he seemed to want to take the issue all over the map.

"There's not a one-word answer," he said. "First of all one of my all-time best Eagle Scouts and Senior Patrol Leaders turned out to be gay when he went to college. A nicer and more dedicated Scout you never would have found. If he had stayed alive and not died from AIDS, and wanted to help with the troop, I would never have hesitated in having him. Some of my sons' best teachers I'm pretty sure were gay. I never had any problem with that. The council has always had an unofficial policy of ignoring leaders who are gay. They claimed they did not want a lawsuit if they accused someone of being gay. So I don't have a problem with any of those situations and therefore I have no problem with gays as Scout leaders." Somehow I knew a "but" was coming.

"The problem with me and the reason national is justified in their lawsuit is what's going to happen when a Scout leader does molest a kid, and it turns out he was gay. Who are the parents going to sue? The deep-pockets B.S.A. Who's going to pay a multimillion-dollar judgment? The B.S.A. So I'd support the position from a liability standpoint, not a moral standpoint. But having said that, I also don't think the government should be mandating politically correct positions. A private organization should be allowed its right to freedom of association. If you don't want Jews in your country club you should be able to say that. With Scouts now we have some companies and national organizations who no longer contribute to Scouts. Do you hurt all the Boy Scouts by not donating because of one principle and ignore all the good assets? I don't know. But the policy is not going to change, because the biggest sponsoring organization right now is the Mormon church, and the Mormon church is adamantly antigay and would withdraw its support if the Scouts ever allowed gays in. You take a look at *Scouting* magazine and all the honorary awards at the national level and it's this elder in the Mormon church and that elder in the Mormon church. It's the most powerful bloc in national."

After going on a while longer, Lester ended up coming back to his favorite subject, which was the depravity of the idiots at Scouting's national headquarters.

"At that level it's not a youth group, it's just a corporation," he said. "What will get us more money and more new members? That's all it's about. No one knows the name of the Chief Scout. Sure, he's in the handbook like Seton or Beard. But those were personalities who kids looked up to and idolized. These guys are just corporate executives. You see their picture in the Handbook and they go to the national jamboree and give some BS speech, but they have no idea what's going on with youth. They're just stuck in their corridors in Irving, Texas. For them it's just money and numbers. Money and numbers."

Lester and Igor are argumentative enough that you could walk by and say, "Good morning," and two hours later still find yourself arguing about whether global warming is real. But you could draw two lessons from their rambling remarks. The first is that Scouting really has a regional problem. These guys are hardly airy New York liberals. But, like the anonymous leader who called the B.S.A. leadership "a bunch of rednecks from Texas," they inhabit a very different culture from the world of Irving, Texas, and like many other leaders in big cities or on the coasts, they really feel alienated from the Scouting leadership. I don't know much about the Shakers after the Civil War, but it's easy to see why a Scouter on the East Coast would worry about

Scouting dying out. Second, for all the moral absolutism on the left and the right, the gay issue in Scouting really does cut more than just two ways. In a court of law, judges have to rule one way or another. But in the real world, there are plenty of opinions and issues somewhere between the two poles of the uniform as a symbol for bigotry and the blue-nose morality police of the national organization. Because Scouting evokes such strong images—pro and con—that complexity never seems to get reflected in the public argument. It's all about the Scouts as the defenders of morality and virtue or the Scouts as hidebound troglodytes, once again hopelessly behind the times.

I'd had enough of Lester and Igor's amicus briefs for a while and headed back to Wolfjaw. Sure enough, there was Dr. Flank packing up his gear in the lean-to. He called the boys over and said we had a great week during Week 1, and he expected things to go at least as well during Week 2. "I leave you in the capable hands of Mr. Applebome and Mr. Walker," he said. We were probably supposed to think of something appreciative and inspirational to say, but instead just tried to exude some indefinable air of authority. "Do I have some volunteers to carry my gear?" Dr. Flank then asked. Several kids stepped forward to grab it. Dr. Flank directed them toward the gear to be transported. He shook hands with Dennis and me and gave a jaunty wave to the assembled masses. And then Dennis and I were in charge.

Without Harry as the designated grownup, we felt a little outmanned. So, as the week progressed under our too-benign leadership, things at times veered a little off course. The ratio of food consumed to food tossed into the forest veered dangerously in the direction of food tossed. There were a few fights, one of which began with a kid spraying water over the monster box and ended with him being sprayed with mustard and other condiments. The malingerers found it even easier to malinger. Our performance in the Waubeeka competition stayed at last year's abominable level.

On the other hand, the rhythms of Waubeeka don't vary all that much from year to year. And, no matter who's around or who's in charge, a huge part of the week is just spent in hanging around and yapping. So we spent much of our time like geezer spies eavesdropping in the land of the Simpsons Generation. We learned this summer's standard retort: "Thank you, Captain Obvious." We pondered questions without answers ("If a man is in the woods talking, and there's no woman around, is he still wrong?") and questions with answers no one was sure of ("What's the plural of octopus?"). We parsed the fine points of the five-second rule, which held that any piece of food dropped on the ground was still perfectly edible as long as it was picked up within five seconds.

The kids' use of the language was often a lot more sophisticated than mine at thirteen and fourteen ("Is there something wrong with him?" "Do you want the summary or the full essay?" "Do you want the précis or the complete text?"). Except, that is, when it consisted of calling everyone else a "lard butt," this year's insult of choice. There was much talk about extreme soft drinks, with the consensus that nothing could top Jolt Cola, which they said had twelve times the caffeine of Mountain Dew and the most caffeine allowable by law, whatever that meant.

There were constant references to *ur*texts like *Monty Python and the Holy Grail,* Starcraft, and the *ur*-est text of them all, *The Simpsons,* whose every episode seemed engraved in their collective unconscious. The episode where Mr. Burns, the mean old guy who owns the nuclear power plant where Homer works, gets shot after building a device to blot out the sun! The one where Homer cheats on his taxes, undergoes an audit, and is forced to become a spy for the FBI! Homer winning a Pulitzer Prize as Mr. X on a muckraking Web site!

The original Handbook, not the Seton one but the by-committee B.S.A. model, begins with a chapter on Scoutcraft. "In all ages, there have been scouts," it reads, "the place of the scout being on the danger line of the army or at the outposts, protecting those of his company who confide in his care." It talks about stalking animals, about virtues like chivalry, loyalty, and obedience. "When he gets up in the morning, he may tie a knot in his necktie and leave the necktie outside his vest until he has done a good turn," it reads. A Scout should take a cold bath often, rubbing dry with a rough towel. And it continues: "A bright face and a cheery word spread like sunshine from one to another. It is the scout's duty to be a sunshine-maker in the world."

Exactly what that had to do with the world of *The Simpsons* and Starcraft was not entirely clear. It was probably a promising sign that Doug and Elliot seemed somehow at home in both Aiur, the distant green world where the Protoss were bred, and at Waubeeka, the distant green world where Sam 'n Eric held sway. Clearly Scouting's genius has been its ability to adapt, Terran-like, to changing times. Left unclear was whether it could still do it, whether the pace of change had become too fast and Scouting had become too slow and ossified to adapt.

The next day I went out looking for Nick, thinking for some reason that he had some insight on all this. I found him at the Waubeeka office, going over some paperwork with an admirably eclectic pile of CDs on his desk—Chopin, the Doors, Woody Guthrie, Peter Gabriel, U-2, Curtis Mayfield, and an album of Gregorian chants. Nick was, of course, an Eagle, and one with a rather distinguished Scouting lineage. His grandfather had started one of the earliest troops in the country and had even met B-P himself during one of the great man's tours of America in the 1930s. Nick had bounced from the University of Alaska–Fairbanks to the University of New Hampshire to Dartmouth. "I'm a theater geek, but I'm studying astrophysics," he said. "I want to be in a position to help develop the first generation of light spacecraft that could operate on the moon. I figure by 2020 I'll be the first Scoutmaster on the moon."

Nick, as it turned out, was a somewhat indifferent manager, whose underlings felt he didn't attend to camp business as assiduously as he should have. But he radiated a knowing sort of self-confidence—in a different time he could have been a young lieutenant you'd follow into battle. And he came across as a Scouting archetype combining different eras, sort of Todd Davis with more of an edge. He talked about Scouting with a striking blend of passion and disdain, as if the Scouting culture wars were washing back and forth in his head even as he was in charge of running the camp. "My parents were divorced when I was four, and my dad didn't live with us," he said. "Boy Scouts put me in touch with people I could respect and learn from, and I couldn't get that anywhere else. It gave me aspirations and goals. But at the same time, it seemed like Scouting was at war with itself, and it gets more so all the time. It's like the best parts of Scouting are contrary to so much of what the organization seems wedded to. It's not just the gay policy, which I find abhorrent. It's the myopia of the national organization in general. It seems to me that what they want is to develop boys who think and feel in a certain way, rather than to develop boys who think and feel intelligently, who think for themselves. The Scout Oath and Scout Law are such powerful ideas. I like to think they're what Scouting's about, not whatever comes from the national organization. I love Scouting, but when the Supreme Court ruling came out on the gay issue I felt like I wanted to rip my uniform off and set it on fire."

Just then Frankie Stanton showed up. He was not having a good day. Stanty, who had been Ted Watson's assistant at the econ lodge, now was over at the Scoutcraft area. He was a high school senior with thick glasses and thick lips, who like Nick had a gift for theatrics. But his grandmother had died suddenly the night before—healthy one day, gone the next. He had talked to her just two days earlier, and when he got the news from his parents he went quickly from disbelief to rage, leading him to destroy an ancient sofa and chair that had withstood untold indignities over the years at the camp office. On top of that, he had developed a painful ingrown toenail that was glowing an excruciating radioactive red that made each step feel like a stroll barefoot over thumbtacks. He needed Nick to drive him to the medical clinic in nearby Chestertown to have it looked at.

We headed toward Nick's green 1996 Volkswagen Golf parked by the side of the parade ground. Stanty was wearing shorts, a T-shirt reading "MIDDIES SWIMMING," and a black baseball cap reading "FRIENDSHIP THROUGH SCOUTING." Nick was wearing a University of Alaska–Fairbanks T-shirt (much cooler than Dartmouth), green carpenter pants, and flip-flops. He turned to a public radio station playing Vivaldi concertos and lit up a Marlboro as soon as we pulled out of the camp.

"Boy, am I an idiot," Stanty said, as Nick drove—faster than I would have—toward Chestertown. "It says right there in the Handbook that you have to cut your nails straight across, and I don't even do that. What a doof."

Nick was not sympathetic.

"You're really gonna be in for it," he said. "You're screwed, man. You can't handle this. When the doctor lances that thing or whatever he's gonna do, you're gonna puke. You'll pass out from the pain."

"I'm gonna be a hobbler," said Stanty glumly. "You gonna hold my hand if I can't stand the pain?"

"No way," Nick said. "We have our limits. You're gonna be out of commission for a week. It's gonna be ugly."

Stanty just looked pained. They were silent for a moment, and then retreated to the default position of Scout camp—Scouting war stories and lore. Nick started off with a scary tale about a leaking propane stove that exploded when he was stuck in two feet of snow in a little camping hut one winter: "There's a candle on the table and as soon as the gas reaches the table BOOOOOOOOMMMMMMMM! There's a fireball in the cabin. It blew the canister up and out to the other side of the room shooting flames. Set the whole front of my sleeping bag on fire, burned my eyebrows off, all my hair, the hair on my nose, the hair on my arms. We threw the canister out the window, beat the flames out of the sleeping bag and were OK." There's a lot more of a don't-try-this-at-home quality to Scouting than people think.

They went on. About the superiority of the patrol cooking at Waubeeka rather than the fancy—by Scout standards—dining hall at Buckskin. The scandal of the new wussified Scout Handbook. "Man, the only one I read is the '76 edition," said Stanty. "I just hate the new one. They ought to call it the Girl Scout Handbook. No semaphore. No Morse code. There's hardly a skill in it they tell you how to do. I don't think you can find the words *Dutch oven* in the whole thing. Man. It sucks."

Finally, we reached the doctor's office, which was decorated with nature scenes from the Adirondacks and helpful bits of medical wisdom ("An overactive bladder can be an accident waiting to happen."). The nurse called for Stanty, and we sat there listening for the shriek of agony. Five minutes. Ten minutes. Fifteen minutes. Finally, he came out, seemingly intact, a mysterious half smile flitting across his face.

"The doctor says I need to take some antibiotics first," he said, failing miserably in his efforts to act as if he wasn't thrilled to get a reprieve. "I need a frappuccino."

From the doctor we drove to Brooks Pharmacy, in a little strip shopping center a few blocks away. Nick and Stanty hung around waiting for the prescription to be filled, checking out the condoms at the rear of the store, then ventured over to the magazine rack, where Stanty picked up five wrestling magazines to read on his trip home for his grandmother's funeral. This was no mere impulse purchase. Stanty announced that he was in training, more or less, to wrestle professionally and needed the magazines to prepare himself for his chosen life's work.

"It's my dream," he said, gazing intently at Chyna's man hands on the cover of one of the magazines. "To make it in wrestling you need three things. You need mike skills, which I have in abundance. You need the physical stuff. OK, I'm a bit lacking there. And you need a gimmick with a finish. I'm thinking of calling myself The Stud, and my finisher would be a hold I'd call VD. You know, I put him out, and I'd go, "'Sorry pal. You've got VD.'"

"Maybe you need to rethink that," Nick said clinically, like a doctor delivering a grim prognosis. "Not sure that one will fly."

"What about just being The Boy Scout, a heroic good-guy character?" I asked.

Stanty gagged and almost spat out his root beer.

"You know what you'd be?" he sputtered. "You'd be the chump. You'd be the guy who came out at the very beginning of Wrestlemania and got your butt kicked. Everyone would hate you. 'You Boy Scout. You pansy. With that prissy little uniform. I hope he kicks your ass.' Stone Cold Steve Austin would come out, give you the finger, drink a beer, and drop you with the stunner. The Boy Scout? Who's gonna be for The Boy Scout?"

And this was from someone who loved Scouting. It made you wonder how an institution can be so revered and so disdained at the same time, so much a part of American life and mythology and so utterly marginalized. When we got back to camp, Stanty hobbled back to his tent to pack up to go home for the funeral. I asked Tim if he had an answer. He thought he did.

"I have friends who say, 'How can you be a Boy Scout? You're supporting discrimination and homophobia.' And I just tell them, 'You just don't understand Scouting.' The real Scouting isn't what the Chief Scout Executive says in the Handbook or the uniforms or the badges. The real Scouting is the covert Scouting. The essence of Scouting is the relationships between boys, and between boys and men of differing ages and backgrounds. The national organization provides nothing more than a platform on which those relationships can occur. And what the Boy Scouts say or do has very little bearing on the actuality. You look around this camp. You've got troops of spoiled suburban brats and troops of big macho working-class Italians. You've got troops that do it by the book and are full of great kids, and you've got troops of kids who stand up straight and are good at getting in line but are a bunch of little thugs. But all of Scouting is about an interplay between the ideals of Scouting and the reality of kids, about what the Handbook says and what kids really do. That's why you can only expend so much energy on what national says. That's symbolic. What happens here is real."

He paused for a moment, as if he hadn't quite thought this through and was figuring it out as he went along. "But here's how the symbol affects the reality. If the B.S.A. keeps drifting to the right, you might have more and more parents who'll say, 'That's probably a group with intolerant values. Maybe I don't want to be part of it.' Then you really can get a change in the organization because of the kind of kids who take part."

That night's campfire began with the usual bonfire and skits and cheers and songs. But then Nick wandered off for a moment and came back with a guitar and a harmonica around his neck à la early Bob Dylan. "Here's an old song by an old folkie that makes a little bit more sense every year," he said. And then he started wailing a twangy, primal version of "The Times They Are A' Changing." What was *this* about? His own commentary on the B.S.A.? A universal statement about change and renewal? He never made it clear. He finished singing and said this was a special summer. It wasn't what he'd expected, because some of the friends he was expecting to work with this year didn't make it to camp. But he'd learned that you never know quite what's going to happen in life, so you make plans and you're always prepared to change them. In the meantime, we were all lucky, he said, to be here, watching this bonfire, sharing the moment, being together. Then he started strumming his guitar again, and broke into Neil Young's "Helpless." Then the campfire wound down, the bugler played "Taps," and it was over.

"There is an impalpable, invisible, softly stepping delight in the camp fire, which escapes analysis," the original Handbook had said. "Enumerate all its charms, and still there is something missing in the catalogue. Any one who has witnessed a real camp fire and participated in its fun as well as its seriousness will never forget it."

I guess I'm a sucker for campfire moments, but this one seemed particularly memorable. The message to me wasn't that Scouting wanted to be a bunch of gay-pride leftists singing Dylan songs and reading feminist poetry. But I was willing to buy into Nick's notion that sometimes it could be—that Scouting wasn't some fill-in-the-blanks production of look-alike troops orchestrated out of Texas, but a reflection of the kids and their communities and their times. There's nothing wrong and much right about the Norman Rockwell imagery of Scouting. In recent years we've developed a renewed appreciation for straight arrows. But Seton and Beard and B-P (though not, alas, West) never wanted a movement of cookie-cutter straight arrows. They were men of extraordinarily rough edges and unconventional ideas, and you would like to think they would have applauded Nick's campfire, which was as unexpected in its way as Baden-Powell's thirty thousand Scouts running full tilt toward King George V.

Or maybe, I began to think later, I was still a little obtuse, too much the observer, not enough the Scout. It's possible, maybe likely, that a subversive political thought was implicit in Nick Does Dylan. But, if so, there was almost certainly a universal statement of what was going on under my nose as well. There was, I realized, plenty of subtle change going on in Troop 1 that I'd barely made sense of. There were new expressions of attitude, like George's two-tone peroxide hairdo that made him look like an adolescent skunk, or Sam's new Gorgonlike Italian Afro. Elliot won the camp's Econ Guru award for outstanding work on the wildlife nature badges. The number of kids taller and considerably more buff than the dads was increasing at an alarming rate. And on the last night, when we had our second annual pig-out campfire to celebrate the end of camp, Dennis and I gave the kids congratulatory speeches and high-fived each other when we were done. Even we geezers had grown as pseudo leaders from the rank amateurs we were a year back.

One other inkling of changing times stuck with me. One afternoon, Ben and I went for a run. Without any prodding from me, he'd begun to work out a little, but I still figured that anything he could do physically I could do better. It was a hot day, and we both began with our shirts on but soon took them off. We started off running together at a moderate pace. About ten minutes into the run, he pulled a bit ahead of me, first a few paces, then several yards, then a good bit more. I decided to catch up, but his lead only increased until finally I could barely see him as he ran ahead, kicking up dust, leaving me, for the first time, far, far behind.

Year III

14: Eagles, Ordeals, and Other Transitions

Nick went back to school, and I never saw him again. But I thought of him often as Troop 1 resumed its kabuki-like routine, each event and season, it seemed, coming from some carefully choreographed script. If Scouting at its best is something reinvented by each troop in its own way, I began our third year of Scouting once again struck by the appeal of Troop 1's version of it. My first year of Scouting was all discovery. The second was mostly rejection. The third began with a renewed appreciation of something that I one day realized with a start was probably already beginning to play itself out, like another part of parenthood that ends before you know it.

Our first hike, after the fall canoe trip, was a District-wide camp-out in Sleepy Hollow along the Hudson. We hiked five miles, at one point getting a lecture from Dr. Flank on the aqueduct we were crossing, which was built in 1842 and brought the first water to New York City. We set up camp along with ten or twelve other troops on a grassy field along a glorious stretch of the Hudson. Dr. Flank, Mr. Toonkel, and Mr. Johnson seemed in particularly good spirits. They critiqued Dr. Flank's honey lime chicken with long-grain and wild rice and drank a covert glass of red wine to his health: "It's for medicinal purposes," Mr.

Toonkel said. "We've got to keep him going, because there's no way in hell either of us is going to run this thing."

The next morning there was a worship service. Attendance was voluntary, and just one adult, who led the service, and seven kids showed up. I was the only one from Troop 1 there, drawn more by curiosity than spiritual yearnings. In another time, or maybe in another part of the country, the service would have been a bigger part of the camp-out. Instead, we looked like a lonely fringe of a fringe as our little group gathered under a big oak tree.

"In this place of worship with thy beauty all around us in the sky, in the trees, in the earth, and in all thy creation, we praise thee and come to worship thee," began the leader, a heavy-set man who said he'd been doing this for twenty-four years. "Blessed art thou, O Lord, our God, who gives us each new day. Amen." We sang a hymn and "America the Beautiful." There was a reading from Exodus, and then a reading of the Scout Law, with a bit of commentary for each item ("...A Scout is helpful: The Good Samaritan showed the spirit of doing a good turn. A Scout is friendly: A real friend is one who remains loyal in victory and defeat. A Scout is courteous: Courtesy is the mark of a true gentleman. It is shown in thoughtful acts and kindly respect for everyone..."). After perhaps twenty minutes, the leader said, "May the Lord bless you and keep you. May the Lord make his face to shine upon you and be gracious unto you. May the Lord lift up his countenance upon you and grant you peace. The service is ended." It felt like a perfect version of B-P's church of the woods, at least as worthy and appealing in its traditionalism as Nick's campfire had been in its iconoclasm, and it seemed a shame so few kids had shown up.

Usually the camporees end with a closing ceremony, but this time the troops just attended to their own business and then drifted off to their soccer practices or homework or video games.

We lingered longer than all but one as the kids made breakfast and packed up and had a final review from Dr. Flank. Ben, Mark, and Jonah lugged their gear up a hill to the parking lot where we were parked and were loading it into my station wagon when Mr. Johnson came by. "I was watching the three of you, and I was really pleased with the way you conducted yourselves," he said. "The way you handled the hike, the way you took care of your cooking and cleaning up, the way you dealt with the other kids. It tells me you're ready for High Adventure. You all interested?" They all looked startled by the invitation, did their best to compose themselves and stammer some version of assent, and then chattered nonstop about it on the car ride home.

This was a very big deal. High Adventure was a week-long canoe trip in which the adult leaders and the most trusted older Scouts disappeared into the wilderness, where they might not see another person for a whole week. In our first year, High Adventure had been a distant, exotic experience reserved for high school kids living on some rarefied grown-up plane. In our second, it was a great temptation, still out of reach but something they'd heard enough about to really want to do. This year they could actually go, if chosen. The adult leaders picked three or four kids from Ben's grade—eighth—to join with about the same number of older ones and perhaps four adults for a trip to northern Quebec. Space was limited by the number of cars and the small size of the camping areas. And it was the one troop activity done on a by-invitation basis—the grown-ups figured that if they were going to spend a week in the wilderness with a bunch of fourteen- and fifteen-year-olds, the kids would have to be able to cook, take care of themselves, and avoid any behavior that would fit in a Tom Green or Adam Sandler movie.

Truth to tell, in terms of skills, Ben was not a Scout of Todd Davis-like proficiency. He was lazy about learning his knots and wasn't an inventive cook like Todd or Allen. But if being a good

Scout at its heart was a way to denote a good kid—someone who lived up to all those worthy, admirably behind-the-times values in the Scout Law—he could not have been much better. Ben had his failings. At times, he lapsed into the none-of-your-business, linguistic minimalism of adolescence in which every question about his companions was answered with "Just some kids," every question about what he was watching on TV elicited "Just a program," and the all-purpose answer to anything else was "Just some stuff." But, so far at least, he'd navigated the shoals of adolescence with remarkable equanimity and good humor. In my whole life, I'd never seen him utter an unkind or hurtful word to anyone. He worked as a caddy at a local golf course, volunteered at a local hospital and community center, and made excellent pizzas from scratch. He knew real-world things I did not, like the difference between a truss and a cantilever bridge or the history and design elements of the space shuttle. He was a serious kid who never took himself too seriously and took his cues from Dave Barry, Dilbert, and *Saturday Night Live* as well as from more straightforward texts. I wasn't sure how much Scouting helped mold Ben and how much it was just a good fit for the way he already was, but Scouting played to his best qualities. If I had been choosing kids to venture into the wilderness with, I'd have chosen him too.

Soon other transitions were in store. Ben became a Patrol Leader, a post rendered somewhat less auspicious by his patrol, which consisted of Mark, his assistant Patrol Leader, a few rookies, and lots of kids who were still on the troop roster but seldom showed up anymore. He'd dutifully call them up before every meeting and hike and still end up presiding over a skeleton crew. He reached the rank of Life, the level just below Eagle, and we spent a few Saturdays at merit-badge seminars at a nearby Mormon church, where kids from across the county took courses that helped them earn the badges required for Eagle.

It's a bit of a scam—in an afternoon kids can get credit for badges that could take weeks of work on their own. But just as there's grade inflation at Harvard, there's a measure of Eagle inflation in the B.S.A. And in the spring, Ben was the first one his age nominated by the other kids in the troop to join the Order of the Arrow, the Scouting honorary society, whose Indian iconography is one of the few explicit reminders of Seton's vision for Scouting. The OA was entirely separate from the advancement path from Tenderfoot to Eagle, and being chosen seemed something of a mixed blessing, since his welcome from the OA began with the cheery salutation, "Dear Ordeal Candidate. . . ."

As we soon learned, to join Ben had go through an overnight "Ordeal," or series of tests, so secret that God would strike me dead if I mentioned any of them here. I drove him up to Clear Lake on a chilly Friday night, figuring that liability law being what it is, the ordeal couldn't be too perilous. But it still felt both alarming and momentous to drop him off, like Abraham taking Isaac to be sacrificed to the Scouting Gods. The last thing I wanted to do was spend the night in the woods without a tent, the one thing we did know he'd have to do. But so far we'd done almost everything together in Scouting. I felt a little diminished, being relegated to mere chauffeur rather than participant. We parked in the lot and picked our way in the dark toward the ranger station, where we spotted Lester's sidekick Igor, who was in some supervisory role. He motioned for Ben to come with him, and Ben trotted off eagerly with a quick farewell and not even a glance back. The ride back seemed a lot longer than the drive up. I spent the next day wondering how he was doing, but when I came up to get him Sunday morning, he was beaming and wearing his white OA sash with a red arrow on it. He chattered all the way back, with requisite discretion where state secrets were involved, about the weekend. Highlights, he said, included something having to do with an orange and an egg;

a fair degree of slave labor; and Ted Watson, the too-serious genius from camp, in full Indian regalia offering assorted OA chants, incantations, and other, mostly indecipherable, mumbo jumbo. It sounded like a junior version of the Loyal Order of the Moose, the Knights of Pythias, or the other fraternal organizations going extinct before our eyes, but it allowed Ben to go someplace new and exciting totally on his own and join a group that he, not we, had chosen.

The troop had a transition too—at least one on paper—that was forced by the competing views of the gay controversy. Troop 1 had been chartered over the years by churches, the American Legion, and its own parents' association. For the last several years, it had been chartered by the Roaring Brook School. But since the ban on homosexuals violated the school district's antidiscrimination policy, Dr. Flank quietly changed the chartering back to Chappaqua Troop 1 Parents' Association, at the same time making it clear the troop did not discriminate. In his letter to the local council announcing the change, Dr. Flank added: "It should be noted that Chappaqua Troop 1 has not, and does not, discriminate against any boy or adult on the basis of race, color, creed, national origin, religion, economic status, citizenship or sexual orientation, in accordance with the laws and policies of our State and community." He was taking something of a risk. Seven Cub Scout Packs in Illinois had been disbanded for saying they would accept gays as leaders. But the local council had no interest in losing a venerable, reliable, and generous troop, so the odds were pretty good nothing would happen. In fact, without backing away publicly, the B.S.A. has signaled that it was clearly not in a mood for its own civil war. The giant Greater New York Council had adopted a policy simply saying: "Prejudice, intolerance and discrimination in any form are unacceptable." And indeed, Dr. Flank never heard a word. Unless it was prepared to see its all-important membership numbers fall off a cliff, the national B.S.A. would have to stick to its philosophical statement without going overboard in enforcing it. Dr. Flank orchestrated the move quietly and efficiently. When it looked like there might be discussion at a school board meeting of the Scouts' use of the school, he asked a bunch of us to attend as a show of support. A half dozen dads sat through an interminable meeting. The issue never came up, but we felt as if we'd contributed through our silent witness.

Certification issue aside, the year progressed at its usual leisurely pace. Once a month, the patrol leaders and other boys in leadership positions met at a different Scout's house at what was called the Green Bar meeting to come up with an agenda for the regular weekly meetings held every Wednesday night. It could be a talk and demonstration tied to some upcoming event (canoeing technique, hiking gear, avoiding hypothermia while skiing). It could be a matter of fundamental Scout training and advancement (first aid, knots, avoiding hypothermia while winter camping). Or it could be a thinly disguised way to kill time (Trivial Pursuit, dodge ball, avoiding hypothermia while playing dodge ball).

One weekly meeting, for example, was organized as a cooking free-for-all. The kids all brought their stoves, set up shop in the parking lot outside the school, and made muffins and stews, pizzas and goulash, chicken stir fry and flaming brownies, which they all shared with each other. Todd made a chicken-and-rice concoction with ginger sauce and then prepared some cinnamon rolls with vanilla frosting for dessert. Allen, the heir apparent as troop master chef, made macaroni and rice and lentils in a vodka-marinated tomato sauce. They shared cooking and culinary wisdom ("Yo, dude. The good thing is if there's too much stew or broccoli you just throw it in the woods. It's biodegradable.")

and exchanged greetings heard nowhere else in their peer group ("So Blitz, how fares the quiche?"). We began at dusk and finished well after dark, and everyone went home fat and happy.

The grandest meetings were the three Courts of Honor, meetings of the kids and their families, where merit badges were given out, advancement was noted, and, in the grandest Courts of Honor of all, Eagles were awarded. As with nearly everything Troop 1 did, there was a time-tested model for each of the three Courts of Honor. The first one, in the fall, featured huge hero sandwiches plus salads and covered dishes brought by each family in the troop. Bob Walker, from the Westchester–Putnam Friends of Scouting, gave an impassioned spiel for contributions. The second, in the winter, was just dessert, fewer badges were awarded, and Bob Walker got the night off. The third, in the spring, featured a gala outdoor hot-dog and hamburger barbecue plus salads and covered dishes brought by each family in the troop; Bob Walker gave his impassioned spiel for contributions.

At the spring Court of Honor this year, Jimmy, the World's Biggest Scout, was getting his Eagle. It's not clear just how much making Eagle means in the world at large—almost certainly less than it did when Scouting was more central to community life. Certainly in the enlightened corridors of liberal America, attaining Eagle may be seen more as a sign of retrograde dweebdom than having the right stuff. But within Scouting, and in the less haughty corners of the country, Eagle still has a mythic, almost totemic power as something that people take with them through life. Eagles, as they will be quick to tell you, are Eagles for life (adults aren't former Eagle Scouts, they're Eagle Scouts). The requirements have changed a little over time. Now you have to have been a Life Scout, the rank below Eagle, for six months. You have to earn twenty-one merit badges, including the mandatory badges of first aid, citizenship in the community, citizenship in the nation, citizenship in the

world, communications, personal fitness, emergency preparedness or lifesaving, environmental science, personal management,
swimming or hiking or cycling, camping, and family life. Troop
1 over its eighty-eight years had produced sixty-six Eagles, beginning with Andrew W. Maxwell in 1936, so each one was a
big deal. After Dr. Flank opened the Eagle part of the evening,
the candidate, Jimmy, was escorted to the front by the current
Eagles in the troop and by some recent alumni, who were in
town or came in for the occasion. "Awarding the Eagle is an important and serious matter," Dr. Flank read in a voice denoting
importance and seriousness. "The Eagle is the highest and most
coveted award in all of Scouting. If, at this point, Scouting has
not achieved its purpose in the building of character—in the
training for leadership—in the practice of service—then it
probably never shall."

The Eagles at the front of the room then read the obligations
that came along with making Eagle. Todd Davis began: "The
first responsibility of an Eagle Scout is to live with honor, which
to an Eagle is sacred. Honor is the foundation of character—
character is what a man really is, down inside, not what someone else may think he is. An Eagle will live so as to reflect credit
upon his home, religious institution, school, friends, upon
Scouting and upon himself." Then it was Jack's turn: "The second obligation of an Eagle Scout is loyalty," read Jack, whose errant tarp ball throw had left Ben with the purple eye at camp.
"Without loyalty, all character lacks a sense of purpose and direction. An Eagle is loyal to his ideals and his values." Rich, my
raftmate from the soggy canoe trip, was on hand and read next:
"The third obligation of an Eagle Scout is courage. Courage
gives character all its force and strength. Trusting in a Supreme
Power, and with faith in his fellow beings, the Eagle Scout faces
each day unafraid, and seeks his share of the world's work to
do." Bob Heller read the last part: "The final obligation of an

Eagle is service. He extends a helping hand to those who toil upward along the Eagle trail he has now completed, just as others helped him in his achievement of the Eagle rank. The habit of the daily Good Turn must take on new meaning and blossom forth into a life of service. The Eagle protects and defends the weak and the helpless. He aids and comforts the oppressed and the unfortunate. He upholds the rights of others while defending his own rights. His code of honor is based upon the belief that real leadership must be founded upon real service."

Then Dr. Flank asked Jimmy to raise his hand in the Scout sign and repeat the Eagle Pledge: "I, Jimmy Francis, believe in the Boy Scouts of America as a movement which has as its aim and purpose character building and citizenship training. I believe it to be a movement that helps a Scout become master of his own powers, helps him get along with other people and helps him find a worthy use for his powers. I, therefore, believe it is my duty to do my best to obey the Scout Oath and Law. I hereby renew my faith in Scouting and promise to do what I can in service to other Scouts who have not come this far along the Eagle trail."

Dr. Flank shook his hand and gave him his Eagle pin, making Jimmy Troop 1's sixty-seventh Eagle, and we all responded with a properly honorable ovation. Most oaths are a little creepy to the modern ear, reeking of lockstep conformity or robotic obedience. When Jimmy was reading his, my mind flashed fleetingly to Michael Corleone at his nephew's christening at the end of *The Godfather* as he piously proclaimed his obedience to the dictates of the Church ("Do you renounce Satan?" "I do renounce him." "And all his works?" "I do renounce them.") while his minions methodically massacred all his enemies. Jimmy didn't seem the massacring kind—though he was big enough to do it himself if the mood struck. And it was hard not to be impressed by the lofty seriousness of it all. When else are kids challenged in quite the same archaically chivalric tones? Paul Fussell once wrote a lovely, admiring essay on the Boy Scout Handbook, calling it, in the end, essentially "a compendium of good sense. . . . Indeed, this handbook is among the very few remaining popular repositories of something like classical ethics, deriving from Aristotle and Cicero." I'm not sure if the ceremony felt quite Aristotelian or Ciceronian, but its choice of values—honor, loyalty, courage, and service—seemed impeccable for a convocation of twelve- to fifteen-year-old boys, and in the end it felt pretty much the way Fussell saw the Handbook—psychologically and ethically on target in a culture woefully short of compendia of good sense.

A few weeks later we returned for a camp-out to Clear Lake, where we had hiked past the old coal-mining railroad the previous year. No one made a big deal of it, but it was a special occasion—Todd Davis's last hike. He was graduating from high school in June and planning to attend Cornell. But he had his prom or some such thing on the date of the overnight canoe trip that always ends the Scouting year, so this figured to be his last outing with the troop. And it wasn't just Todd that was leaving. He was the third of three brothers who had made Eagle. His mother had helped organize every Court of Honor for as long as anyone could remember. It was hard to think back on a time when Troop 1 didn't have one of the amazing Davis brothers in the thick of things. Back in A. Lewis Oswald's heyday in Kansas he could assume an eternal crop of new Scouts, one following another in the Great Game. That was then. As we began the hike, Fly Guy, who had a daughter finishing her junior year in high school, was walking along with Todd, quizzing him on our generation's version of the Great Game, getting into college. Where had he visited? When had he started? Who was his counselor? How involved was she? What did he think of Hopkins or Penn or Dartmouth? Even in the woods, it was hard to avoid the real world kids inhabited. And while there were, no doubt, plenty of kids as remarkable as the Davis brothers out there, it was no longer certain that many of them were headed for the Boy Scouts.

When we reached our campsite, the kids set up their tents and then hiked down to the lake, where Fly Guy was going to give one of his fly-fishing exhibitions. Todd and Mr. Johnson and I stayed in camp. The afternoon sun was just beginning its descent as we sat on a huge slab of granite facing west. I asked Todd where he thought Scouting was headed. He wasn't too optimistic, less because of any gripes with Scouting than because of the dictates of suburban life. "The young ones start at such an early age now," he said. "What do the Tiger Cubs start at? Six? Seven? Maybe the B.S.A. feels like it's got to compete for the kids' attention, but the little kids spend all that time making paper, or whatever they do, they're burned out before they get to camp or do their Wilderness Survival merit badge. We had a peak back in the '70s, I think, and, honestly, I don't see us getting back to it anytime soon, or maybe at all. Kids just do so much. And I include myself. I started private music lessons after the first grade. Kids used to do that in the fourth grade. They start music and sports and everything so early. I do too much too, but I always knew Scouting was going to be part of my life. Most kids aren't that way."

The troop was coming back, and a bunch of them joined us on the rock. We sat in the sun, talking about the hike, Mark's new tent, Todd's ability to cook anything on an outback oven, Leatherman versus Swiss army knife. The day felt long and slow, like the ones I remembered when we played ball all day and hoped no one's mother called him in for dinner so we could keep playing till dark. After a half hour or so, Ben and his friends began drifting off. Todd grabbed his one-man tent and ventured out into the undergrowth, far from everyone else, to set up his tent, alone.

15: Summer Camp 3: Going for the Gold

Maybe it's just paternal pride, but I'd like to think our one brief, dazzling, totally unexpected, semimiraculous eleventh-hour ascent into Scouting Greatness began with Ben's Deucer Improvement and Beautification Project.

There were plenty of reasons not to sign up for a third tour of duty at Camp Waubeeka. I viewed Year One as a mandatory part of my recruitment contract, sort of like a tour of Nam that you couldn't get out of. I signed up for Year Two before I decided I would rather have stayed home, and then enjoyed it anyway. But Year Three was different. I didn't have to go, and I had plenty of time to get out of it if I chose to. And, after two years, I had pretty much done Scout camp. I was a little old to make Eagle. What was the point?

But, in the end, I signed up for a simple reason. I did it because I wanted to—for me, not for Ben. There's no way in the world I could have anticipated that when I ventured into the world of Troop 1 three years earlier. But I did it because the week in the woods with no fax, no e-mail, no phone, no communication with home or office was the most relaxed I got all year. I did it because I treasured the time with Ben and, despite all logic, found the whole ragged lot of kids more likable than not. I did it because I liked arguing with Lester, listening to Igor play his harmonica, seeing the Mohawks on the Bellmore kids, hearing the echoes off the lake during the campfires. I would have felt something missing from my summer if I hadn't been able to check in at Chez Wolfjaw for the week. And I did it because, in the subliminal way we get invested in things without quite knowing it, I liked being a part of the troop and its rhythms, and I was happy to be thought of as part of the reliable corps of Troop 1 Volunteer Regular Irregulars.

As usual, the cast of characters was both old and new. Harry was long since gone from the troop, pining for Scoutdom while his kids sailed blithely through their youth as far from Baden-Powell as they could get. Eric was doing only the first week, so Dennis didn't make it either. Instead, I was to be joined by the all-Italian tag team of Vince Farrentino and Robert Lombardi, the fathers of Sam and Mark, whom I had met back at my first Scout outing at the Paul Bunyan Camporee. This was fine with me. The two were among my favorite dads in the troop and seemed to present an appealing contrast. Vince, I assumed, could play tough guy, and Robert was reputed to be a good cook, no small attribute in the woods. And it meant something else. Since neither of them had been there before, I was, by default, the senior dad, Scouting veteran, and experienced leader. Once Dr. Flank left after completing the first week, the Troop 1 Scoutmaster for the week was—of all people—*moi*.

We met at Vince's house at seven on a cool, clear July morning, gassed up, and took off, Vince and Robert in Robert's pale blue Volvo station wagon and me in my black one. We arrived to find Dr. Flank and the rest of our troop awaiting our arrival.

It soon became apparent the previous week had not been the troop's best week ever. I shrewdly figured this out when everyone gave me the same evasive answer when I asked how the week had gone.

"I'll tell you later," said Fly Guy, so the kids wouldn't hear what he had to say.

"I'll tell you later," said Ben, so as not to be seen consorting with the enemy.

"I'll tell you later," said Dr. Flank, like 007 waiting for the right moment to brief 008.

In truth, I learned, it hadn't been all that atypical a week. Many merit badges were earned. Many vegetables were thrown into the woods rather than cooked. One patrol, in the interest of minimizing KP duties, had set a record for doing the least possible cooking per pound of food meted out. Sam 'n Eric had sung "Scout Socks" at all hours of the night. Dr. Flank and Fly Guy had logged countless hours fishing on the Waubeeka Lake, with the Fisherman of the Week Award going to Fly Guy for his eighteen-inch bass.

That said, the week had not done much to rebut our reputation as Scouting's answer to *Animal House*. Thanks to the helpful and courteous efforts of a Scout from another troop, who was a CIT and thus able to go into town without adults around, six Scouts spent the better part of the first week amassing quite a little weapons cache. This consisted of two blow guns with four-inch-long hypodermic needles that you shot through a foot-long black steel canister, three butane lighters, two butterfly knives, and one lock-back knife, each item capable of keeping squadrons of personal injury lawyers employed for the rest of the decade. Some of the weapons purchasers, wanting to be sure their investments did not go to waste, decided to try out the knives on one of the tarps at the campsite, slicing it neatly like a side of flank steak. This was a very bad idea. It said right in the 2001 Troop Leaders Guide, "Every Scout and every Adult Leader must know that deliberate damage to camp property may result in the person or persons responsible being immediately sent home without return of fee in part or whole." The "may result" left us an out—barely—in terms of expulsion, but Dr. Flank was furious when he found out what had happened, his wrath extending to the innocent as well as the guilty. He confiscated the weapons and made it clear that this offense went way over the line.

There were those at camp, Lester among then, who felt the offenders should have been summarily dismissed, rather than reprimanded and disarmed. But the truth was that if every transgressor were removed from camp, it would turn into a pretty quiet place. So all guilty parties got to stay, but with the knowledge that they had screwed up big time and would sin again at their peril.

Still, despite the fallout from the weapons of mass destruction, it didn't take us long to get into the swing of things. First we drove down to Lake Luzerne, where we dined at our usual eatery, a riverfront restaurant and milk bottle museum, which had mannequin cows in their crisp aprons perched out front to greet us. Then we roamed the streets like a feral band of mall-deprived shoppers, ducking in and out of the Luzerne Market and the local drugstore scooping up junk-food necessities, particularly twelve-packs of Cokes, Sprites, and root beer.

Then we all rendezvoused at the Hudson River Rafting Company for 3.5 miles of rafting on the Sacandaga River. We divided up into three rafts, with eight of us in each raft and Dr. Flank kayaking down behind us wearing a yellow helmet that made him look like some kind of E.T.-like watery alien. Our guide was a young woman with sundry body piercings who was a student at a local college, and the older kids, in particular, clearly liked having this exotic woman, just a few years older than they were, as their guide. The day had stayed cool and the skies had turned overcast. My main goal was to stay dry, something I accomplished just barely by sternly invoking the wallet-and-keys defense ("I can't get in the water. I have my wallet and keys in my pocket"—even though I had left them in Fly Guy's van) while almost everyone jumped or was dragged into the river. It's hard not to enjoy tubing down Class 2 and Class 3 rapids, but I was still half in work mode, my brain stewing over one or another minicrisis from the previous week, so I felt more like observer than participant.

After the trip ended we had nothing to do until dinner, so we just hung out in the parking lot of the outfitter's building. George and Tom threw a tennis ball back and forth. Ben, Mark, and Jonah wandered down by the river. Dr. Flank spent at least a half hour counseling Hal, who was upset because some of the other kids had teased him. Mr. Farrentino and Mr. Lombardi sat on the tailgate of a station wagon talking with some of the kids about the last week's events. It evoked summer at its indolent best, and as I sat there, listening to Doug's analysis of the latest developments in the Starcraft cosmology, I could feel my metabolism reverting to its Waubeeka mean. Finally, we headed out in the general direction of Warrensburg, a motley jumble of roadside commerce, where we got to choose between a generic diner, Gino's Pizzeria, and the Dragon Lee Chinese Restaurant. After dinner, most of the first-week dads and the kids who were returning with them headed south for home, and the rest of us headed back to Waubeeka.

It was eerily quiet. One set of troops leaves Saturday morning and the next arrives Sunday afternoon, so Saturday night is the interregnum between the different weeks of camp. The staff gets the night off. There are no activities. The waterfront and commissary are closed. There's no evening retreat, no blasts from the rifle range, no bugler to play "Taps." Wolfjaw was utterly unchanged. The only unfamiliar item was a letter posted on the bulletin board, red ink on lined notebook paper:

> Dear The Members of Chappaqua Troop 1, We would like to express our sincerest apologies for the embarrassment which was caused by the damage caused to the tarp at one of the patrol cooksites. The responsible parties will gladly pay for the replacement of the tarp and participate gladly in the hanging of a new tarp. We hope you accept our apologies and not hold a grudge. We hope that together we can put this incident behind us.
> Regretfully,
> Wolfjaw 3 and
> other responsible parties.

Dr. Flank was staying overnight, so he still had the lean-to. I ended up, Todd Davis-style, in the most distant tent, situated between Wolfjaw and the nearby Polaris site in what I liked to think of as suburban Wolfjaw. About a half dozen of us, including Ben, Doug, George, Mark, and Jonah, played cards—hearts, spades, an Italian card game called Scopa—for hours on the upstairs picnic table by the light of Dr. Flank's Coleman lantern before we went to bed.

The next morning we had our annual all-foods-known-to-man breakfast at Buckskin and prepared to do our laundry in the small town of Bolton Landing. It was then that deucer lightning struck. All in all, Ben's leadership record thus far had been spotty. He had done his best with his skeleton patrol, but there usually weren't enough kids to make it a real test of leadership. So when he and Jonah were made Patrol Leaders for Week 2 of camp, with Allen, our master chef, as the Senior Patrol Leader, he was determined to take his duties seriously. That very morning he decided to go ahead with his first major management initiative—a fundraising campaign to create an endowment for air fresheners and bug strips for the deucer. He hit up each of the kids for a few dollars, and then went to the adults as well.

"Mr. Farrentino, Mr. Lombardi, have you visited the latrine during your short stay at camp?" he asked.

Indeed they had.

"Did you like what you smelled?"

No, come to think of it, they were less than enchanted by the aromas wafting through the deucer.

"Well, wouldn't you like to replace that horrific stench with a nicer fragrance? Gentlemen, I'm here today to tell you that with a small donation of one or two dollars to the Deucer Beautification Project you can make that dream a reality. Your donation will go toward the purchase of air fresheners and fly traps for the latrine. So, what do you say?"

Needless to say, they were glad to contribute. By the time his fundraising was completed, Ben had $15. He made his purchases at the supermarket in Bolton Landing and installed them immediately upon our return. The change sent shock waves through Wolfjaw. Sam himself was soon seen striding manfully from the latrine, hollering words never before spoken at Camp Read and probably never before spoken on the planet.

"Yo, guys. Have you been in the deucer? It smells awesome."

Campers came up to Ben to congratulate him on his achievement.

"Hey, Ben. Nice job on the crapper."

"Your tax dollars at work," he modestly replied.

At the same time, Allen was hatching plans of his own. Mr. Lombardi, who was never really off duty as a teacher, sat down with him to ask him what his goals were for the week as SPL.

"Well, I'd like to win the Waubeeka Award," he said.

This was a truly novel thought, on the order of a declaration that he'd like to grow a second head or have everyone spend the week speaking Russian and doing campfire skits based on

Dostoyevsky novels. We had finished dead last among the troops in attendance the previous week. Troop 1 was totally absent from the many signed W's that adorned the Scout office in honor of previous Waubeeka Award honorees. No one could remember Troop 1 ever winning the award. Instead, we took pride in our status as The Troop Least Likely to Win the Waubeeka Award.

Still, the idea had some appeal. For leaders Allen, Ben, and Jonah, it seemed the kind of challenge that Scouting, even Troop 1's version of it, was supposed to be about. About half the kids were perfectly happy to go along with whatever the troop agenda was going to be. And even some of the more contrary ones—still smarting from Dr. Flank's weapons confiscation— saw a reason to buy in. Dr. Flank was leaving early Monday, and winning the award when the troop's official authority figure wasn't around would be like getting good grades but managing to piss your parents off at the same time. It was a way to be trustworthy, loyal, helpful, and all that, but something of a wise guy as well. And before long, as if a benign computer virus had wormed its way into every camper's mental hard drive, Troop 1 had achieved a rare degree of unanimity. We had decided to go for the Gold.

Of course, no one knew quite how one went for the Gold, but we started where we could. A big part of the score came from the daily troop inspection report, the document that tallied how well we did at cleaning the site, putting all tools and sup- plies in their proper place, and showing up more or less re- spectably attired at the retreat each evening. We bustled around Monday morning cleaning the site in anticipation of the daily in- spection, and all the kids showed up at retreat that evening in their Scout shirts and the closest things to khaki shorts they could come up with. Sure enough, after the prior week's daily scores in the mid-to-low 20s (it's hard to get less without incur- ring fatalities or engendering widespread intestinal distress), we scored an encouraging 34 of 36—not the perfect scores of Bronxville 4 and Scarsdale 2, but pretty damn good. The next day we corrected Monday's shortcomings—saws improperly stowed in the axe yard and water cans for fires improperly placed at the tents instead of a central area—and lo and behold, we scored a perfect 36, which set off a round of high-fives at retreat. In addition, Allen tied the fastest timber hitch knot in the evening Scouting Challenge. The next day we scored 36 again, putting us, according to reliable sources, in the lead after three days.

Having tiptoed toward competence, we felt emboldened to do more. Robert, in a fit of enterprise that deserved a Waubeeka Award on its own, had masterminded a service project that saw the kids construct a majestic WOLFJAW sign out of two long tree limbs and twenty-three beech logs lashed together to spell out the name of the campsite. The kids sawed the logs to size and tied them together with taut square lashing, proving that the knots and lashing can really be used after all. The complete assemblage was hoisted ten feet high above the entrance to the camp, making use of a ladder the kids had made as a side project, and it will no doubt stand for years to come as a monument to Troop 1's enterprise and grit.

While this competition was playing out, a second was also beginning, a new event called the Scoutmaster's Challenge. We Scoutmasters were to undergo a grueling series of challenges designed to test what was described as our mental, physical, and spiritual capabilities as mentors to America's youth. Well, maybe grueling was going a bit far. What we had to do was find the answer to five trivia questions about Camp Waubeeka—things like how many working rifles are there at the rifle range? (10); How many camp staff members have worked at the econ lab? (4); Who is Waubeeka's Waterfront Director? (Nicole Wicks). Then we had to come up with a new camp cheer and compete in a boccilike game using rocks instead of balls to see who could throw the rock closest to a line of rope without going past it. I got most of the answers from Warren, the same CIT who had sold the weapons during Week 1 and was around when the staff came up with the questions. Allen, the SPL, came up with the cheer, which he said was to the tune of the horrid pop song "Lady Marmelade," though you could have fooled me. It went like this:

Hey-beeka, Ho-Beeka. Waubeeka.
Hey-beeka, Ho-Beeka, Probeeka.
Waubeeka. Probeeka.
WAUBEEKA!

It wasn't "The Love Song of J. Alfred Prufrock," but it wasn't any worse than the lyrics to "Lady Marmelade," whatever they were supposed to mean. We had to throw the rocks ourselves. OK, it was neither the Ironman Challenge nor a Mensa exam, but Vince, Robert, and I all competed for the Greater Glory of Troop 1.

Still, we were a mere sideshow. It wasn't as if the Waubeeka Award competition sucked up everyone's attention. Kids continued to pile up merit badges. George and Hal, two kids the same size and age who had turned into a dysfunctional couple, whined and wheedled and fought with each other all week over who had taken out more wood, or made more food pickups, or had started better fires. Sometimes Herb chimed in to add to the cacophony. We took a trip to the Zip Line, the trolley over the water at the Buckskin Lake, where even I got in the water. Upstairs at the campsite Doug was constantly organizing card games, which were augmented by a Scrabble game Mr. Lombardi contributed to the cause. In The Underworld, life was a little quieter because Sam decided it would be sacrilegious to do "Scout Socks" without Eric, so he retired the song for the week.

The deucer continued to serve as an inspiration to latrine management experts around the globe. And Ben and Allen, in a heartwarming tribute to Ben's southern roots, came up with a new camp delicacy: gourmet grits. They got up as early as 6:00 A.M. to have the proper time to do the cooking just so. First they cooked up a pot of grits. Then they added garlic, onions, grated sharp cheddar cheese, and salt and pepper. Voilà! Super Grits strong enough to give your fillings a cheesy radioactive glow. You wouldn't want to start every day that way, but, to be perfectly honest, it was pretty damn good.

Maybe it was because the kids were older and there were fewer discipline issues, but as the week wore on, the dads felt less and less like authority figures and more and more like fellow travelers. Ben would be found sitting in one of the deluxe camp chairs with footrest, backrest, armrest, pillow, and drink holder, directing cleanup by offering Cokes and Sprites as rewards for undesirable tasks. Tom, now fourteen going on twenty-one, was constantly disappearing and hanging out with the staff, particularly the female members. Warren, the weapons dealer from Week 1, joined us every day for lunch in The Underworld, his past sins long since forgotten. Doug prowled around for card partners or soulmates to ponder the mysteries of Starcraft. Kids pored through Campmor catalogs, compiled merit badge notebooks full of leaf or tree drawings, and debated which sleeping bags would be best to have if you found yourself atop Mount Everest. Mark came up with more Seinfeldian questions ("If manatees are the cows of the sea, how come you can't tip them?"). Jonah had developed into an assertive leader with a touch of Todd Davis's cockiness. Even Sam took on the slightly unsettling quality of a respected elder statesman, perhaps humbled by the burdens of leading his faction without Eric. He spent much of his time, like a pilgrim anticipating life in the Promised Land, contemplating a new and loftier existence next year at Staff City. At one point, he shocked the world by expressing interest in attending MIT.

Vince and Robert added their own distinctive touches. Both were born in hill towns in southern Italy, Vince in Muro Lucano,

Robert in Campobasso, and moved to the United States when they were about eight, so they shared not only a similar life story, but the same Italian dialect. And as the week went on, they increasingly found themselves conversing in Italian, which gave our campsite the feel of a commedia dell'arte version of a Boy Scout outing:

ROBERT: Chi è il direttore delle frecce?
VINCE: Non lo so ma penso che si chiama Chris. È l'unico là in ogni caso. È come in Italia—ognuno ha il titolo. Professore, Direttore, Commendatore.
ROBERT: Come gli Italiani, i Boy Socuts amano la burocrazia.

(Who is the archery director?
I don't know. I think it might be Chris. He is the only
one there anyway. It's like Italy, everyone has a title:
professor, director, commander.
Like Italians, the Boy Scouts like bureaucracy.)

Another morning, they were watching as a new cooking regimen at the upstairs campsite didn't seem to be any more efficient than the old one it replaced:

ROBERT: A che punto stanno con la colazione?
VINCE: Molto meglio. Si sono svegliati più presto stamattina.
ROBERT: Ma ancora non hanno cucinato...
VINCE: Forse era meglio quando era peggio!

(How is breakfast going?
Much better. They woke up earlier today to get things
started.
But they still haven't cooked...
Maybe it was better when it was worse.)

By Thursday, the Waubeeka competition was mixing the thrill of victory with the agony of defeat. We suffered a severe setback that day when Steve, the camp commissioner, reported that we had fallen short on inspection. In a fateful twist worthy of Greek tragedy, someone had left the deucer lid up, losing points for cleanliness. It would be just our luck to lose on a deucer technicality after the greatest advances in latrine hygiene in Waubeeka history.

That unexpected setback was particularly worrisome because we'd suffered an even more costly one the day before. We'd had five kids, Sam among them, complete the mile swim—about half the total who completed it in the whole camp—as a way to pile up more Waubeeka points. But as virtuous and impressive as the mile swim no doubt was, we were belatedly informed it did not count toward the Waubeeka Award. Suddenly, fifty points we'd thought were ours had just evaporated. Maybe we just weren't destined to escape our fate.

After retreat that night came the next big event, the staff hunt, where campers had to round up staff members hiding across the vast reaches of Waubeeka. Ben and Mark had prepared for the event by coming up with a precise plan for how to deploy our forces. Unfortunately, they had never got around to actually conveying it to the rest of the troop, so the kids tore off willy-nilly in search of staff members, who were accorded points based on their importance or notoriety and brought once apprehended to the waterfront for summary dunkings. Vince, Robert, and I scurried over to the waterfront to see the warriors return with their spoils.

First came two Bronxville 4 kids with Stanty. Then some little Mohawk kids with Bonnie, the femme fatale from the econ lodge. Some Rye 2 kids showed up with Dolan, one of the lords of Scoutcraft, and then a Scarsdale kid brought grumpy Ted Watson. *Where were we? This was turning into a disaster!* Finally,

Tom showed up with some twit from handicrafts, worth maybe five points, but others, returning to their old desultory form, were wandering back to the waterfront empty-handed before the hunt was even over. *What were they thinking? The hunt was still on! Get back out there, you yo-yos!* Meanwhile, Bronxville had scored an incredible coup—they had bagged Tom Logan, back again as the camp director, which meant fifty points, more than a whole day's worth of deucer cleaning and monster box maintenance.

We felt like we were watching our chances for Waubeeka immortality leech away. Someone clanged the bell at the top of the waterfront watchtower, signaling the end of the hunt, and we glumly headed back toward Wolfjaw.

"Bummer, man," I said.

"Che sfortuna," Vince muttered in Italian.

"Peccato," Robert said in agreement.

And then down the road we saw a sight so startling that at first it seemed an apparition. Sam and Jonah were toddling along next to Steve Silvers, the camp commissioner, like Peter triumphantly bringing home the wolf at the end of *Peter and the Wolf.* Of course! The bell meant the game was over, but it took kids as long as ten minutes to make it back to the waterfront with the staff members they had already caught. *Fifty points. We're still alive!*

Friday, the day that would decide our fate, dawned bright and clear. There were two big events left, the water carnival and the final campfire, and we knew we needed to do well in both. Using my executive powers as acting faux Scoutmaster, I quietly decreed a third event, our now-traditional last-night troop campfire. I mentioned the plan to Robert and Vince (and Ben, who seemed like a quasi adult by this point) and then sneaked out of camp late in the morning to shop for graham crackers, Hershey's chocolate, and marshmallows for s'mores, along with Cokes, Sprites, pretzel rods, and other sources of excess salt and empty calories. I stowed the stuff at the commissary and walked next door to the camp office, where I saw Steve Silvers and asked how we were doing in the competition.

He hesitated for just a moment.

"I can't tell you too much," he said, "but if you kick butt in the water carnival you'll be in great shape."

Yesss!!

"Who else is up there?"

"Bronxville and Scarsdale."

I rushed back to the site, where the kids, of course, had the same information I did only in more detail. At the appointed hour, we all trooped over to the waterfront. There were a few kids from Rye. An enormous gaggle of macho Bellmore Mohawks showed up, which was fine, because they had assumed the mantle of Troop Least Likely to Win the Waubeeka Award and thus posed no threat. Then a contingent showed up from the troop from Glen Cove, Long Island. We waited. And waited some more. It seemed hard to believe our luck could be this good, but Bronxville and Scarsdale had not shown up! Lester sometimes made a point of stressing troop activities over competitions or badges, but whatever the reason for his totally unexpected absence, all we had to do was win a few awards and we were all but in.

Sure enough, like clockwork, we won the first award, the T-Boat Rescue, which consisted of one kid swamping a canoe, two more canoeing out to him and righting his canoe and emptying out its water, and then the first kid rowing back. Next came three challenges: diving and making the biggest splash, diving and making the smallest splash, and best belly flop. We lost the first. We lost the second. We looked to Sam, our obvious candidate for the belly flop.

"I don't know, guys," he said nervously like a rookie para-trooper contemplating his first jump. "I'm worried about hurting my balls."

I stepped forward.

"We need you this time, big guy," I said. "Even if it means a little . . . discomfort, you've got to take one for the troop."

He looked me straight in the eyes, and nodded almost imperceptibly. Then he took off his shirt, flung it behind him, and strode toward the dock, where he proceeded to displace half the lake with a full frontal, zero gainer, zero tuck, classic belly flop. We figured that we were golden until Steve announced, "For the last event we'll need one of your smaller kids."

Last event? Already? The water carnival other years had featured eight or ten events. Just our luck that the one year we were in shape to clean up, the whole thing consisted of only five. Which meant, after the Mohawks had won the previous event, a totally lame exercise that involved blowing a ping-pong ball back and forth the width of the shallow area of the waterfront, we still didn't know who was ahead.

We went into the evening tense but ready. We got a perfect score at our final retreat. We signed up for the maximum two skits. It was now in the hands of the Big Scout in the Sky.

The campfire started late, because we had to wait until it was totally dark to begin. It soon became clear why. As we entered we saw a canoe containing two mock Indians in buckskins and headdresses gliding across the lake, where they lit a big yellow W that had been carefully placed for the evening in the shallow water. Two other Indians, faces stern, arms folded, stood on the banks. They lit two enormous bonfires, and the campfire began. First an Order of the Arrow ceremony, the excuse for all the Indian costumes, welcomed six new potential inductees who had been selected to be ordeal candidates. They were applauded by the troops and then led off into the woods, where presumably their skin was cut with rusty kitchen knives for a fraternal blood oath. Then we did the Waubeeka cheer with the "CAMP, CAMP, CAMP," providing a particularly resonant echo off the lake. Gussie, Lester's SPL, who happened to be one of the few black kids at camp, led everyone in the Waubeeka fight song. Many skits were performed and songs sung.

Finally, Steve called for everyone's attention. "I've got two last special announcements," he said. The kids suddenly became absolutely quiet. "First, I want to award the Scoutmaster Challenge to the Scoutmaster who has excelled in the moral, mental, and physical competitions over the past week."

He looked around the amphitheater to drag the moment out. A whisper of breeze blew off the lake. Then he said, "The winner is . . . Peter Applebome of Troop 1 Chappaqua."

If there had been voting booths, they should have been impounded. If there had been punch cards, someone needed to check all the dimpled, pregnant, and hanging chads. Of all the awards in the world I was not qualified to win—a very long list—the Scoutmaster's Challenge would have ranked near the top. Truth to tell, even in our little band, Robert was definitely the best teacher and motivator. But, on the other hand, a challenge is a challenge, and I had not won anything since winning the International Bad Hemingway competition for the worst Hemingway parody perhaps fifteen years ago, so I was delighted to be honored, however comically unworthy I was. I rushed to the front to shake hands with Steve, delivered a properly humble victory speech, crediting my victory entirely to the boys of Troop 1, and returned in triumph to my perch on a log near the back of the semicircle facing the water. The troop responded with high-fives, and expressions of "You go, Mr. Applebome." Ben gave me a look that was part congratulations and part amused recognition of the illogic of it all.

Everyone quieted down in anticipation. The big moment was at hand.

"We have had many tight races for the Waubeeka Award," Steve said, "but I don't know if I've ever seen one as close as this one. Three troops were divided by five points and the fourth was only ten points behind. So we had many troops that worked hard and did a great job here and easily could have been the winner. But the winner of this week's Waubeeka Award is... (the pause seemed to last forever)...Troop 1 Chappaqua."

I'm not sure who was more excited—the kids or Vince, Robert, and me. We hollered like maniacs in English and Italian. We exchanged high-fives, low-fives, and mid-fives. We did chest butts and butt butts and other suitable expressions of manly enthusiasm. We quieted down for "Taps" and then floated back to Wolfjaw, the kids singing that god-awful "We Are the Champions" song as they marched up the rocky path to the site. It was the Cubs winning the World Series, Gonzaga winning the NCAA basketball tournament, Ball State beating Florida State in football, the Devil Rays beating the Yankees.

We already had the campfire made. I brought the bags of goodies to the upstairs picnic table, opened up the pretzel rods, and gave one to each kid as a victory cigar. Then, with everyone puffing away in contentment, Robert lit the fire, and in a few minutes it was our own small-bore facsimile of the roaring blaze at the lakefront. We hunted for sticks to make s'mores, broke out the chocolate and marshmallows and graham crackers, and relived our moment of triumph.

I had one more duty to perform. I hadn't learned my knots or lashes. I never got around to memorizing the Scout Law. I still didn't know much first aid. Still, there was something exhilarating about being the purported leader of our exultant little band. Like Cochran, the well-meaning Scoutmaster in *Be Prepared*, I felt that something good had rubbed off on me, and I didn't want to blow it. I had never worn the Scout uniform, always feeling a bit of comfortable distance in my familiar old T-shirts and worn-out shorts. But at this moment, for the first time, I found myself wishing I had a Scout shirt (Scout socks and shorts never entered my mind) as a way to erase any vestiges of cool, ironic distance I might have had left. I might have been a temporary, accidental Scoutmaster, but at this moment, it felt really important that I was a good one.

During the afternoon I had taken out my laptop and written an award ceremony, seventy or eighty words on each kid. Not Dr. Flank's Indian tales. Not Mr. Johnson's saga of Great Chief Leknoot. Not Mr. Toonkel's ghost tales. Just Mr. Applebome's Week 2 Award Oration. I figured it was my only chance to be Grand Wizard of the campfire, and I wanted to be certain it was a success. The kids had earned our respect. At this moment, I wanted to be sure I earned theirs.

"OK," I barked in my most authoritative voice. "It turns out we have a few more awards to give out. Listen up. There'll be a test afterward to make sure you were paying attention."

Total quiet. So far so good.

"One Troop 1 Scout has shown a particular affinity for inter-acting with the females in camp," I began. "He's at the commissary hanging around with Carrie. Joanna always seems to show particular interest when he shows up at the econ lodge. So in recognition of his selfless efforts as an ambassador to the females in camp, his dedication to the worthy cause of furthering intergender relations, and his natural skills as a ladies' man, our honorary Girl Scout Award goes to . . . Mr. Thomas Edwards."

Tom, proving my point, turned out to be the only Scout who wasn't there, which made the award that much better. We toasted him in absentia. Next came the Dream Couple Award: "Throughout history, there have been couples whose undying love for one another changed the course of human events—Romeo and Juliet,

Antony and Cleopatra, Gatsby and Daisy, Bill Clinton and Monica Lewinsky..." It went to Hal and George, the kids who had spent the whole week nagging each other. The two stood up together and beamed as everyone gave them a round of applause. Allen, our peerless master chef, the overlord of onions, the sultan of salt, the greengrocer of garlic, the minister of mustard, one of our first two inductees into the Order of the Arrow and the Royal Order of the Grit, won the Julia Child Award for outstanding cookcraft. Ben, our other inductee into the Order of the Arrow and the Royal Order of the Grit, won the W. Edwards Deming Management Award, for his creative use of Coke and Sprite cans as motivational tools and his groundbreaking innovations in latrine management and maintenance.

By this point all the kids were into the spirit of the event, sucking happily on their pretzel rods, waiting their turn to be recognized, and issuing titters of recognition when it was clear who each lucky recipient would be. Sam deserved and received something of a special citation: "It must be said that in the grand scheme of things, most of us are bit players at Camp Waubeeka. This is not true for our next honoree. Other than Dr. Flank and his absent partner, Mr. Eric Walker, no Troop 1 member is as famous—or infamous—in camp as our next honoree. But we have to ask the question, has this former bad boy gone good? No annoying renditions of 'Scout Socks.' No breaking skeets against his head. No behavior incurring threats by angry Scouts from Greenwich, Bronxville, or Bellmore. Instead, we had a master of cookcraft, an awesome performance in the mile swim, the signal success of finding Steve Silvers in the staff hunt, and his critical victory in the belly-flop competition. Gentlemen, a legend in his own time, the winner of this year's Sam Farrentino Award for Farrentinian behavior is...Sam Farrentino."

Sam got a richly deserved standing O, and I felt like a comedian who knew he had his audience. Everyone got his moment of recognition. Jonah got the Todd Davis Award for exemplary patrol leadership, maintaining peace and tranquility in The Underworld. Mark joined former Waubeeka campers Immanuel Kant, René Descartes, Sören Kierkegaard, and Friedrich Nietzsche as the winner of the year's Transcendental, Existential, Aristotelian Award for creative thinking and contributions to world philosophy. I ended with a heartfelt tribute to Doug: "It was hard to know if our final honoree came to us from Las Vegas or whatever planet it is in Starcraft. On the one hand, he was the master dealer of every card game known to man. On the other, he was always one step away from blasting Terrans or Zergs or Protoss. So for outstanding service in two dimensions, the earthly and the extraterrestrial, and for exemplary service to the peanut growers of America, who would be bankrupt without his business, our award for the Scout most likely to be at home in the bar scene from *Star Wars* goes to Mr. Doug Newton."

We hung around until eleven or so, pigging out, telling jokes, toasting our worthy rivals from Bronxville and Bellmore, and evaluating which of us would look best in one of the Bellmore Mohawks. Then we applauded Tom when he sheepishly returned in time for a command repeat performance of his award. Finally, the kids began to look like they were beginning to slow down. A few were clearly ready to nod off. We poured water on the fire, stumbled to our tents, and called it a night.

The next morning we all got to sign the W in our victory lap as Waubeeka Award winners. Then the kids riding the bus home piled in, and the bus pulled out in a billowing pillow of dust. Mr. Farrentino and Mr. Lombardi and their kids pulled out in Robert's Volvo. Ben and Jonah got into my car. I offered a crisp salute to Lester, who was jawing with Steve over something or other, and we pulled away and headed for home. As we lumbered down the dusty road out of camp, I had a fleeting thought: I wondered if I'd ever see this place again.

16: A Final Trip

One spring day about eight months after my last summer at Waubeeka, I took a different kind of Scouting expedition—a visit to the B.S.A.'s National Headquarters, situated in a nondescript brown brick office building in a pod of low-rise office buildings on the featureless prairie between Dallas and Fort Worth. The Boy Scout and American flags flew out front. A famous bronze statue of a Scout from the 1930s stood there too, looking lost and forlorn in this bland corporate landscape. Immediately inside the lobby was a wall of thirty-nine plaques honoring big donors, including the Amoco Foundation, IBM, Burlington Industries, Murphy Oil Corp., Quaker Oats, and McKinsey & Co. On the walls of the reception area were reproductions of four Scout paintings, two by Norman Rockwell, two by his student and successor Joseph Csatari. In a narrow hallway was a large portrait of B-P. It looked totally incongruous, as if there was no place to put it, so they stuck it on a wall and forgot about it.

I had written to Chief Scout Executive Roy L. Williams, who succeeded Jere Ratcliffe, requesting an interview, making the case that I was no mere writer but the distinguished winner of the Camp Waubeeka Scoutmaster Challenge. I guess he wasn't impressed, since I never heard from him. Instead, I met with Gregg Shields, a Senior Account Supervisor with the giant Edelman Public Relations, who handles the Scouts' PR. He met me in the lobby and then took me down to an empty conference room on the lower level. Shields had the rather thankless job of trotting out the Scout line on the gay issue or responding to allegations like the Circle Ten Ghost Troop fiasco. I had heard the Scouts were famously unhelpful to the press, but Shields did his best. He said he wasn't surprised that Williams wasn't available. "He doesn't do interviews," said Shields, a pleasant enough midwesterner transplanted to suburban Dallas. "I think I can remember maybe one he's done since taking office. It's just not what he does. There's some logic in the Chief Scout Executive for the B.S.A. nationally not taking a public role, but letting the success of the organization speak for itself."

Shields affected a tone that was measured but upbeat. "Gallup did a study five years ago on men who were Boy Scouts," he said. "And men who were Scouts are significantly different, more likely to have leadership roles in the community, more likely to go to church, more likely to espouse values of family, positive values. So we see lots of signs of vitality. Our camp at Philmont is sold out two years in advance. I wish you'd been at the jamboree this year. I don't want to get too schmaltzy, but one of the senior volunteers was a guy who played a saw. Most kids had never seen anyone play a saw, and here he was with forty thousand kids watching him play 'Somewhere Over the Rainbow.' At first I was kind of concerned for the old boy. But he didn't take himself too seriously and he played it and then took a big bow. And then he said, 'For my next piece I'd like to play something we all know,' and he sat down and played 'God Bless America,' and three bars into it, I could hear behind me forty thousand young voices. I could see all these kids, hats off, singing 'God Bless America.' And it was really something. When it was over, we evacuated the site—forty thousand boys—and the only garbage was in the garbage cans."

Other things were not so rosy. Yes, enrollment was steadily dropping, but, he said, there is much more competition for boys' time than there was in the past. I asked Shields how well he thought Scouting had done in reaching out to minority communities, and he said there was no way to be sure. "That's our Scoutreach Program," he said. "We don't know how successful, because we don't have the data. The organization has the belief that you don't need a pedigree to be a Boy Scout. So until just a year or two ago there was no ethnic information on your application. There's still no income information. So it would be hard to say how far we've come because we don't know where we were. But we do know the Boy Scouts are making a very serious effort to reach those populations that have been underrepresented in the past. Today we print literature in thirteen languages." Nor could he say anything about the investigation of the Circle Ten Ghost Troops and other incidents of inflated rolls. "There's currently an open investigation by the Postal Service; that's about all I know," he said in standard flack-speak.

As for the gay controversy, Shields patiently repeated what I'd read elsewhere, that Scouting's essence was its core values and that endorsing homosexuality was inconsistent with them. "There are people who don't agree with it, and we accept that," he said. "But just as we respect their point of view, we ask their tolerance for our values and our ideas. Families who agree with our values embrace Boy Scouting. Those who don't are free to do other things." Then he said something I didn't expect: "One of the biggest growth markets for Boy Scouting has been and will continue to be—and we need to capitalize on it—non-denominational Christian churches who share many of these values—belief in God, belief in family, belief in serving others."

I'm sure it was true, but focusing on the most reliable bastions of the religious right seemed to be a form of niche marketing carrying a pretty clear message of where Scouting thought its future lay. I felt like my friend who had considered pulling her son out of Cub Scouts—being dared to play elsewhere if I didn't like their rules.

"We did a poll in January 2000 asking people if they supported the Boy Scouts policy on gays," Shields continued. "Seventy percent said 'yes'; the other 30 percent either said 'no' or were undecided. This was asked of all parents, both Scouting parents and non-Scouting parents. So we've got a majority, a strong majority. It's certainly a lot stronger than any presidential election we've had recently. You have to separate the essentials from the nonessentials, the mission from the method. The uniform has been changed I don't know how many times. That's not essential. The Scout Oath and Law has not changed. That's essential. The values of Scouting, that's essential."

I asked for a tour, but Shields said there wasn't much to see. Instead, we took the elevator back up, joined by six well-scrubbed young men in white shirts and ties and name tags identifying the towns they were from (workplace casual has not exactly swept through the B.S.A., though there is a Casual Thursday, which means sport coat, no tie). Then we drove five minutes to a nearby strip mall, where we had a buffet lunch at the Veranda Greek Café, with rugs and paintings—*The Last Supper,* flamenco dancers, Dutch still lives, brooding waterfronts—in every genre known to man. Over lunch, Shields mentioned something that I barely took notice of—that there were twice as many Cub Scouts as Boy Scouts. When we came back, he gave me a copy of the B.S.A. annual report. On the cover was a Tiger Cub, a cute black or Hispanic kid who looked like he was just past the age of riding in a car seat. Except for the Learning for Life programs, in which the B.S.A. contracted with schools to teach children about values and character development, all the Scout enrollment totals had dropped for the year, with the total at 3.351 million, down from 3.392 million. (It dropped again to 3.325 million the next year.) But there were 2.1 million kids in the three Cub-age programs and just over a million in Boy Scouts and Varsity Scouts, which enrolled more advanced Scouts ages fourteen to seventeen. This seemed a little shocking. The B.S.A. had resisted the creation of Cub Scouts for two decades, feeling Scouting was meant for older boys. Now, for two-thirds of boys, Scouting ended by the time they were eleven or so. Instead of Scouting's vaunted values and service, the Scouting experience for most kids was doing the Pinewood Derby in elementary school, getting their first camping experience, and then dropping out before the meaningful parts of Scouting could sink in.

We came back and chatted outside in the parking lot for a few minutes, the headquarters no different than any other corporate office except for the Scout posters you could see in the offices. Then I drove off, still thinking about the membership numbers.

Maybe Scouts getting younger was inevitable. Sociologists talk about the compressed lives that kids now lead. Girls who used to play with Barbie dolls until ten might now stop at seven, so maybe Scouting for most boys now ends with Cub Scouts. But the number of kids in the population is exploding because of the baby boomers' "echo boom." If Scouting can't grow now, it never will. If a corporation dropped from 4.9 million customers, the number of boys in Scouting in 1972, to 3.3 million, it would be judged a disaster. But Scouting seems to sail smugly along, secure in its legacy and its mythic, if diminished, place in public life.

Closer to home, recruitment seemed to be looming as a big issue with Troop 1 as well. Dr. Flank professed not to be concerned. The troop's membership had waxed and waned over time, and when we joined, just four years ago, the leaders felt it was getting too many kids, so maybe I was overreacting. But after Ben's first year, new membership fell off a cliff. There were several kids the year ahead of him, and his class of ninth graders so far had retained a solid core of about eight kids from the twelve or so kids who had started out when he did. But there were only five kids left in the eighth-grade group below and none at all in the year after that. Kids like Dave and Marty, the little survivors of our disastrous rafting trip, showed up a few times, maybe spent a summer at camp, and dropped out before I knew their names. We had a great little kid named Sahil, who the big kids identified as his year's star Scout, but he moved to Chicago. So as the next year wore on there were still plenty of Scouts for the meetings and hikes, but they were mostly high school kids, and it was hard to keep them interested in the meetings covering material they'd already learned. We were in danger of becoming a troop with many chiefs and few Indians. A highlight of every year was the last outing before camp, the overnight canoe trip on the Delaware. But this year the trip coincided with the day the high school kids had to take their subject-matter SAT-2 tests. For the first time, the outing had to be cancelled. Getting a dad for the second week of camp was suddenly a huge struggle. For a while we had only Mr. Lombardi until another dad was coaxed into volunteering. And who knew what was going to happen when Dr. Flank finally called it quits? Nearing our ninetieth birthday in 2003, I was beginning to wonder if we'd be around to hit one hundred.

True, the troop had seen similar membership dips in the past. But it felt like Scouting faced a steeper hill all the time, and I wondered if the controversy over the gay issue had, at least in communities like ours, added a glaring new disincentive to joining Scouts. We weren't going to quit Troop 1, but if we had been just beginning, the image of Scouting as harsh and intolerant would have been a reason not to join, as it was for the terrific young son of some friends of ours. In another era, he would have been the archetypal Eagle Scout. In this one, he followed the B.S.A.'s expulsion of James Dale, told his parents that maybe Scouting wasn't his kind of organization, and on his own decided to drop out of Cub Scouts. It wasn't a case of politically correct adults making a political statement. It was an ethically acute fifth grader looking at the B.S.A.'s values and behavior and deciding he did not like what he saw.

The Scouts locally said their research showed their biggest problem in recruiting is not politics but competition for boys' time. But maybe the Boy Scouts needed to learn some lessons from the Girl Scouts. In our two-county Boy Scout council, membership was plummeting, dropping over the past decade from 17,624 in 1992 to 9,450 in 2002. Meanwhile the local Girl Scouts, who quite explicitly mandate no exclusionary standards for religion and sexual preference, had doubled their enrollment since 1984 and grown by 25 percent since 1992. Whatever the cause, as the number of Boy Scouts continues to drop, it reduces the pool of adults likely to be interested in running troops or pushing their kids toward it in the future. It felt like a downward spiral. No wonder national is so solicitous of those eager-beaver Mormons.

Once I was at Harry's house, and he was showing me memorabilia of the Brooklyn camp-out he had put together. One of his sons wandered over to idly poke through the old badges and patches and photographs, amused at his dad's ancient keepsakes. "Dad, if you did that in Chappaqua probably no one would show up," he said dismissively. "Everyone I know hates Scouting. I don't think anyone in the whole middle school does it anymore. They think it's cheesy, uncool, and old-fashioned. Why does anyone need to tie knots and read a compass? If you're in the woods and you need something, you call your dad on your cell phone."

But if Scouting is a harder sell for suburban kids, it's not going away. Membership is down, but 3.3 million scouts is still a lot of kids. Its position in America's collective unconscious and as a recipient of corporate donations remains secure for now. And there are at least three reasons to believe this can be a fairly auspicious time for Scouting. First is what I think of as the North Face Moment—the vogue for hiking and climbing into distant, unpleasant, or inaccessible places in expensive, synthetic outdoors gear. When I was a kid, we played ball. Now, kids still play ball, but they also dream about hiking the A.T. in their Merrell hiking boots, North Face Gore-Tex shell, and Capilene underwear. That's a huge opportunity for Scouting. Second is the breast-beating about endangered boys and absent dads. I'm not sure either is true, but why quibble? The fact is we're at one of those cyclical moments of societal panic about how we're raising boys and the role of dads in the process. Scouting didn't exactly begin as a New Age bonding experience, but there are very few activities in modern life that bring dads and sons together the way Scouting does. You can coach Little League or AYSO soccer, but it's still the kids playing and the adults watching or yelling from the sidelines. In Scouting—at least in Troop 1's version of it—you're all along for the same trips and outings. Third is the world after 9-11. The instant cliché that everything changed after the terror attacks is demonstrably not true. But, if 9-11 put a dent in the primacy of irony as a worldview, if it reminded us of the heroism that can come from men (and it mostly was men) doing tough, unglamorous jobs in fire departments and police stations and the military, that can't hurt Scouting and could help it. A bunch of Boy Scouts carrying the flag in the Memorial Day parade seems a lot more relevant, even to liberal sophisticates, now than it did prior to September 11, 2001.

But whether Scouting can capitalize on any of that is another question. I had asked a few people, like Nick and Dr.

Flank, for their thoughts on how to reinvigorate the B.S.A. Using their ideas and my own, this is what emerged:

1. **Stop the discrimination:** The B.S.A. defends its exclusionary policies against gays and atheists by saying Scouting is entitled, indeed required, to stand up for its fundamental values. Quite right. But Scouting is undermining its core values—teaching young men to be tolerant, kind, helpful, decent, and friendly—by taking a stand in favor of discrimination. And the real disaster of both policies is that they make Scouting look backward and narrow at a time kids increasingly think of Scouting as something that's already behind the times. The real charm of Scouting has always been its fundamental decency and sense of inclusion. You have never needed a degree in philosophy to understand the Scout Law or the ethic of fairness and tolerance that resonates through Scouting. You don't need one now to see that both policies make the Scouts seem unfair and intolerant. And there's nothing in the writings or the lives of Baden-Powell, Seton, or Beard to think they would have endorsed the B.S.A.'s moral litmus test. Scouting needs to continue to develop and refine rigorous zero-tolerance policies on any kind of sexual abuse or inappropriate behavior. But kicking out gay Eagle Scouts does not help achieve it. Scouting once caught the vast middle of American life. It would be a supreme tragedy if it evolved into a politically laden movement catering to Mormons, Catholics, or the Christian right and writing off everyone else.

2. **Find a dynamic leader:** Scouting was built by three charismatic, idiosyncratic visionaries—Baden-Powell, Seton, and Beard. Their presence drew generations of kids to Scouting. Now no one knows who they were, and Scouting is led by invisible careerist bureaucrats even the Scouts don't know. If not a new Baden-Powell, Seton, or Beard

(though it could use one), Scouting needs its Steve Jobs or Lee Iacocca or Ray Kroc—maybe someone like an astronaut who was a Scout as a kid—a leader who can put a vibrant face on a declining enterprise and make the case for why Scouting still matters.

3. Throw out the uniforms: One of the quotes from B-P on the wall of the office at Waubeeka began: "For the boy, a uniform is a big attraction." Up until the 1950s, a vaguely military uniform was a source of pride. But for middle school and high school kids now, it's just a source of embarrassment, something no one wears in public. Nick suggested doing what, say, the NFL does, licensing its logos and putting them on outdoors clothes. You could have shells and fleeces with the Boy Scout logo, in whatever color a troop wanted, that would give troops uniformity and identity without saddling them with outdated uniforms no one wants to wear.

4. Embrace diversity: They're trying. Scouting makes a good-faith effort at courting minorities, but it can do better. Baden-Powell was a revolutionary. His idea of a movement that joined both tony public-school boys and working-class ones in an organization that spanned class lines struck some as ingenious and others as heretical. There's no longer anything revolutionary in the idea, but no one puts it to work. Scouting has the potential to unite inner-city black kids, rich suburban white kids, and working-class exurban kids in a common movement. The trouble is, it never happens. Scouts, for the most part, interact only through their own troop. Scouting needs a concerted push to get different troops together—something beyond the District Camporee or even the National Jamboree, the huge national gatherings of Scouts held every four years. For instance, a program pairing our troop with a black or Hispanic one from the same county, or one from overwhelmingly white North Atlanta with one from overwhelmingly black South Atlanta, would be a revelation for both groups. It would transform Scouting into what B-P envisioned, a challenge rather than a predictable bromide.

5. Commit to service projects: This is another one where Scouting's values are perfectly aligned with the moment. When I was a kid, public service was a largely obscure notion, left for grown-ups or do-gooders. Now, it's part of the daily vocabulary of youth, a staple on every college campus and college résumé. Scout troops do some of it, but they are perfectly positioned to do a lot more. An obvious area is the environment, which is nonideological and probably has more innate appeal to kids than any other issue. It's also an issue at the heart of Scouting's roots and current culture.

6. Focus on keeping older kids: This has been a problem for Scouting since it began, and it gets harder all the time. It's not easy to keep older kids in Scouting. But make no mistake: Getting first graders involved in Tiger Cubs may keep the B.S.A.'s numbers up, but it won't do much toward realizing the worthy, serious goals that Baden-Powell, Seton, and Beard had for Scouting.

7. Advertise: That's how we spread a message in America. Scouting is saddled with an image so dull and deadly, it's amazing it still has a pulse. Like the U.S. Army did with "Be All That You Can Be" or the Marines with "The Few, The Proud, The Marines," Scouting needs to aggressively put across a positive, contemporary message or it's going to continue to decline.

Maybe a resurgence is impossible. Scouting is a century-old movement that began before there was radio, let alone television or computers. It had peaks of relevance during the World Wars and the Cold War. Now it seems to be becoming a niche product, a movement that is almost aggressively behind the times, where kids get to hear old-timers playing "Somewhere Over the Rainbow" on a saw. And the truth is, for all our egalitarian rhetoric, there's not much interest in a movement that's open to everyone. Our dominant cultural values are all about exclusion and prestige—the fancy Lexus, the Park Avenue address, the Yale sticker on the rear windshield. We're not that interested in something that's as accessible to the kid in Harlem as it is to the kid in Chappaqua. And the biggest hurdle may not be recruiting the kids; it may be finding the adults with the time, energy, and devotion to run a troop and put together a good program for it. It's an enormous commitment few working parents these days are willing to make.

That said, Scouting isn't doomed to continued decline. In my desk at home I have five patches I was awarded for participating in events during my hapless tenure in Scouting. There are two from Camp Read, one from that first Paul Bunyan Camporee, one from a dimly remembered Manitoga Trek 2000, and, my favorite, a lovely pale blue Klondike Derby patch, with whip-wielding driver, dogsled, and huskies from the year we had the Klondike Derby sans snow. They were given to everyone who showed up, but I've come to see them as treasured keepsakes, and sometimes I take them out when I'm working at night and idly ponder them the way I once would have flipped through a stack of baseball cards. This is not a part of dad-dom I ever envisioned or sought, but if Scouting could win me over, it could recruit anyone. Shields, the Scout's PR guy, is right, at least in part. Scouting's core values—as embodied in the Scout Law, not the case law—are wonderful building blocks for a movement and a life. Scouting's genuinely egalitarian goals and instincts are more important now—for poor kids on the bottom and for rich kids on the top—than they've ever been. It's one of the only things that kids do that's genuinely cooperative, not competitive. If my kid starts at quarterback, yours does not. If he finishes first in the class, yours can only hope to finish second. But while the troop is a cooperative venture, kids succeed or don't in Scouting on their own. One kid making Eagle doesn't make it any harder—or any easier—for another to do the same. And at a time when few middle class kids join the military, it's a truly egalitarian activity that's good precisely because it's not exclusive—everyone gets to join, and kids have to get along with each other whether or not they're in the same clique, play on the same team, or exist in the same social niche.

The Harvard sociologist Robert Putnam made a splash a few years ago with the book *Bowling Alone,* which said we're suffering from a loss of social cohesion because institutions that used to knit people together no longer do. We don't join bowling leagues; we bowl alone. But we don't Scout alone. Back in Don Vanderbilt's day, one of his assistant Scoutmasters, John Ripley, gave the same talk to the fathers at the beginning of each year. "This is a golden opportunity that every father here will never have again," he said. "You and your sons do this as equals. You camp, you cook, you hike; everything you do in the woods, you do as equals. You'll never have this opportunity again. You should take advantage of it. If you're planning just to drop him off Wednesday night and not get involved, don't bother. That's not what we're about."

One of the nicest Troop 1 events each year is the spring barbecue and Court of Honor for past and present members and friends of the troop. The Scouts gather in clumps sorted largely by age, the sisters and younger siblings form their own age and gender-appropriate posses, and the parents get to mingle in relative peace. The spring Court of Honor the year after our Waubeeka triumph felt like the flashback at the end of *The Godfather* 2, with Sonny still alive, Fredo still a part of the family, and Michael still young and idealistic. John Ripley was there, serving up hamburgers with Mr. Johnson. Todd Davis came back from college with a scraggly goatee and strolled in with his brother Jeff, also an Eagle, who had his hair in some kind of weird samurai bun. Bob Heller was there too, as was Jack the tarp-ball star. Even the old Scout Hut was sort of there, its image at the center of the huge blue Troop 1 seal that Dr. Flank brings to all the ceremonial occasions. The rest of the cast sauntered in: Sam (minus Eric, who was still active in the troop but a no-show that night) sporting his billowing Italian Afro, Ben's Amigos, Dr. Flank, and Messrs. Toonkel and Johnson. Fly Guy was fretting because he had to miss camp this year, but Mr. Lombardi was planning to be back for a return engagement. There were even a handful of new kids, who looked as impossibly small and young now as the older kids looked impossibly large and old when Ben and I started three years ago. We would have to see how many of them decided to stick around.

The evening went by the familiar Troop 1 script. Dr. Flank gave out the merit badges, talked about camp and High Adventure, and announced the date and time for the planning meeting for next year. Bob Walker made his pitch, passed out pledge cards, and thanked us fulsomely for our support. Mr. Toonkel and Mr. Johnson came up with a tooled leather belt for the outgoing Senior Patrol Leader. Dads and moms who had contributed to the year's events were thanked. Many burgers and hot dogs and plates of pasta salad and chips were consumed.

Before the watermelon and chocolate chip cookies and brownies for dessert, Dr. Flank called all the current and former members forward—from Todd Davis to the tiny sixth graders—to join him in the circle. They linked hands. "I challenge you to be your best and to give Scouting your best personal effort," Dr. Flank said. And they all repeated together: "May the Great Master of all Scouts be with us until we meet again."

Seeing the little kids made things feel a little bittersweet. Just as grownups always think of themselves as younger than they are, we do the same with our kids. And seeing those little kids reminded me how far Ben was from being one. Not that I should have needed the reminder. A few weeks after our triumph at Waubeeka, Ben had gone on High Adventure, his week in the wilds of northern Quebec. I'm not sure I would have been invited, since my cooking and camping skills had stalled around Tenderfoot level, but a week canoeing and hiking through the Canadian wilderness was more outdoors adventure than I had in mind. He went. I stayed. I was glad he had Dr. Flank, Mr. Toonkel, and Mr. Johnson to guide him along. But it felt like we had walked down a road together and had finally reached a point where he kept going, and I turned back.

And, without my quite realizing it, Ben had become a different creature than he was when we started Scouting. One day in eighth grade he had dragged out our old NordicTrack, which we never used, and started working out. Then we got a treadmill, and he started buying hand weights, first fifteen pounds, then twenty, twenty-five, and thirty, which he began using with religious regularity. He bought a book on weight training and drew up intricate tables of the sets and repetitions he did on assorted curls, squats, crunches, lifts, and lunges. Within a few months most of his flab was miraculously gone, and before long he was fit and buff enough to look like the models on the covers of *Men's Health* and *Maxim*. We used to play at a blocking drill where we'd bang into each other like opposing linemen, but hitting him now is like running into a brick wall, so that game has been retired for my protection. So much for worrying he'd be a wuss. One day, Ben picked up one of my Miles Davis CDs and put it into a Sony Discman. He'd never shown much interest in music, but he liked it and asked for other suggestions. Before long, he was listening to Davis's "Kind of Blue," "In a Silent Way," "Jack Johnson," and "Porgy and Bess"; John Coltrane's "My Favorite Things," "A Love Supreme," and "Blue Trane"; Duke Ellington, Herbie Hancock, and other surprisingly sophisticated and unfashionable stuff. He was now bigger than me, so I started wearing his hand-me-downs. I also wore the outdoor watch with the braided leather strap he got me one year for Father's Day, and took to carrying around as a sort of talisman the red Swiss army knife he bought me another year as a birthday gift. It was hard to know how much of Ben was a result of his parents, his genes, his schools, Scouts, happenstance, his horoscope, or dumb luck. But, using the Scout Law as a yardstick, I calculated that by the time he took off for High Adventure, he was very loyal, usually helpful, extremely friendly and courteous, exceptionally kind, reasonably obedient, usually cheerful, fairly thrifty (with the exception of all that camping gear), probably no more or less brave than most, quite clean (if you don't count his room, in which case he's a disaster), and not particularly reverent. Seemed fine to me.

I was almost right about never returning to Waubeeka. I did make one more trip to Camp Read the next winter when the troop took a ski trip to Gore Mountain, about twenty miles away. The temperature was about 10 degrees and everything was covered under a foot of snow with a hard, icy glaze on top. We stayed in one of the fancier (by Scout standards) cabins at Buckskin, and, proving I had learned nothing in three years, I somehow showed up without a sleeping bag. I slept on a bunk bed above Ben's in my clothes and used my coat as a blanket. I woke up cold, stiff, tired, and feeling terminally stupid. If they had ever given me my Scoutmaster Challenge Award (supposedly there was a trophy or plaque, but I never got it), I would have sent it back and told them to give it to Mr. Lombardi or Mr. Farrentino.

But I never made it back to Scout camp. As Ben got older, he didn't lose interest in Scouting. He still appreciated the hikes and camp-outs the way he had when he was younger. In fact, as schoolwork got more stressful with the lethal doses of AP courses that kids take these days, he came to appreciate the outings all the more, signing up for almost every camp-out and hike as natural restoratives. But instead of making it to Waubeeka for a fourth year, Ben moved onto other things his next summer. He spent two weeks on one of those too-expensive wilderness trips, hiking through the Blue Ridge Mountains; took a two-week course in Forensics at the University of Virginia, and then did the troop's High Adventure for the second time. He didn't seem to miss Waubeeka, but I did. It had been a long year working at the *New York Times* post 9-11, and I'd like to have seen if Waubeeka would have had the same restorative powers it did in the past. And Scout camp was something Ben and I shared. I wasn't ready for it to end.

One of Baden-Powell's favorite paintings was a maudlin oil by a London Scoutmaster named Ernest S. Carlos entitled *If I Were a Boy Again*. It shows a wasted man with hollow eyes, sitting slumped in a chair as he watches his son, a radiant young Boy Scout, prepare for an outing. The father sits at a table crowded with books, a teakettle and teacup, staring at the boy. The son jauntily prepares for his adventures oblivious (or indifferent) to the melancholy old coot sitting behind him. I've often wondered why Boy Scouts seems to be invested with so much more cultural significance than Girl Scouts—the one full of powerful metaphorical resonance, the other pretty much identified with cookie sales. In part, of course, it's a reflection of the different opportunities, expectations, and burdens put on boys and girls in the past, and, to some extent, in the present. But I think it's something else as well. Men, as women often remind us, seem fixated on being boys. The most coveted jobs for men are the ones they dreamed about as boys. I'm sure it's fun to play in the WNBA, but it's not as much fun as being Kobe Bryant or Michael Jordan or Barry Bonds or Brett Favre. It's impossible to appreciate the almost spiritual attachment men put on being, say, firefighters or cops without realizing it allows men, in some ways, to always be boys. Baden-Powell's favorite play was—what else?—*Peter Pan*, which he saw twice during the first month it was produced in London. And for this man who never really outgrew being a boy, the Scouts, on whatever level you want to look at it, was always something of an adventure in eternal youth. As long as the boys stayed young, he could too.

Scouting never worked quite on that level for me, and it doesn't work that way in the culture anymore—its symbolism is too out of date. But the melancholy message of Carlos's painting has a tinge of universal truth. You're not a parent for very long, and you do what works for as long as it works before your son takes off to live his own life on his own terms. I feel lucky to have had this unexpected vehicle to share my son's youth, to shape it, and to be shaped by it as well.

We like to think of our kids as extensions of ourselves (*the heirs apparent!*), but that's a parental conceit. Sometimes we lead our kids, sometimes they lead us; sometimes we mix and match, and eventually we just go our separate ways. I hope I led Ben in some good directions, but Scouting turned out to be one rich, revealing, totally unexpected way he has led me, even if he could lead me only so far. It's still his world more than mine.

On spring and summer nights when I get off the train, the field by the station is usually full of other dads' kids playing Little League games in the dwindling sunlight or under the lights at the Rec Department field. I sometimes stop and watch for a few minutes, taking in the busy green pageant and listening to the chatter of the kids, the ping of the balls flying off the aluminum bats, and the familiar thud of ball meeting glove. Invariably, I get a wistful pang of remembrance and regret. How did that end so fast?

I didn't choose Scouting, but I'm glad Ben did, and I'm sure before too long I'll feel a similar shiver of remembrance and regret when it's over too.

Bibliography

I was able to make use of a wide variety of materials in writing this book. Some were especially helpful. The single best source on Baden-Powell is Tim Jeal's *The Boy-Man: The Life of Lord Baden-Powell,* the definitive Baden-Powell biography to date. Less balanced and complete, but also valuable, was Michael Rosenthal's *The Character Factory: Baden-Powell and the Origins of the Boy Scout Movement.* The best source I found on the history of the Boy Scouts of America was Carolyn Ditte Wagner's 1978 doctoral dissertation, *The Boy Scouts of America: A Model and a Mirror of American Society.* Particularly valuable on contemporary Scouting issues and controversies are Jay Mechling's *On My Honor: Boy Scouts and the Making of American Youth* and Chuck Sudetic's "The Struggle for the Soul of the Boy Scouts" in *Rolling Stone.* For Troop 1's history, I was extraordinarily fortunate that Doug Rohde had decided to research the troop's history for his Eagle project in 1989. And Patrick Boyle's *Scout's Honor: Sexual Abuse in America's Most Trusted Institution,* while hard to find, is a powerful, troubling, important look at sexual abuse within Scouting, worthwhile for its insights into pederasty both within and outside Scouting. I did not list every newspaper, magazine, and Internet site I made use of, but the following is the list of the main reference materials I consulted.

Baden-Powell, Lord Robert S. S. *Paddle Your Own Canoe: Or Tips For Boys From the Jungle and Elsewhere.* London: Macmillan and Co. Ltd., 1939.

———. *Scouting for Boys.* Scouts' Edition. London: C. Arthur Pearson, Ltd., 1963.

Beard, Daniel Carter. *The American Boys Handy Book: What to Do and How to Do It.* Rutland, Vt.: C. E. Tuttle, 1966.

———. *Hardly a Man Is Now Alive: The Autobiography of Dan Beard.* New York: Doubleday, Doran & Co., 1939.

Bensman, Todd. "Scouts' controversy similar to '70s flap. Group says it's serious about resolving charges of padded membership rolls." *Dallas Morning News,* 4 June 2000.

———. "Government investigates Scouts' membership figures." *Dallas Morning News,* 14 May 2000.

———. "Boy Scouts' rolls decline by 25%." *Dallas Morning News,* 25 February 2001.

Birkby, Robert C. *Boy Scout Handbook,* 10th ed. Irving, Tex.: Boy Scouts of America, 1990.

Boy Scouts of America. *The Official Handbook for Boys,* 1st ed. Garden City, N.Y.: Doubleday, Page & Co., 1911.

———. *Boy Scout Handbook,* 11th ed. Irving, Tex.: Boy Scouts of America, 1998.

Boyle, Patrick. *Scout's Honor: Sexual Abuse in America's Most Trusted Institution.* Rocklin, Calif.: Prima Publishing, 1994.

Brenna, Susan. "Does My Son Have to Quit the Boy Scouts?" *Salon,* 7 July 2000.

Chappaqua Historical Society. "The Early Quaker Hamlet of Old Chappaqua: its houses, its people, its way of life." Chappaqua Historical Society, 1973.

Cloud, John. "Can a Scout Be Gay? The Boy Scouts' Battle to Stay Straight Goes to the Supreme Court." *Time,* 26 April 2000.

Cochran, R. E. *Be Prepared! The Life and Illusions of a Scoutmaster.* New York: William Sloane Associates, 1952.

Bibliography

Cohen, Randy. "The Ethicist: Demerit Badge." *New York Times Magazine,* 23 July 2000.

France, David. "Scouts Divided." *Newsweek,* 6 August 2001.

Fussell, Paul. *The Boy Scout Handbook and Other Observations.* New York: Oxford University Press, 1982.

Garst, Shannon. *Ernest Thompson Seton, Naturalist.* New York: Messner, 1959.

Gibson, J. *Manual of Drill for Boy Scouts.* Glasgow: James Brown & Son, 1912.

Greenhouse, Linda. "Justices Explore Scouts' Exclusion of Gay Members." *New York Times,* 27 April 2000.

———. "Supreme Court Backs Boy Scouts in Ban of Gays from Membership." *New York Times,* 29 June 2000.

Hanley, Robert. "New Jersey Court Overturns Ouster of Gay Boy Scout." *New York Times,* 5 August 1999.

Jeal, Tim. *The Boy-Man: The Life of Lord Baden-Powell.* New York: Morrow, 1990.

Keller, Betty. *Black Wolf: The Life of Ernest Thompson Seton.* Vancouver: Douglas & McIntyre, 1984.

Letcher, Gary. *Canoeing the Delaware River: A Guide to the River and Shore.* New Brunswick, N.J.: Rutgers University Press, 1985.

MacDonald, Heather. "Why the Boy Scouts Work." *City Journal* (Winter 2000).

Macleod, David I. *Building Character in the American Boy: The Boy Scouts, YMCA, and Their Forerunners, 1870–1920.* Madison: University of Wisconsin Press, 1983.

Mechling, Jay. *On My Honor: Boy Scouts and the Making of American Youth.* Chicago: University of Chicago Press, 2001.

Meyer, Kathleen. *How to Shit in the Woods: An Environmentally Sound Approach to a Lost Art.* Berkeley, Calif.: Ten Speed Press, 1994.

Murphy, Dean E. "Pinning Demerit Badge on Chief Boy Scout S.

Bibliography

Africa: Blacks Seek Amends for Founder Baden-Powell's Alleged
Misdeeds a Century Ago." *Los Angeles Times,* 24 July 1999.

New Castle Historical Society. "A Bicentennial History of the Town
of New Castle 1791–1991." New Castle Historical Society, 1991.

Oswald, A. Lewis. *Troop One Marches On!* Hutchinson, Kans.:
Rotherwood Press, 1934.

Peterson, Robert W. *The Boy Scouts: An American Adventure.* New
York: American Heritage, 1984.

Putnam, Robert D. *Bowling Alone: The Collapse and Revival of
American Community.* New York: Simon & Schuster, 2000.

Rohde, Doug. "Chappaqua Troop 1 and Scouting in Chappaqua:
Seventy-five Years." Unpublished Research Project, 1989.

Rosenthal, Michael. *The Character Factory: Baden-Powell and the
Origins of the Boy Scout Movement.* New York: Pantheon, 1986.

Samson, John G., ed. *The Worlds of Ernest Thompson Seton.* New
York: Knopf, 1976.

Seton, Ernest Thompson. *The Book of Woodcraft and Indian Lore.*
Garden City, N.Y.: Doubleday, Page, 1921.

———. *Wild Animals I Have Known.* New York: Scribner, 1926.

Sudetic, Chuck. "The Struggle for the Soul of the Boy Scouts."
Rolling Stone, 6–20 July 2000.

Thompson, Tracy. "Scouting and New Terrain." *Washington Post
Magazine,* 2 August 1998.

Wade, E. K. *The Piper of Pax: The Life Story of Lord Baden-Powell of
Gilwell.* London: C. Arthur Pearson, Ltd., 1924.

Wagner, Carolyn Ditte. *The Boy Scouts of America: A Model and a
Mirror of American Society.* Doctoral dissertation. Baltimore:
Johns Hopkins University, 1978.